ML
1015

7

THE
Fender
ELECTRIC
GUITAR
BOOK

THE FENDER ELECTRIC GUITAR BOOK
A Complete History of Fender Instruments

BY TONY BACON

ocm 72868606

A BACKBEAT BOOK
This new third edition 2007
First edition (as The Fender Book) 1992;
second edition (as The Fender Book) 1998
Published by Backbeat Books
(an imprint of Hal Leonard Corporation)
19 West 21st Street,
New York, NY 10010, USA
www.backbeatbooks.com

Devised and produced for Backbeat Books by Outline Press Ltd
2A Union Court, 20-22 Union Road, London SW4 6JP, England
www.backbeatuk.com

ISBN: 978-0-87930-897-1

CREATIVE DIRECTOR: Nigel Osborne
EDITOR: Siobhan Pascoe
DESIGN: Paul Cooper

Origination and print by Colorprint (Hong Kong)

07 08 09 10 11 5 4 3 2 1

CONTENTS

the fender story

Sotheby's auction house, London, England, April 1990. The star of today's Rock'n'Roll & Film Memorabilia sale is a 1968 Fender Stratocaster said to be the one that Jimi Hendrix played at the Woodstock festival. Iconic is an overused word, but this time it might even be the right one. The room is buzzing and the excitement builds as we get closer to lot 490. Sotheby's says the Jimi Strat "has belonged to [ex-Hendrix drummer] Mitch Mitchell since … September 1970 and is now estimated to sell for £60,000–70,000".

Hilary Kay, who will become better known for her appearances on BBC TV's Antiques Roadshow, is the auctioneer. She starts the bidding at £48,000. Immediately a bidder comes on the phone and nudges it to 50 grand. Then the battle takes off as two rivals, each on the end of a phone, push the price ever upward. Everyone else in the room is aghast as the bidding streaks through £100,000 and eventually comes to a halt, on the second phone, at £180,000.

With the buyer's premium, that brings the price-tag to £198,000 (about $375,000). Kay shakes her head and declares the guitar sold to bidder number 270. It is by far the most money anyone has ever paid for an electric guitar. It will be upstaged by another Strat, almost 15 years later, when Eric Clapton's 'Blackie' goes for a staggering $959,500 plus premium.

What would Leo Fender, founder of the Fender guitar company, have made of all this? Back in the 1970s, a reporter told him that players were beginning to think of old Fender guitars in the same way as the hallowed and valuable Stradivarius violins of 17th century Italy. The 65-year-old Leo Fender paused, as well he might. Then he said: "Well, I'm sure a lot of musicians feel just like that about 'em. Now I'll give you an example. In 1929 I bought a Model 12 Remington. I mean, I could really hit a target with that old rifle. One time I got a jack rabbit at better than 300 yards. You see, some pieces of machinery just suit people."[1]

Clarence Leonidas Fender was a practical man, proud of his work. He was born in 1909 in a barn near the Anaheim–Fullerton border in the Los Angeles area. His parents ran a 'truck farm', growing vegetables and fruit for market, including the area's famous oranges. The Fenders had put up the barn first before they could afford to build a house. Leo's father had come to California from Illinois, and Leo's ancestors were American right back to his great-great-great-great grandfather, who emigrated from Auerbach in Germany to the United States.

Leo's second wife recalled a telling episode from the young Leo's upbringing. "When he was a little boy his father told him that the only thing worthwhile in this whole world was what you accomplished at work, and that if you were not working you were lazy, which was a sin. So Leo judged himself and everyone else by that ... and himself hardest of all." [2]

The Fender company's simple, elegant guitar designs graced millions of instruments around the world – not only the enormous quantities built by Fender themselves but also the countless copies and approximations that have been made by other manufacturers. Virtually every innovative pop musician has used a Fender guitar at some point, and the famous Fender logo has long been a familiar sight to musicians – from the western swing and rock'n'roll stages of the 1950s to the present-day scene. No other organisation would contribute more to the look and sound of the solidbody electric guitar than Fender.

Virtually every innovative pop musician has used a Fender, and the logo has long been a familiar sight to musicians.

Leo Fender's original company changed the course of popular music by revolutionising the design and manufacture of electric guitars. So successful did they become that in 1965 the Fender business was sold to the giant CBS conglomerate for no less than $13 million, an unprecedented sum. Yet the whole affair had started some 20 years earlier when Leo made some electric steel guitars with a few thousand dollars earned from a record-player design. From those humble beginnings grew one of the largest, most influential and splendidly original musical instrument companies in the world. Despite spectacular later successes, during its early years the southern California company came perilously close to failing. It was Leo Fender's sheer determination, combined with his luck in surrounding himself with clever, dedicated people, that helped pull the Fender company through difficult times.

As a young man, Leo studied accountancy and began his working life in the accounts sections of the state highway department and a tyre distribution company. But his hobby was always electronics. In his 20s he built amplifiers and PA systems for public events: sports and religious gatherings as well as dances. He took a few piano lessons before trying the saxophone, but was never serious, and he never learned to play the guitar.

When Leo lost his accounts job in the depression he took the bold step of opening his own radio and record store in Fullerton, around the end of the 1930s. The Fender Radio Service, as he called the new retail and repair shop, seemed a natural step for the ambitious, newly-married 30-year-old. Leo advertised his wares and services on his business card as "electrical appliances, phonograph records, musical instruments & repairs, public address systems, sheet music". For now, instruments were in third place. But the new store on South Spadra brought introductions to many local musicians and to characters in the music and electronics businesses.

During the first few years of the store, Leo met several people who would prove important to his future success. First among these was a professional violinist and lap-steel guitarist called Clayton Orr Kauffman, known to everyone as Doc. The story goes that, around 1940, Doc brought an amp into Leo's shop for repair, and the two got chatting. Doc had

Kauffman & Fender began production of electric lap-steel guitars and small amplifiers in November 1945.

amplified his own guitars and worked on designs for an electric guitar and a vibrato-arm. By this time Leo had already begun to look into the potential for electric guitars and to play around with pickup designs. Fender and Kauffman built a crude solidbody guitar in 1943 purely to test these early pickups, one design for which was patented in '44.

DOC AND THE LAP

Doc went to work for an aircraft company during World War II. The two incorrigible tinkerers still found time to get together and came up with a design for a record-changer good enough to net them $5,000. Some of this money went into bolstering their shortlived company, K&F (Kauffman & Fender). They began proper production of electric lap-steel guitars and small amplifiers in November 1945.

Lap-steel guitar playing, often known as Hawaiian style, had been fashionable in America since the 1920s and was still tremendously popular. The steel had been the first type of guitar to go electric in the 1930s. Several innovative companies, with Rickenbacker in the lead, experimented with electro-magnetic pickups, fixing them to guitars and connecting them to small amplifiers. The steel had become popular as an easy-to-play instrument suitable for beginners, but the electric version had also appealed to professional musicians, especially in Hawaiian music and country and western bands.

Musicians play steel guitars on their lap (or sometimes standing, with the guitar mounted on legs). The name comes not from the construction – Fender's steels were mostly wooden – but from the metal bar used in the player's left hand to stop the raised strings, which were generally tuned to an open chord. During the 1930s and later the term 'Spanish' was used to identify the other type of guitar (less popular at the time) which was played upright against the body. Leo would call this the 'standard' guitar.

Doc Kauffman wrote later about the early days of K&F. "[Leo and I] would go down to the store, and at the rear was a metal building that housed the guitar department, and we would work till midnight." This description of a guitar "department" is certainly optimistic. Most people who saw the "metal building" remembered it as a tin shack hastily and cheaply assembled behind Leo's radio store. Doc continued his account: "I used to assemble all our instruments and string them up and play a few steel licks, and Leo used to say he could tell how production was coming along by counting the tunes I was playing." [3]

Leo met another significant person at this early stage, one who would become a key contributor to the later success of the Fender company. Don Randall was general manager of Radio & Television Equipment Co (known as Radio-Tel), based in Santa Ana, just 15 miles south of Fullerton. One of Randall's customers was the Fender Radio Service.

FENDER ELECTRIC INSTRUMENT CO.

Leo had not served in World War II, because of a childhood illness that cost him his right eye. Randall, who spent three years in the army, said that Leo was able to expand his shop's trade in those war years. Randall recalled: "During that period there weren't too many people about to do that kind of business. When I got out of the service I came back and started doing business with Leo again, selling parts and equipment."

It was around this time that Leo and Doc Kauffman decided to split. "It seems Doc was afraid to carry on with the business," said Randall.[4] Leo was happy to work into the middle of the night at the tin shack making the K&F lap-steel guitars and amps, but Doc wasn't so keen to spend long hours locked away from the world.

Leo said later: "It costs a lot of money to get into large-scale production, and the 1930s depression was still fresh in Kauffman's mind, so he didn't want to get involved. He had a ranch or farm … and he was afraid [that] if we got over-extended on credit he might lose it. He thought he'd better pull out while he had a full skin, so in February of '46 he left it all with me."[5]

According to one colleague, Doc – who remained lifelong friends with Leo – was asked later if he resented selling out, given the subsequent success of the Fender business. "And Doc said no, he was never sore, because Leo would have killed him before he got through with it anyway," referring to the exhausting hours. "Doc liked to spend time with his family, he didn't like staying down the shack till 10 or 11 at night, seven days a week. Anyone that worked with Leo had a hard time not over-working, because Leo expected you to be on call all hours." [6]

So Leo and Doc parted. Leo said later: "His worry was right. We had quite a few hard years ahead." [7] In 1946, Leo called his revised operation Fender Manufacturing, renaming it the Fender Electric Instrument Co in December 1947. He continued to make lap-steels and amps as he had with K&F, but would gradually develop new products. He'd appointed Don Randall's Radio-Tel, owned by Francis Hall, as the exclusive distributor of K&F products early in 1946, with salesman Charlie Hayes heading the push to persuade dealers to stock Fender gear.

Leo expanded into larger premises on nearby Pomona Avenue in Fullerton, at the corner of Santa Fe Avenue, separate from the radio store. One observer described the new property as two plain steel buildings and "not very handsome". Another remembered that the Pomona buildings did not have their own toilets. Consequently, Fender workers had to cross the nearby railroad tracks to use the facilities in the Santa Fe station. Eventually, one rather elderly employee couldn't make the treacherous trans-railroad journey, and the next day Leo had no choice but to hire a portable lavatory.

Dale Hyatt was another important new member of the gradually growing Fender team. He joined the company in January 1946 and would later become a crucial member of the Fender sales team. One of his early tasks, in late 1947 or early 1948, was to take over the radio store business, because Leo was trying to get things started at Pomona Avenue. However, business was slow and Fender had to rely on a loan from Radio-Tel's Francis Hall to keep going.

Leo was an introverted, hard-working man, happiest by himself, drawing up designs for new guitars and amps.

Leo was an introverted, hard-working man, prone to long hours and selfless application to the task in hand, happiest when by himself and drawing up designs for new projects. He thought that if there was a product on the market already, he could make it better and cheaper – and make a profit in the process. Despite spectacular later successes, during the early years the new Fender company came perilously close to failing. It was Leo's sheer determination combined with his luck in surrounding himself with clever, dedicated people that would help pull through these difficult times.

Now that the war was over, there was a general feeling that a fresh start was possible, and American businessmen began to exploit mass production, a key process in this new beginning. Leo's particular application of this technique to guitar manufacturing was to be his master-stroke, but in these early days he still needed outside expertise in the mass-production of parts. And so another piece of the jigsaw came into place.

Karl Olmsted and his partner Lymon Race left the services in 1947 and decided to start a much-needed tool-and-die company in Fullerton, making specialist tools and dies for customers to use to stamp out metal parts on punch presses. "We were looking for work," Olmsted explained, "and Leo had reached the point where he needed dies to be made for production work. They'd been making parts by hand, cutting out the metal any way they could. But he was getting to the point where they wanted to make several of each thing." Race & Olmsted continued to make Fender's tooling and most metal parts for the next 30 years and more. "As it progressed, so we progressed to more complicated, sophisticated, high-production tooling," said Olmsted. [8]

> "Exclusive new patented pickup unit affording greater brilliance and presence. Equal volume output from all strings without compensating adjustments."

Next to join Fender's company was George Fullerton, who was to become what one co-worker described as "Leo's faithful workhorse". The two had met at one of the outdoor events for which Leo was still supplying sound systems. Young George – who was "going to school, playing music, repairing radios, and delivering furniture" – started to help Leo with these events. Gradually, Fullerton's radio repair turned to fixing amps and lap-steels, and he started working at Pomona Avenue in February 1948. "It was only a small place then," he remembered, "only two or three people, a couple of girls." [9]

Not only small, but precarious. Lack of cash was an almost ever-present problem at Fender in those early days. One employee said that there were times when it was hard to cash Fender cheques in Fullerton – especially if Leo's first wife, Esther, was late receiving her wages from her job at the phone company.

A very early ad for the new Fender company's wares in 1947 showed just three lap-steel guitars and a couple of amplifiers. Fender stressed the plus points of the guitars: "Exclusive new patented pickup unit ... affording greater brilliance and presence. Equal volume output from all strings without compensating adjustments."

THE LEO AND DON METHODS

Leo and Randall were two highly motivated men with very different ways of working. Dale Hyatt: "Leo sometimes was very resistant to change: you had to prove everything to him. Nothing wrong with that: you just had to do it. Randall, of course, was much the same way: he was also rather stubborn in his realm of thinking. It's been said that they fought like cats and dogs, but I don't believe that's true at all. They couldn't fight – because they just didn't talk to each other, period. But I think one was as good as the other – and they were good for each other. I don't say that Leo Fender was the greatest thing that ever happened to Don Randall or vice versa. No, I think they were the greatest thing that happened to each other." [10]

Leo was certainly single-minded. He would have been happy if he could just continue to slave away in his workshop, sketching out pickup designs or enjoying a new piece of machinery. As far as he was concerned, the fewer people who got in the way of all this, the better. And generally speaking, Leo was – according to Leo – the only one able to get such things done.

A FETISH FOR MACHINES

One of his colleagues said: "Leo might come in one morning and buddy, he had something in his mind that he wanted to try. The place is burning down? Let it burn down. He wanted to do what he was on. And he wasn't one to give any compliments. You could tell Leo something and you'd give him an idea; you could tell he was looking straight at you and thinking [about it]. Wouldn't say a thing, wouldn't agree that you'd even told him anything. Then later on your idea would show up on something."[11]

Randall had a good sales head: he wanted a good product at a competitive price that would rock the market, and often he had to shake things up at the factory to get results. Leo, meanwhile, would be changing a particular wiring scheme for the seventh time. He was constantly trying to perfect this guitar or that amp. Randall said: "Leo was a strange man, in a way. He had a fetish for machinery. Nothing was done economically, necessarily. If you could do it on a big machine, let's buy the big machine and use it – when you might have been able to buy the part the machine made a lot cheaper from a supplier."[12]

Karl Olmsted agreed. "Leo would say that he'd like a certain part, and we'd take it back to our workshop. Then I'd say Leo, we'd have to hand-make every one of these, there's no way you can mass-produce it, it's going to be slow and expensive. He'd say, well, what can you come up with that's cheap and that'll make me happy? Almost every job was that way."[13]

> By 1950 Fender was well known throughout the country and yet almost anonymous in its home town.

Fender's electric lap-steels began to enjoy local success, on the West Coast and into the Southwest, and increasingly eastwards. The local Fullerton paper reported in November 1949 that the Fender firm was "well known throughout the country" and yet "almost anonymous" in its home town.[14]

Leo began to think about producing an electric 'Spanish' guitar, in other words one of standard shape and playing style, in contrast to the lap models he currently made. He had converted a few regular acoustic guitars to electric for individual customers, but wanted to go further. There's no hard evidence of who first thought of a Fender Spanish-style electric, although salesman Charlie Hayes may have suggested it to Leo. If he did, then it was by far the most important contribution he made to the company's prosperity, way beyond all the amps and instruments he sold and the dozens of dealers he signed up and encouraged.

Guitar-makers and musicians didn't yet understand or appreciate the potential for electric guitars, which were still in their infancy. Rickenbacker, National, Gibson, and Epiphone had made regular 'Spanish' archtop hollow-body acoustic guitars with f-holes and built-in electric pickups and controls since the 1930s, but to little effect. Rickenbacker was located in Los Angeles, not far from Fender, and had been the first with a pickup employing the novel electro-magnetic principle – the type used since on virtually every electric guitar.

Gibson set the style for the best hollow-body electrics, and for example had launched the accomplished ES-175 in 1949. And while demand was rising from dance-band guitarists who found themselves increasingly unable to compete with the volume of the rest of the band, these early electric-acoustic guitars were mostly experimental, only partially successful from a technical standpoint, and still to become a great commercial sensation.

A solid guitar reduces the body's tonal interference and more accurately reproduces and sustains the sound of the strings.

A number of instrument companies, players, and amateur inventors in America were wondering about the possibility of a solidbody instrument. Leo himself had already made one: the pickup testbed he'd built with Doc Kauffman in the early 1940s. The attraction to players of a solidbody guitar was that it would cut the annoying feedback that amplified hollow-body guitars often generated. At the same time, a solid instrument would reduce the body's interference with the guitar's tone and so more accurately reproduce and sustain the sound of the strings.

Rickenbacker had begun marketing a relatively solid Bakelite-body electric guitar in 1935 – the type that Doc Kauffman had played – but the guitar, offered in lap and Spanish styles, was small and awkward. Around 1940, in New York, guitarist Les Paul built his 'log', a personal testbed electric cobbled together from a number of instruments and centred on a solid through-neck block of pine. A little later he concocted a couple of similar instruments for regular playing, his 'clunkers'.

As ever, Leo consulted many local musicians, trying out prototypes with them, putting testbed instruments in their hands, constantly asking their opinions on this pickup arrangement or that control scheme. He remembered: "About 25 percent of every day was spent with visiting musicians, trying to figure out what would suit their needs best."[15] One guinea pig said how he'd often turn around on stage at a local gig to see Leo "oblivious of musicians, audience, club management, and disruption generally," busily changing amp controls or suggesting guitar settings – and usually in mid-song.[16]

George Fullerton recalled spending many long hours at Leo's side as the design for the new solidbody Fender came together. He said: "How do you design something that's a brand new item, a brand new thing, that will fit people and be desirable? We tried a lot of different things and finally came up with the basic design. It seemed to be the most suitable thing we had found: easy to hold, easy to play, you could get to all the frets. Leo was very strong for building something that was very serviceable, durable, easy to repair, and, like he used to call it, 'built like a tank,' to stand up to rough treatment. We tried to design something that would be strong and do a good job for a playing musician. We made lots of different things that we tested and tried. We didn't just decide what to do and do it; it had to be proven."[17]

Two single-pickup prototypes for the new guitar have survived. The first one dates from the summer of 1949 and has a two-piece pine body. The headstock was based on the existing lap-steel guitars – symmetrical, slightly tapered, and with three tuners each side. The integral steel bridge/pickup assembly, the two-knob control plate, and the bolt-on neck were all in place. A second prototype from around the autumn or winter of 1949 was made from ash – which became a key timber for early Fender solidbody guitars – and had the remarkable six-tuners-on-one-side head that we know and love today as the Telecaster headstock. The new solidbody was nearly there.

HEADS UP ON BIGSBY

In Downey, California, about 15 miles to the west of Fender's operation in Fullerton, Paul Bigsby had a small workshop where he spent a lot of time fixing motorcycles and, later, making some fine pedal-steel guitars and his famous vibrato units. He also ventured into solidbody electric guitars and mandolins. He hand-built a limited number of distinctive instruments, starting in 1948 with the historic Merle Travis guitar, a solidbody with through-neck construction (like Les Paul's and Leo's testbed guitars) and a headstock with the tuners all on one side.

It seems unlikely that the design of the Fender solidbody was influenced very much by Bigsby's slightly earlier instruments. George Fullerton said that he and Leo knew Paul Bigsby and saw Merle Travis playing his Bigsby guitar, and Don Randall too said Leo had seen it. Travis himself has said that Leo borrowed his Bigsby, though Leo denied it. Dale Hyatt was probably right in doubting that Leo copied Paul Bigsby. "They just both made something at the same time," said Hyatt.[18] Leo had his own ideas; the Bigsby simply proved that a guitar of this type could attract good musicians.

Some of the most important aspects of the design of the new solidbody Fender guitar were adapted from the company's existing lap-steel instruments. The wonderful bridge pickup – arguably the key component of its sound – was based on the unit already fitted to the Fender Champion steel, launched in 1949. The pickup was slanted to emphasise bass tones – just as Gibson had done with the pickup on their ES-300 model, introduced in 1940. The Fender bridge pickup would come to be recognised as one of the company's finest achievements, with a tone all its own that would attract generations of players to the Telecaster and the Esquire.

Leo decided to base the solid construction of the new guitar on the way he made his solid-wood steels. He wanted to maintain the advantages of these relatively easy-to-make guitars. There was absolutely no point, as far as he was concerned, to even consider the relatively complex methods used by contemporary electric guitar makers like Gibson and Epiphone. Their workers had to deal with multiple parts and spent a great deal of time and skilled effort to construct the hollow-body instruments. It's often been said that Fender's workshop was more like a furniture factory than an instrument factory. Expediency and straightforward practicality ruled Leo's head and, therefore, the Fender shop.

We know that Doc Kauffman had a Rickenbacker semi-solidbody guitar. The inquisitive Leo must have studied the design of his friend's instrument in detail and couldn't have failed to notice that the Rick had a detachable neck. He realised this made sense for easy repair and service – returns of some early Fender products told

> It's often said that Fender's workshop was more like a furniture factory than an instrument factory.

him how important this was – and a detachable neck must have appealed to his love of simple, economic methods of working. National and Dobro also made their guitars with detachable necks, but along with Rickenbacker they were in the minority. Most mainstream makers employed the more time-consuming glued-on neck that, again, needed the attention of skilled workers.

Leo was well aware that he could manufacture a solidbody electric guitar practically and cheaply. He knew that such an instrument would make sense to musicians and offer them musical advantages. He explained later: "I guess you would say the objectives were durability, performance, and tone." He looked again at his existing steels when he considered the kind of tone that the new 'standard' guitar ought to have. He said: "We wanted a standard guitar that had a little bit more of the sound of the steel guitar."[19]

THAT CLEAN FENDER TONE

Hollow-body electric guitars of the time generally delivered a warm, woody tone, reflecting the construction of the instrument and the pickup's position near the neck. Jazz guitarists loved that sound. Leo had something quite different in mind. Not for Fender the fat Gibson and Epiphone jazz voice. His lap-steels had a cleaner, sustained tone, and that's what he wanted for the new solidbody, something like a cross between a clear acoustic guitar and a cutting electric lap-steel. Leo explained later: "I wanted to get the sound you hear when you hold the head of an acoustic guitar against your ear and pluck a string."[20]

Meanwhile, Don Randall was frustrated. Leo did not have a finished sample of the new solidbody Fender good enough for Randall to take over to New York City to the NAMM show in summer 1949. At these important regular gatherings of the National Association of Music Merchants, major manufacturers would show off their new models, usually in advance of them appearing on the market. Store owners would visit from all over the country to decide which of the new wares they would eventually stock in their outlets.

With time on his hands, the Fender sales boss took a good look around at the other makers' products. Randall lost no time in telling Leo his conclusion: a single pickup was simply not enough for the new guitar. He saw that Gibson was launching a new ES-5 hollow-body electric with no fewer than three pickups, and several other companies had two-pickup models at the New York show. Randall battled with Leo over the

> "The Esquire guitar is something entirely new ... the features found are far in advance of all the competition."

need for a two-pickup guitar. Fullerton said: "Leo was a really strong minded person with the ideas he had: you didn't change him. If he had an idea to try something, the only way you'd ever change him would be to prove that what he had would not work."[21] Reluctantly, Leo would end up with two new solidbody guitars: the single-pickup and (briefly) two-pickup Esquires and, slightly later, the two-pickup Broadcaster.

But in the meantime, by April of 1950, Fender had the new single-pickup instrument to promote in their catalogue. "The Esquire guitar is something entirely new in the electric Spanish guitar field," wrote Randall, who named the new Esquire himself. "The features found in this new guitar are far in advance of all the competition." Today we're used to advertising hype; back then it was more or less the truth. Randall went on in Fender's Catalogue No.2 to highlight the attractions of the new-fangled construction. "Because the body is solid, there is no acoustic cavity to resonate and cause feedback as in all other box type Spanish guitars. The guitar can be played at extreme volume without the danger of feedback."

Fender salesmen received their first samples in April 1950, but production of solidbody guitars in any great numbers was yet to start at the Fender factory. The first appearance of the Esquire on a Fender pricelist came with the August 1st document, and by now it had two pickups. Sitting alongside six steel guitars and five amplifiers, it was pegged at $139.95. A case added a further $39.95. In May, Fender had added a new concrete building alongside the two steel ones on Pomona Avenue, presumably with increased production in mind.

But the new instrument did not prove immediately easy to sell, as Don Randall soon found out. This time when he went to the NAMM show – in Chicago in July 1950 – he had a sample of the new guitar with him. Fender was represented by Randall alongside salesmen Charlie Hayes and Don Patton at distributor Radio-Tel's display in Room 795 at the Palmer House. "I just got laughed out of the place," said Randall. "Our new guitar was called everything from a canoe paddle to the snow shovel. There was a lot of derision."

Randall did have at least one useful meeting at the Chicago trade show, however, when Al Frost from National explained that the lack of neck strengthening in the sample would be likely to cause problems later for neck stability. "So I contacted Leo," Randall recalled, "and I says, Leo, we've got to have a neck [truss] rod in there. [Leo said,] 'No we don't need one, it's rock maple.' I said I tell you one thing: either we put a neck rod in there or we don't sell it. Now make up your mind!

> ## National said the Fender sample's lack of neck strengthening could cause problems later for stability.

"And this was the way I had to handle Leo. He was actually kind of afraid of me. I don't know why. I was the only guy who could handle him and make him do things. Rest of them it was, Oh yes Leo, yes Mr Fender. But Leo was about two-thirds afraid of me, because I really leaned on him to get him to make changes that were necessary. So we put out just a few of them without a neck rod, and then we put a neck rod in."[22]

ESQUIRE: THIRD TIME LUCKY?

Salesman Dale Hyatt also had to struggle against a less than serious view of these new Fenders, which he was trying to sell further north. He had his Esquire samples and was out selling them in Manteca, a few miles inland from San Francisco. Hyatt's brother, who lived in the area, had tipped him off about the dozens of country musicians playing around town – and it was country players who were showing most interest in the new Fender electric guitar.

"They had these nightclubs going and guys playing honky-tonk and country-western," Hyatt remembered of Manteca. "I'd taken five guitars with me. So I got a guy playing one. He quite liked it – and all of a sudden it just quit, didn't know what was wrong with it. It was embarrassing. So I went out to the truck, got another one. It lasted about 30 minutes and it quit. Then they started saying: 'There he goes again, ladies and gentlemen, wonder how many he's got?' Anyway, the third one kept on going and worked for the rest of the evening."

Hyatt had stumbled on a weakness of the new Fender's pickup shielding in the most public way imaginable. This was the cost of trying to sell what were still in effect pre-production versions, or working prototypes. "But anyhow, that was the start of it," Hyatt laughed. "That gentleman came down to my brother's house the next day and brought his son's electric train set, which he wanted to trade for one of the guitars. Another of the first ones I sold of what we now know as the Telecaster – it might have been the second or third I sold, I'm not sure – was to a gentleman in Long Beach. He was one of the very first people to buy Leo Fender's solidbody guitar, and I know he played that thing for years and years."[23]

For now, the Esquire was put aside until proper production of the single-pickup model began in January 1951. In October or November 1950 production started of a two-pickup Fender, now with added truss-rod following the trade-show advice and some more badgering of Leo by Randall. Randall came up with a new name, Broadcaster, and the retail price was set at $169.95. This put it around the same level as Gibson's fine ES-175 hollow-body electric, which sold for $175. In today's money, that would be equivalent to about $1,400, underlining the fact that these were not cheap guitars. The most basic new hollow-body electric from a budget brand such as Silvertone could be had for around $45 ($380 in today's money).

The Broadcaster was really the first Fender solidbody electric to be made and sold in any reasonable numbers. Leo said later: "The single- and double-pickup guitars overlapped ... but the Broadcaster was the first one we built."[24] In other words, we can presume he meant this was the first one to be built in significant numbers. Fender historian and author Richard Smith found out that Fender sold 152 Broadcasters in the first two months of 1951. All this makes the Fender Broadcaster the historically significant solidbody electric guitar.

But the Broadcaster name was shortlived, halted in February 1951 by Gretsch, the large New York-based instrument manufacturer. They indicated their existing use of 'Broadkaster' on drum products (and earlier on banjos) and their 1937 trademark registration of the name. Gretsch had already stopped another drum company, Slingerland, from using it, and for some reason were sufficiently troubled by a guitar to block Fender's use too.

Fender complied with the request, as Dale Hyatt explained. "There was a sense of camaraderie between the manufacturers in the early days. No one was trying to beat the other to a patent or anything like that. So Gretsch just pointed it out and we agreed to do it."[25] This was echoed in a letter that Randall sent to Fender salesmen towards the end of February 1951 outlining the necessity for a name change. He told them that Gretsch had

In October or November 1950 Fender started production of the two-pickup Broadcaster, which soon became the Telecaster.

▲ 1950 BROADCASTER

▼ 1953 ESQUIRE

■ Soon the Broadcaster became the Telecaster, seen in a proud 1952 ad (opposite page, far right) that boasts about "wide range tone effects" and "pickups adjustable for tone response" as well as "no feedback" and "modern design". The Esquire was revived from its earlier pre-production role and became the one-pickup version of the new Fender solidbody, illustrated here by a wonderfully careworn '53 example (above). It's worth reminding ourselves this early in the book that these guitars – despite soaring values on the collector's market – are designed to be played. And these two certainly have been. Long may they run.

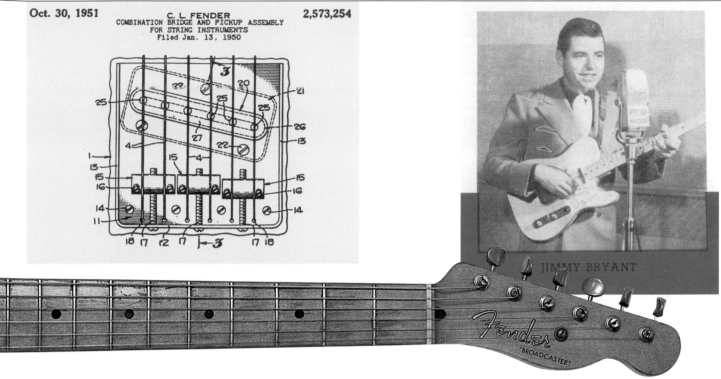

JIMMY BRYANT

■ The Fender Broadcaster (main guitar) was the shortlived production model of Fender's newly designed solidbody electric 'Spanish' guitar. An important early player of the Broadcaster was country wiz Jimmy Bryant (above right). Leo and his team took the best ideas from existing lap steels, including that angled pickup at the bridge position, based on the unit in the company's Champion steel guitar (patent drawing filed January 1950, above left). The 'Spanish' term means that it wasn't a lap steel, a distinction that had to be made at the time to distinguish them from the popular lap steel types. Fender's main business at the start of the 1950s was still in lap steel guitars and small amplifiers, as seen on the catalogue cover and inside page (below). This 1950 Fender Catalogue No.2 includes inside the first appearance (below, centre) of the new solidbody, in early Esquire guise.

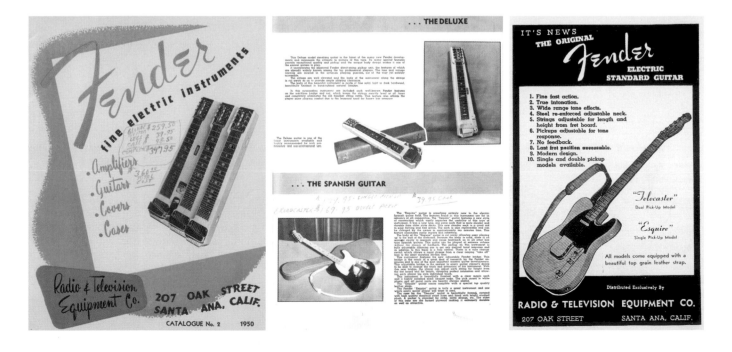

advised Fender of the infringement. "We have checked this and are inclined to agree that they are fair in their request. Consequently, it behooves us to find a new name. ... If any of you have a good name in mind I would welcome hearing from you immediately."

At first, Fender simply used up their existing Fender Broadcaster decals on the guitar's headstock by cutting off 'Broadcaster' and leaving just the Fender logo. These no-name guitars are known today as Nocasters.

A few days later, Don Randall coined the new name for the Fender solidbody: Telecaster. (He subsequently came up with virtually all the well-known Fender guitar model names.) The Telecaster name certainly seemed appropriate, fresh from the new age of television. Radio people made broadcasts, so the TV equivalents were telecasts. Leo himself was well aware of the drawing power of the medium, as George Fullerton explained. "When that was brand new, Leo's store was probably the only place in town that had televisions, and he used to have one that he'd put in the window facing out into the street, speaker outside. At night there'd be a crowd of people around watching wrestling or whatever was on. Sometimes it would be cold and foggy, but there'd still be this crowd of people."[26]

The Telecaster name was on headstocks of the two-pickup model by April 1951, and at last Fender's new $189.50 solidbody electric had a permanent name. The proper single-pickup Esquire was also available by now and priced at $149.50. Again, a solid case for either model would add $39.95.

The simple, effective Telecaster had a basic, single-cutaway solid slab of ash for a body and separate screwed-on maple neck. It was designed for mass production. The angled single-coil pickup was mounted into a steel bridge-plate carrying three adjustable bridge saddles – for two strings each – and a further metal-covered pickup sat near the neck. The body was finished in a yellowish semi-transparent colour known as 'blond' and the pickguard was black. The guitar was plain. It was like nothing else and ahead of its time. It fulfilled Leo's aim to have a standard guitar that was easy to build and, as such, underlined one of the reasons for Fender's coming success. It was a relatively simple, unadorned guitar that served a practical purpose: it did exactly what the player wanted as soon as he plugged it into an amp.

One of the earliest players to appreciate the new Fender sound was Jimmy Bryant, best known among fellow musicians for his remarkable guitar instrumental duets with pedal-steel virtuoso (and Fender player) Speedy West. Bryant was also a busy Los Angeles session player and a regular on Cliffie Stone's country TV showcase, *Hometown Jamboree*. (For a sample of his work, try 'Bryant's Bounce' from 1952 by Speedy West & Jimmy Bryant, or Tennessee Ernie Ford's 1953 'Catfish Boogie', or even the 1952 cut 'Oakie Boogie' by Ella Mae Morse, each a glimpse at Bryant's clean, clever, and sometimes wild playing that ever since has had us all wondering quite how he did it.)

Leo and George Fullerton had taken an early Broadcaster out to the Riverside Rancho, a western-music nightclub in Glendale, California, where Bryant was playing. He took a look at the strange new instrument, picked it up, and started playing.

Fullerton remembered: "He got to do a lot of neat things on this guitar, and pretty soon all these people who'd been dancing were crowding around listening to what he was doing. It wasn't long before the whole band was standing around too. He was the centre of attention. Jimmy played things on guitar that nobody could play. And of course this was an electric with low action – and with that cutaway he could go right up the neck.

"So naturally we put one in his hand, and this was like starting a prairie fire. Pretty soon we couldn't make enough of those guitars. That wasn't the only reason, but it was a lot of it, because Jimmy was on television shows, personal appearances, and everybody wanted a guitar like Jimmy Bryant's. That was one of the starting points of that guitar."[27]

Bryant died in 1980, but his son John remembered an important event in early Fender history. "The Roy Rogers movie *In Old Amarillo* shows my dad playing the first guitar that Leo gave him. It was filmed in early '51. Leo was on the set that day, off camera, and he was very happy his new guitar was going to be shown in a Roy Rogers movie."[28] This 1951 movie must mark one of the earliest (if fleeting) celluloid appearances of a Fender solidbody.

COWBOY DREAMS

George Fullerton said that Fender guitars were aimed at the working musician. "Think of a movie cowboy and you might remember Roy Rogers, Gene Autry: the big silver screen, and here they are in their fancy hats and shirts and boots and their shiny gold-plated guns. But did you ever see a real working cowboy? He's dirty and got rough boots on and heavy leather on his pants. So we kind of looked at the guitar players as being working cowboys. If you're gonna go out on stage and it's a personal appearance and you're a top-notch entertainer, well, you might want a flashy guitar and flashy clothing. But you're not a working musician, and that's not your dress code. See, this Telecaster was so popular – still is right today – and it's part of the dress code of the musician. Take that out of their hands and put something else there and you're taking off part of their dress, part of their appearance. It's like taking Roy Rogers and not putting the hat on him."[29]

Fender launched another very important instrument in 1951, the Precision Bass – the first commercially successful solidbody electric bass guitar. (This was the exception to Randall naming the instruments; 'Precision' was Leo's idea.) The P-Bass too was typical of Fender's early products, with an elegant simplicity and geared to easy, piece-together construction.

Leo would always opt for function over looks. "I had so many years of experience

■ Broadcaster player Jimmy Bryant was almost certainly the first musician to appear on film playing a Fender guitar. He was a phenomenal, untamed player, heard to best effect on record when teamed with (Fender-playing) pedal steel man Speedy West. Bryant appeared in the corny 1951 Roy Rogers Western movie *In Old Amarillo* (poster top left), playing his Fender solidbody in the band (above) at a local funfair as various unlikely plot devices unfurl around Pepita Martinez in the foreground. Leo Fender was on set for the day of the filming and must have been a proud man.

▼ **1951 NOCASTER**

■ When Gretsch pointed out their prior use of Broadcaster – actually Broadkaster, and on drums – Fender decided to change the name of their new guitar. In the interim they simply snipped the model name from the existing headstock decals, resulting in what are known today as Nocasters (main guitar).

TURN ON THE TELE

◀ 1953 TELECASTER

■ The new name for the Fender solidbody was, of course, Telecaster, and here's a gorgeous 1953 example (right) to drool over. It's typical of the earliest style of Tele, with black five-screw pickguard. The Spaniels (above) hit big with their doo-wop pop in the 1950s, notably the memorable 'Goodnite Sweetheart Goodnite' in 1954, and decided a Tele was a good reward for all that success.

with work on radios and electronic gear," he said, "and my main interest was in the utility aspects of an item – that was the main thing. Appearance came next. That gets turned around sometimes."[30] His second wife, Phyllis, who would live with him for the last 11 years of his life, said: "Leo would sit in his room for hours playing with his cameras, and then he'd go outside and take pictures of trash cans. I'd say honey, why are you taking pictures of these? 'Oh, I was just trying out these lenses and filters.' So why not take a picture of a tree? 'They were just something to photograph,' he'd tell me. 'They were near the back door and I didn't have to go far.' Convenient, you know?"[31]

Business began to pick up as news of the Telecaster spread and as Randall's five Radio-Tel salesmen – Art Bates, Mike Cole, Dave Driver, Charlie Hayes, and Don Patton – began to persuade store owners to stock the company's new solidbody instruments. Early in 1953, Fender's existing sales set-up with Radio-Tel was re-organised into a new distribution company, Fender Sales, which was operational by June. Based like Radio-Tel in Santa Ana, Fender Sales had four business partners: Leo, Don Randall, Francis Hall, and Charlie Hayes (the latter three coming from Radio-Tel).

In fact, this marked the start of a power shift away from Hall. Hayes, who had been Radio-Tel's first salesman, was killed in a road accident in June 1955. Dale Hyatt took over his sales patch. Late in '53, Hall had effectively sealed his own fate by buying the Rickenbacker guitar company – a potential competitor. So in 1955 Fender Sales changed to a partnership between Leo and Randall. Randall actually ran this pivotal part of the Fender business. As Hyatt said, "You can make the finest guitar in the world, but if you don't sell the first one you're not going to get the chance to make another."[32]

Despite the exciting new developments with the solidbody guitar and bass, during the early 1950s Fender's main business remained in amplifiers and electric steel guitars. They were vitally important to the reorganised Fender operation, and the lines were rapidly expanded. Fender's single-neck steels before 1950 included the Organ Button – an odd name derived from a switchable muted 'organ'-tone effect – plus the cheap Princeton with hardwired cord, the long-lived Deluxe, which survived in various guises until 1980, and the Champion. The latter was renamed Student in 1952 as a come-on to the booming guitar-teaching 'studios' of the time that Randall recognised as a ready-made market (and of which more later).

Fender had made multi-neck steel guitars from the earliest days: the two-neck Dual 8 Professional, for example, was launched in 1946, and the triple-neck Custom followed three years later. They provided players with the means to change quickly between tunings, although the pedal-steel guitar would soon dispose of this rather unwieldy arrangement.

Western swing was a lively dance music that had grown up in Texas dancehalls during the 1930s and '40s, and its guitarists popularised the electric instrument in

America, at first mostly with steel guitars. Many of the genre's steel guitarists played their driving electric runs on Fender models such as the Stringmaster – notably Noel Boggs with Spade Cooley and Leon McAuliffe with Bob Wills. There were also some 'Spanish' guitarists like Telecaster-wielding Bill Carson with Hank Thompson's Brazos Valley Boys, who played a commercial fusion of western swing and honky tonk and had a Number 1 country hit in 1952 with 'The Wild Side Of Life'. Spade Cooley's guitarist Jimmy Wyble was pictured with an Esquire in an early Fender ad.

Another important addition at Fender came in 1953 when steel guitarist Freddie Tavares joined the California guitar maker, mainly to help Leo design new products. Tavares was best known for his swooping steel intro over the titles of the *Looney Tunes* cartoons. One interviewer typically came away from the factory remembering Tavares as a "big, friendly, native-born Hawaiian", while a co-worker described Tavares as "one of the best musicians I have ever known, and just as good at engineering. A very talented man".[33]

In June 1953 Fender acquired a three-and-a-half-acre plot at South Raymond Avenue and Valencia Drive in Fullerton with three new buildings. Fullerton's City Council was on a programme of rapid and significant industrial development. "Prior to 1950," reported the *Los Angeles Times*, "Fullerton was a citrus area with its industries primarily devoted to citrus products and food processing." The paper quoted a Fullerton official on the moves being made in the new decade. "Everyone liked the peaceful area geared to country living. But some began to realise that industry was needed to balance the economy as more and more people came in. Now there's almost 100 percent support for [the changes]."[34]

Clearly, the new Fender buildings in the heart of Fullerton's development area indicated that expansion of the firm's products was imminent. As well as the two electric guitars – the Telecaster and Esquire – Fender had a line of seven amplifiers (Bandmaster, Bassman, Champ, Deluxe, Princeton, Super, Twin Amp), five electric steel guitars (Custom, Deluxe, Dual, Stringmaster, Student), and the Precision Bass. But the company wanted to produce even more. *The Music Trades* magazine reported that with the new property Fender "hoped that production will be upped by almost 100 percent in the next few months".[35] First, however, their rather haphazard production methods had to be organised more efficiently.

This job fell into the very capable hands of another newcomer, Forrest White. He had worked as an industrial engineer at an aircraft firm in Akron, Ohio, but during a business trip to Los Angeles in 1944 he'd fallen in love with the area and decided to move there as soon as he could practically do so. He had built several guitars in his spare time, including an early solidbody electric ("way before Leo did," he claimed later).

White's opportunity to move out west came in 1951 when he was hired by a Los Angeles company. He'd already met Leo a few times, and in spring 1954 they had

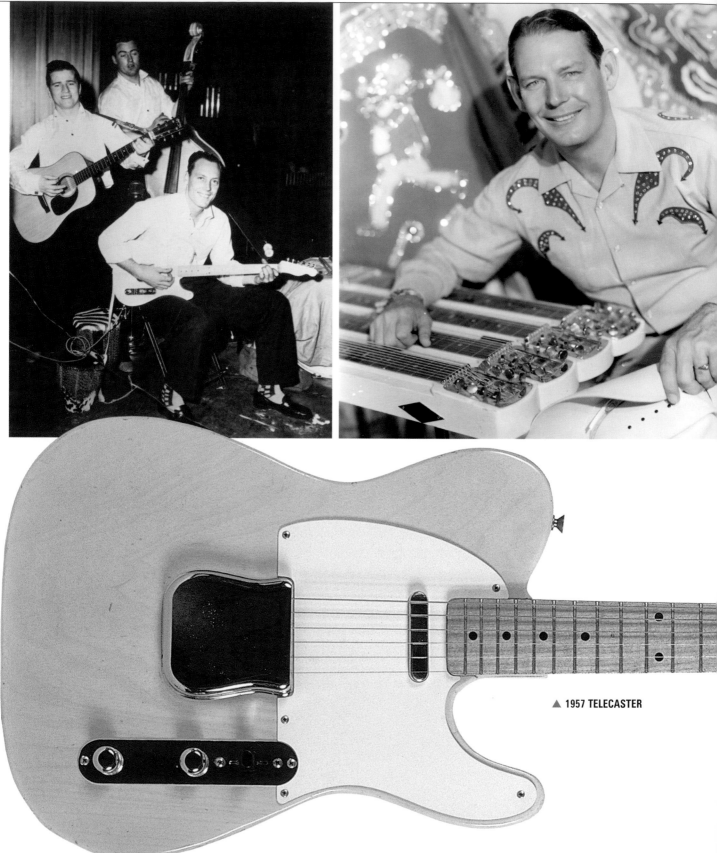

▲ 1957 TELECASTER

By the mid 1950s, new Esquires and Telecasters had a fresh look as the Fender solidbody instruments began to change from black to white pickguards and came with a paler, less yellow finish to the body. Fenders were beginning to attract the attention of up and coming R&B and rock'n'roll musicians in the States. Clarence 'Gatemouth' Brown (above) played an attractive Texan mix of R&B and western swing on his old black-'guard Tele and clearly had access to a natty tailor. Paul Burlison let rip during the 1950s in The Rock 'N Roll Trio (opposite page, top left), discovering an angrier voice for his white-'guard Tele with the aid of a distorted amplifier, best heard on the Trio's classic 'The Train Kept A-Rollin'', which was later covered by The Yardbirds. Meanwhile, Fender ensured their loyal western swing and country customers were supplied with new lap steel guitars. Leon McAuliffe (opposite, top right) had joined Bob Wills' Texas Playboys at age 18 and played a splendid four-neck Fender steel.

lunch. Leo asked White if he'd be interested in helping him sort out some "management problems" at Fender. White remembered their conversation. "Freddie Tavares had told Leo that the company was ready to go down the drain, it was that bad. Leo had no credit whatsoever and had to pay cash buying any material and so on. Some of the employees' cheques were bouncing. Freddie had said that Leo didn't have anyone in the plant who could do what needed to be done. So it just so happened that my timing was right."[36]

Karl Olmsted of Race & Olmsted, Fender's tool-and-die maker, recalled how close Fender came to going broke at the time. "He tried to buy us with stock, to get out of paying our bills, and like idiots we didn't take the bait," Olmsted said with hindsight. "But actually I'm not sorry that I didn't, because I'm not sure that I could have worked for Leo day in, day out. At least we had the advantage of occasionally being able to say, 'Leo, this is all we can take,' and stepping back. As good as the relationship was, once in a while you had to do that – and I couldn't if they'd taken us over. We just gave him credit and credit and credit – practically to the point where we couldn't make our payroll and bills and everything else. If this guitar craze hadn't taken off, he wouldn't have made it. So genius has to have some luck – and he had genius *and* luck."[37]

Meanwhile, Leo took an intrigued Forrest White to look at Fender's set-up at the new South Raymond buildings. "And it was a mess," White recalled. "There was no planning whatsoever, because Leo was not an engineer, he was an accountant. Things had just been set down any place. Man, everything was just so mixed up, you can't believe it. There was no planning whatsoever, because in all fairness to him he didn't have any experience in things like that."

So White agreed to come in and work for Leo, beginning in May 1954. "But I said it depends on one thing. If I can have a free hand to do what I know has to be done, fine. Otherwise I'm not interested. He gave me that free hand. When I stepped in, from that point on I ran the factory. He stayed in design, but I ran it."

One of the most important aspects of production that White sorted out was an incentive scheme tied to quality control, where assemblers on the production line did not accept a product from the previous stage unless they were happy that it was perfect – effectively making each operator an inspector. "The reason for that," White explained, "was that if something had to be re-worked, it was on their own time. If someone loused up, hey – once they accepted it, then it's their problem. But as long as they turned out good production that passed, they made good money, darned good money."[38]

Now Leo had able men – Forrest White and Don Randall – poised at the head of the production and sales halves of the Fender company. He had a new factory and a small but growing reputation. And he had the start of a fresh generation of guitars – the solidbody Telecaster, Esquire, and Precision Bass – with Freddie Tavares ready to help him design new ones.

Leo being Leo, he was not content to stay still. Soon, he and the team and their musical quinea piqs were working on a new guitar – the one that would be released in 1954 as the Stratocaster. George Fullerton remembered that planning for it had begun before the move to South Raymond in summer '53, and others recalled Leo and Freddie Tavares making the original sketches of the instrument around that time. Leo seems to have viewed the Tele and the Strat not as individual instruments but as a sort of single work in progress, a developmental whole. He thought that the new, improved model would necessarily replace the Telecaster. Not quite, Leo.

Don Randall was typically unsentimental in his recollection of the birth. "You know, the Esquire and Telecaster are pretty ugly guitars when it comes right down to it. In the days of Gibsons and others with bound necks and purfling, they were plain vanilla. But we thought they were beautiful because we were making money with them."[39]

This pressure from the sales arm of Fender makes sense now when you look back at what was going on at the time. We've already seen how other makers at first mocked Fender's unique solidbody guitars. But soon Gibson had joined in with their Les Paul, Gretsch with the Duo Jet, Kay with a K-125 model. Harmony had a new electric solidbody model, too, and they called it the Stratotone – a name that someone at Fender must have noticed. Competition was building. "We needed a fancier guitar, an upgrade guitar," said Randall.[40]

Leo and Freddie Tavares, meanwhile, were listening hard to players' comments about the "plain vanilla" Tele and Esquire. Some were complaining that the hard edge of the Telecaster's body was uncomfortable, so the team tried shaping parts of it with gentle contours. Among the dissenting voices was Western Swing guitarist Bill Carson. He'd moved to California in 1951 and sought out Leo Fender – Carson had tried a Broadcaster, loved its feel, and wanted one. He was given a Telecaster and amp and, as he didn't have enough to buy them outright, agreed to pay $18 a month and act as a musical guinea-pig for new products.

Carson gradually came to the conclusion that he wanted something more than his Telecaster. In later years, with the benefit of hindsight, he described his early-1950s dream guitar as follows: "Six bridges that would adjust vertically and horizontally, four pickups, the guitar should fit like a good shirt, with body contours, and stay balanced at all times, have a Bigsby-style headstock, and a vibrato that would not only come back to exact string pitch after use but that would sharp or flat half a tone at least and hold the chord." Not far from what became the Stratocaster, in other words. "And according to Leo," said Carson, who died in 2007, "that was tough to do."[41]

Someone else who helped with user feedback was musician and entertainer Rex Gallion. George Fullerton described Gallion as "a big man who complained that his guitar used to cut into his body a lot. He worked the Las Vegas, Reno, and Lake Tahoe circuit, but occasionally was in the Los Angeles area. He always tried to spend time at the factory, talking about new ideas and improving some things".[42]

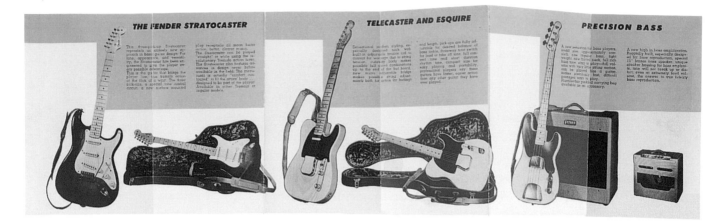

THE FENDER STRATOCASTER   TELECASTER AND ESQUIRE   PRECISION BASS

■ Fender's catalogues and ads were still relatively conventional in the mid 1950s. This example (above), which marks the first inclusion in a promo flyer of the brand new Stratocaster guitar, illustrates the functional nature of the Fender literature at the time, with the company's striking and stylish material still a few years down the line.

THUMBS CARLLILE

BUDDY MERRILL

ALVINO REY

■ Early Fender catalogues may still have been functional, but already the idea of featuring well-known players was underway. The notion of a name guitarist prompting potential owners to grab a particular maker's instruments was not new, but Fender quickly saw the advantages. Here (above) are three Strat endorsers from the 1950s, Thumbs Carllile, Buddy Merrill, and Alvino Rey – players then fairly well known but today almost forgotten.

▲ 1954 STRATOCASTER #0001, CUSTOM FINISH

▲ 1954 STRATOCASTER

■ The flowing curves of the standard sunburst Stratocaster (main guitar) and its beautifully proportioned body are stunning enough today. When they first appeared in 1954, like this first-year instrument, it must have seemed as if an alien spacecraft had just made a special delivery. Guitar design would never be quite the same again. The famous Strat pictured above is part of the impressive collection of David Gilmour. It has a non-standard colour finish, gold-plated hardware, and an anodised metal pickguard. It also bears serial number 0001 but is unlikely to be the first ever made, since its neck date of June 1954 places it alongside other Strats from the earliest months of tentative production.

The Stratocaster was eventually launched during 1954. Fender probably made some samples early in the year, and then, following the first ads for the guitar in April and May, some sporadic production began around May, June, and July. (Dave Gilmour's famous 0001-serial Strat has a neck dated June.) Randall said in a letter to dealers that "shipments are expected to begin May 15th". Forrest White said the first proper production run was in October, for 100 Stratocasters, filling an order from Fender Sales dated October 13th.

Once again Randall named the new model, and he said later that his inspiration was the dawning space age and the lure of the stratosphere. As a keen pilot, he'd probably noticed that America's brand new B-52 bomber was called the Stratofortress, and it was around this time that Pontiac launched their sleek Strato-Streak car. Randall had almost certainly seen Harmony's new-for-1953 Stratotone electric guitar, too.

The Fender Stratocaster looked like no other guitar of the time. Carson's four pickups didn't quite make it, but the new Fender was the first solidbody electric with three. Freddie Tavares said later: "Leo would say ... let's put in three pickups. Two is good, but three will kill them!"[43]

The three identical pickups each had six individual polepieces, staggered in height to compensate for string volume. The bridge pickup was angled like the Tele's; overall there were more tones and an even greater dose of top end for those who wanted it. The guitar's three knobs controlled overall volume, neck pickup tone, and middle pickup tone, and the three-way switch selected each pickup individually. (Players soon discovered it was possible to lodge the switch between settings to give neck-and-middle and bridge-and-middle combinations for further tone qualities.)

The Strat featured a newly-designed built-in vibrato unit, erroneously called a 'tremolo' by Fender and many others since. The Synchronized Tremolo provided the player with pitch-bending and shimmering chordal effects. It was "Leo's pride and joy," said Randall, but it provided the Fender team with a series of headaches during its development. The first version of the vibrato was completely scrapped. George Fullerton said: "When the first one came off the line I grabbed it, but it was terrible – it sounded terrible, tinny, and wouldn't sustain sound. So I rushed down to the lab, where it was all set up for production, and I said, 'Leo, we've got to stop this.' Well, that whole thing was thrown out, all the parts, all the tooling, many, many thousands of dollars worth." Leo put the damage at $5,000. "It had to be redesigned," said Fullerton, "not only to sustain notes but to give a solid sound."[44]

The result of all this work was the world's first self-contained vibrato unit, for which Leo applied for a patent at the end of August 1954. It consisted of an adjustable bridge, a tailpiece, and a vibrato system – all in one. Not a simple mechanism for the time, but a reasonably effective one. It followed the Fender principle of taking an existing product (in this case the Bigsby vibrato) and improving it.

The unit is fixed to the top of the body by six screws (in front of the saddles) on which it pivots. From the base of the bridge comes a long 'inertia block' or 'sustain block' that goes through a hole in the body to a cavity in the rear. The strings travel through the base of the bridge and into the block, and are anchored at its base, visible in that rear cavity. The tension of the strings is balanced by up to five springs fixed to the block in the cavity. Adjusting the number of springs and their fixing point allows the player to fine-tune the feel and efficiency of the vibrato system. It's an ingenious device.

NOW WITH INTONATION

The new Strat vibrato's six bridge-pieces, or saddles, could be adjusted for height and length, which meant that the feel of the strings could be personalised and the guitar brought more closely in tune with itself. Bill Carson again claimed importance in bringing the idea of separate saddles to Fender's attention. "I was having trouble with the Telecaster, because I was playing several hours each weekend on record sessions and in clubs, and the intonation for recording was a real problem. As you know, the Tele has three sets of two strings each going over a common bridge, so you just cannot intonate it. You couldn't then and you can't now.

"I sawed each of my Tele's three bridges in two and made me six bridges, and pretty clumsily propped up each half section with a striker-strip section from a bookmatch packet – I had that little sandpaper grit on there and it helped to hold it in place. That way I could intonate the instrument and play in tune. A lot of the recordings that were done in those days were with big-band arrangements where the guitar player would probably be playing a part with a reed or brass section, and if you couldn't play in tune, the producer wouldn't call you back for other record dates. So you'd lose money if you couldn't do that."[45]

Fender's Strat wasn't the first to attempt a six-way bridge with string-length adjustment: Gretsch's Melita had appeared around 1952 and Gibson's Tune-o-Matic a little later. But the Strat's bridge offered height as well as length adjustment for each string. All in all, it was a master-stroke, a brilliant example of Leo's ability to think through an idea and, with the help of his team and guinea-pigs, to make it work practically and musically.

As an object, the Stratocaster was the embodiment of tailfin-flash '50s American design. Just imagine the impact this gorgeous object must have had at the time! That radically sleek, solid ash body (later alder) was based on the outline of the company's earlier Precision Bass. It was contoured for the player's comfort and finished in a yellow-to-black sunburst finish. Even the jack mounting was new, recessed in a stylish plate on the body face. Bill Carson said it was George Fullerton who suggested this practical new idea.

The neck followed Fender's bolt-on principle, but the headstock was new. Or was

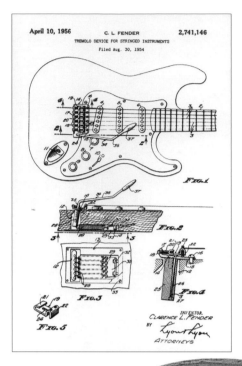

■ Paul Bigsby is best known today as the inventor of a basic but effective vibrato system, but back in the 1940s and '50s he also built guitars on a limited custom-made basis. He made steel guitars and some early solidbody electrics, including one for Merle Travis (main guitar), which some say influenced Fender. The few musicians who played Bigsby 'Spanish' electrics loved the necks in particular, and some added them to other guitars, including Travis himself (with Bigsby-necked Martin, left).

■ The stylishness of the Stratocaster soon became a mark in its favour beyond the more important attributes of playability and musicality. The vibrato patent (opposite) underlines the thought that went into each and every detail, while this later ad (right) placed the Strat in its peak iconic period of Americana. The entire collection here, from guitar to shoes to clothes – and probably that mailbox too – are a modern eBayers' dream.

You won't part with yours either*

Wherever you go, you'll find Fender!

For your personal selection see the complete line of Fender Fine Electric Instruments (like the popular "Stratocaster" guitar shown above) on display at leading music dealers throughout the world.

Fender
SALES, INC

SANTA ANA, CALIFORNIA

▼ 1948 BIGSBY MERLE TRAVIS

■ Paul Bigsby made this early solidbody for Merle Travis in 1948, about 15 miles from Fender's HQ. Many since have pointed to that headstock shape and say it influenced the Strat head (and perhaps even more the later Jazzmaster). But as we'll find on the next picture spread (see page 39) there were earlier precedents that both makers may have drawn upon. All great artists borrow and adapt, as you'll know if you've ever written a song. So why not guitar-makers too? The jury is out.

it? Considered alongside Paul Bigsby's 1948 solid through-neck guitar made for Merle Travis, you'd be inclined to say there was some influence from the earlier instrument. Yet both Bigsby and Fender could have been influenced by the headstock shape of 19th-century acoustic guitars by Martin and others, which in turn derived from a German design. Leo himself said he saw a touring Croatian group with instruments (probably tamburitsas) with that head design and that he'd spotted an ancient African instrument in a New York museum with the same style of head. It must have seemed safer to credit these distant people than a potentially litigious alive-and-well Orange County resident.

Influences aside, the Fender Stratocaster was a stunner. It looked and played like no other guitar around – and in some ways seemed to owe more to contemporary automobile design than traditional guitar forms, especially in the flowing, sensual curves of that beautifully proportioned and timeless body. The Strat's pickguard complemented the body lines perfectly, and the overall impression was of a guitar where all the components ideally suited one another.

It's no surprise that the Strat is still thriving today, well over 50 years since its birth in the Fender company's functional buildings in Fullerton, California. The supreme Fender Stratocaster has become the most popular, the most copied, the most desired, and very probably the most played solid electric guitar ever. On its 40th anniversary in 1994 an official Fender estimate put Stratocaster sales so far at between a million and a million-and-a-half guitars. By the late 2000s it had climbed to well over two million. But we can still only play one at a time.

In the beginning, however, during the mid 1950s, the Strat wasn't a world-beater. Only later in rock'n'roll would it find its true home. Fender historian Richard Smith has calculated that during 1954 and '55 Fender sold 720 Strats but 1,027 Teles and Esquires. As we'll see, those proportions would fluctuate during the coming years.

Salesman Dale Hyatt: "Let me tell you, the dealers didn't just grab the Stratocaster, they didn't take 'em away from you. The vibrato system was something that was very difficult for most of them to get used to. They said, 'It'll never work. Who needs it? You can bend the neck to do this kind of thing.' But it caught on, nevertheless. It forced the musician to create a brand new wave of sound, a different style of playing."

The Strat did indeed become famous later in the 1950s in the hands of players such as Buddy Holly, Carl Perkins, and Buddy Guy. "After rock'n'roll started," said Hyatt, "of course all the dealers who had been so hesitant began teaching the electric Spanish guitar."[46]

Fender priced the new guitar at $249.50 (or $229.50 without vibrato; both plus $39.50 for a case). This put the Strat above the $199.50 Precision Bass, the $189.50 Telecaster, and the $149.50 Esquire. All the innovation did not come cheap: that $249.50 for a Strat in 1954 would have the same buying power as $1,900 of today's money.

With the Stratocaster joining the Telecaster and Esquire in the line, Forrest White said that the manufacturing process for electric guitars remained simple and effective at Fender. "We bought our lumber in long lengths, 18 or 20 feet, ash or alder, depending on what we were making. You'd cut the wood and glue it together so you'd have a block of wood that was the size of a guitar body."

To continue the process, White said they used router plates made from quarter-inch steel in the required body outline. "You'd attach one to the bottom with a couple of screws, and you could drill on that side, where the neck plate and everything went. On the other side went the plate where the pickups and everything ran. So you always had a minimum of two plates, sometimes three depending on how sophisticated the instrument was – some might have more cut-outs and so on. You'd screw those on, trace around them, bandsaw the body roughly to shape, then take off the excess on the router, and on it would go for sanding."

White next described how Fender made necks. "For ovalling [shaping] you had a couple of holders swinging back and forth, and then there was a mandrel that had the holes cut out for the frets. Leo designed almost all of the tooling himself. It was very simple, but it was a case of having to walk before you ran. We didn't have any computerised routers and so on like they have now, where they can cut out many necks at a time. It was one at a time back then, and everything was simple. Crude, really, but it got the job done."[47]

There were further crude machines throughout Fender's buildings. Some were for winding pickups – ramshackle affairs with wheels and pulleys – while in another area a few informal finish-spray booths stood alongside a wall of racks for drying sprayed bodies. There were punch presses for making metal parts and benches for final assembly. One worker would screw on pickguards and pickups and tuners; another would take over and solder the electronics together. Finally, new guitars would be strung up and tested through a handy amplifier lifted from the line.

Musical instrument stores at the time found a clever way of increasing their sales of guitars and many other musical instruments by running a school or 'studio', usually on the same premises after-hours, offering lessons to would-be players. These schools were well situated to sell a start-up instrument to the beginner – and equally attentive when the new musician felt his or her skills demanded a better and more expensive instrument with which to show off this new-found talent.

Fender were as aware of these marketing tactics as any go-ahead American instrument manufacturer and sales outfit of the 1950s. So in 1956 the company introduced a pair of new 'student' electrics. The guitars had a 22.5-inch scale-length as opposed to Fender's customary 25.5-inch scale, and the 'three-quarter size' one-pickup Musicmaster and two-pickup Duo-Sonic were described in the company's literature as being "ideal for students and adults with small hands".

They were clearly designed for players on a tight budget, ideal for those starting

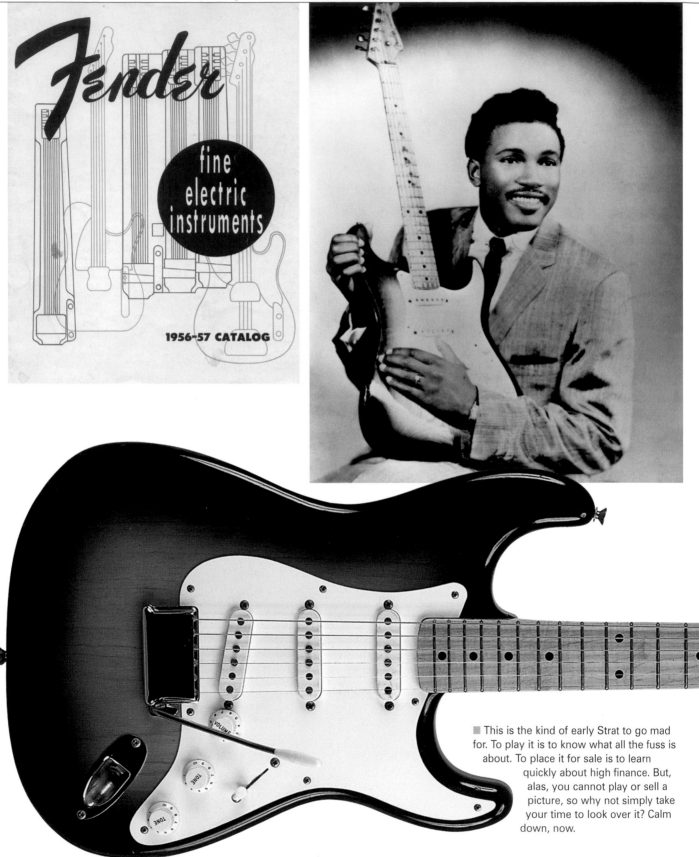

Fender

fine electric instruments

1956-57 CATALOG

■ This is the kind of early Strat to go mad for. To play it is to know what all the fuss is about. To place it for sale is to learn quickly about high finance. But, alas, you cannot play or sell a picture, so why not simply take your time to look over it? Calm down, now.

◄ **1850S MARTIN**

▲ **1957 STRATOCASTER**

■ As the 1950s progressed Fender's fortunes improved (1956/57 catalogue opposite) and the Stratocaster began to reach the hands of some talented players, not least a cadre of key bluesmen. Pictured here are two great Strat-playing Chicago blues heroes: Otis Rush (opposite) and Buddy Guy (above).

■ Remember about the supposed influence of Bigsby's headstock shape on Fender? Maybe both Bigsby and Fender saw the headstock shape of 19th-century acoustic guitars by Martin (above) and others, which in turn derived from a German design, mainly by a guy named Stauffer. Leo said he saw a touring Croatian group with instruments (probably tamburitsas) with a similar head design and that he'd spotted an ancient African instrument in a New York museum with the same style of head.

out on electric guitar who flocked to the retailers' schools. The two guitars certainly looked cheaper than Fender's Strat, Tele, and Esquire – and indeed they sat at the bottom of the pricelist. In February 1957, the Strat with vibrato listed at $274.50, the Tele was $199.50, Esquire $164.50, Duo-Sonic $149.50, and Musicmaster $119.50.

One apparently attractive feature of the Duo-Sonic and Musicmaster (and a few early Strats) was what Fender called "gold-finished pickguards". These metal 'guards were produced by an oxidation process called anodising. The result provided excellent electrical shielding, meaning less extraneous noise. However, the electrolytic anodised 'skin' wore through quite quickly to the aluminium below as the player strummed and picked, leaving unsightly grey patches, and the idea did not last too much longer.

An unusual solidbody electric Mandolin was also new in the company's catalogue. By now there were over 50 people working at Fender and the factory hummed with constant activity. Work would sometimes spill out into the alleyways, a distinct advantage of the California climate. Leo was almost always inside, and would often burn the midnight oil. His solidbody electrics were proving themselves useful musical tools. Soon it would no longer be a matter of Fender trying to sell the guitars, but of making enough to meet the apparently ever-growing demand. With rock'n'roll around the corner, Fender's place in music history was but a few short years away.

We've already met one notable Tele player, Jimmy Bryant – but for all his untamed dexterity he could hardly be described as a rock'n'roller. Neither could B.B. King, who used a Telecaster around 1950 when he first went out on the road, nor Gatemouth Brown on early-'50s instrumentals such as 'Okie Dokie Stomp'. But the most visible player of the Tele in the late 1950s was James Burton, seen almost every week playing alongside Ricky Nelson on the *Adventures Of Ozzie & Harriet* TV show.

Back in 1953, the 13-year-old James had persuaded his parents to buy him a brand new Telecaster that he'd spied in a local store. He's been a top Tele man ever since and became a prime influence on many other key players. Burton may well have had the first Telecaster-fuelled Top 40 hit when his guitar lick turned into Dale Hawkins's raw 'Suzie Q', a song that crashed into the chart in July 1957, bursting with Burton's earthy playing. At the end of that year came the offer to join Ricky Nelson on the TV show. Burton, already a busy session player in Los Angeles, played rhythm guitar on his first Nelson sessions; the earliest on which he played lead was 'Believe What You Say'. It was a Number 4 hit for Ricky Nelson in April 1958.

Back at Fender HQ, now a growing and clearly ambitious operation, the team must have looked enviously at the market leader, Gibson, whose list of electric models ran from the Les Paul Junior at $120 right up to a natural-finish Super 400CES at a dizzying $700. It was obvious that some players would buy expensive electrics. The models at the head of the Gibson list were luxurious hollow-bodies, aimed at and played by the top jazz guitarists. Fender decided they would make a solidbody instrument for these well-heeled jazzmen.

So along came the Fender Jazzmaster, launched towards the end of 1958 at $329.50 and clearly the company's top-of-the-line model. Some prototypes have survived that lend a little insight into the design process: one has Fender's regular fretted maple neck of the period, rather than the new rosewood fingerboard that would grace the production model; another had a Strat neck and black-cover pickups.

When the production Jazzmaster appeared in 1958, Fender couldn't resist plugging it as "America's finest electric guitar ... unequaled in performance and design features". Freddie Tavares, as usual responsible for some of the design input, said later: "When we built the Stratocaster we thought that was the world's greatest guitar. Then we said let's make something even better – so we built the Jazzmaster."[48]

Immediately striking to the electric guitarist of 1958 was the Jazzmaster's unusual offset-waist body, which became the subject of one of Fender's growing number of patents. And for the first time on a Fender, the Jazzmaster featured a separate rosewood fingerboard, glued to the customary maple neck and aimed to provide a comfortingly conventional appearance and feel for the jazzers. There was a bigger, even more Bigsby-like headstock, too.

The guitar's floating vibrato system was another new feature, with a tricky 'lock-off' facility designed to prevent tuning problems if a string should break. This vibrato was quite different from the earlier Strat unit, with a separate tailpiece and bridge, and did not succeed nearly as well, proving a difficult and sometimes buzzy beast.

The Jazzmaster had a couple of large, flat pickups, unlike any of Fender's others and with a smooth, thick sound, still quite cutting at the bridge but suitably jazzy at the neck. Fender's Don Randall recalled a major criticism of the Jazzmaster. "It never met with very much favour because those big, wide pickups were not shielded, so you'd come on stage among all the wires and cables and pick up too much hum and noise from the lights, static, and all."[49]

The pickguard was at first one of the anodised gold-coloured types, but this gave way in 1959 to white or tortoiseshell plastic. The Jazzmaster's controls were certainly elaborate for the time. The good idea was that you could flick the small slide-switch to select between two individual circuits that you'd preset: one for rhythm; the other for lead. But the system was over-complicated for players brought up on straightforward volume and tone controls (in other words, pretty much everyone).

The dual-circuit idea was adapted from a layout that Forrest White had devised back in the 1940s when he built guitars as a hobby. He'd put a switch into his steel guitar to flip between preset rhythm and lead tones. "I saw Alvino Rey at the Paramount Theater in Akron, Ohio, and he had to keep fiddling with his guitar when he wanted to change from rhythm to lead," said White. "I thought well, there's no reason he should have to do that. Later, I said to Leo, 'What you need is a guitar where you can preset the rhythm and lead.'

"Leo didn't play guitar, he couldn't even tune a guitar, so he didn't think this was

▼ **1957 MUSICMASTER**

■ Fender's new 'student' guitars, the Musicmaster (above) and Duo-Sonic (main guitar), first appeared in 1956. They had smaller, lighter bodies than the principal Fenders, shorter necks, and basic appointments. Fender used the term "three-quarter size" in publicity for these new guitars, but only the neck and the resulting scale-length were smaller, designed for younger hands just starting to play. The Musicmaster was the single-pickup version, offered at first in an unexciting beige finish. The guitar pictured has the later sunburst finish but retains the anodised 'gold' pickguard of the original. Despite their cheaper price and vibe, the student models were playable then and now. Fender seemed to have cut the right corners.

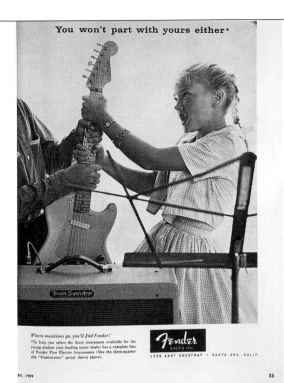

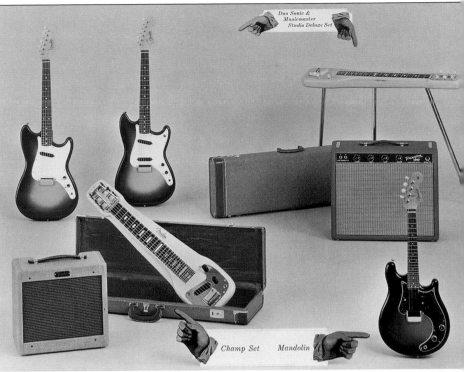

Fender certainly tried new things, even with the Tele and the Strat in place. A bizarre newcomer for 1956 was the electric solidbody Mandolin, pictured (above, far right) in a later catalogue. Fender's advertising was getting better, exemplified by the new series headed 'You Won't Part With Yours Either' (left, Musicmaster ad).

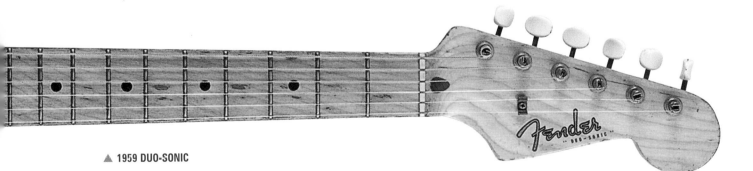

▲ 1959 DUO-SONIC

The second of the two new 'student' electrics was the Duo-Sonic, which was in effect a Musicmaster with an extra pickup added at the bridge position. This model too had the cheaper vibe of the Musicmaster as well as the shorter scale, which reduces string tension and so makes it easier for new players to fret notes.

important. Rey came in the plant one day, and I said, 'How would you like not to have to mess around with the controls, just flip a switch?' He says, can that be done? I says, well sure, I already did it. So Leo brought the Jazzmaster out, and that guitar was the first where you could switch between rhythm and lead."[50]

JAZZMASTER: THE MISSING JAZZ

The sound of the Jazzmaster was generally richer and warmer than players were used to from Fender. "Leo was trying to get more of a jazz sound than the high, piercing Telecaster sound," explained White. The new model certainly marked a change for the company and an effort to extend the scope and appeal of their guitar line. Ironically, this has been partly responsible for the Jazzmaster being less popular than the Strat and Tele, mainly because many of us aren't struck by the model's sounds and playability.

Despite the model's name and apparent intention, jazz guitarists found little appeal in this new, rather awkward solidbody guitar, and mainstream Fender fans largely stayed with their Strats and Teles. Bob Bogle in The Ventures played a Jazzmaster for a while in the early 1960s, and a few surfers, including The Surfaris of 'Wipe Out' fame, seemed to like the guitar's ability to switch from snap to smooth with the presets. Accomplished American instrumentalist Roy Lanham favoured a Jazzmaster for a while too. About the only 'real' jazzers who ever tried the new Fender were the esteemed Joe Pass and the lesser-known Eddie Duran, but these too were brief flirtations. Jazzmen kept hold of their hollow-body electrics, and Fender had to come to terms with what seemed like their first dud.

Most of the work on the early Fender publicity and ads had fallen to Don Randall, but during the 1950s they needed help to take the brand to a new level. Advertising in America was becoming a more sophisticated affair, and smart agencies were adept at convincing firms to spend more on slick ads that provided a consistent identity for a set of products.

Fender turned to Bob Perine from the Perine-Jacoby agency of Newport Beach, California, in 1957. He would continue to shape the look of Fender publicity until 1969. Perine, a keen amateur guitarist himself, transformed Fender's image and in the process created some of the most stylish and memorable guitar ads and catalogues ever printed. Some collectors today value prime 'Fender paper' of the 1950s and '60s almost as highly as the instruments themselves.

One of Perine's early tasks was to devise and shoot a series of press ads with a single theme: a Fender product in an unlikely setting, set off with the tag line: "You won't part with yours either." In other words, your Fender guitar or amp is so important to you, you'll take it anywhere. One of the very first appeared in print toward the end of 1957 and showed a gent in a sharp suit on a bus holding on tight to his white-finish white-'guard maple-neck Tele. Many ads followed in the series, along with some bearing the alternative line: "Wherever you go you'll find Fender." Guitars were seen perched on army tanks, erect at the drive-in cinema, in mid-air around a skydiver's neck, strapped to a surfer … in fact, pretty much anywhere. Perine and his team must have had a lot of fun.

The Fender catalogues too suddenly became beautiful objects under the new man's direction. The 1958/59 catalogue was Fender's first with a full-colour front-and-back cover, which opened out to display a luscious panorama of prime gear, including a red Strat with gold hardware and a blond Tele and Esquire, all eyed up by a couple of cool crewcutted chaps. The booklet was a model of clear, simple design. No matter that the pictures of the Tele and Esquire inside were of obsolete black-'guard models: you couldn't help but want everything, whatever the details. One new fact that might have caught the stylish guitarist's eye was a small announcement that instruments were "available in custom color finishes at an additional 5% cost".

Some Fenders were now officially offered in 'custom colors' beyond the regular finishes. This would explain that red Strat proudly displayed on the front of that colourful 1958/59 catalogue. Most Fenders of the 1950s came in a standard finish only: blond for Teles and Esquires, sunburst for Strats and Jazzmasters. Nonetheless a few guitars, specially made at the factory effectively as one-offs, had been finished in solid colours. The rare surviving examples indicate that this practice was underway by 1954, but few players back then seemed interested in slinging on a coloured guitar, and Fender's main production remained in blond and sunburst instruments. A handful of rare '50s Strats were finished in solid colours, but Telecasters hardly at all, although some special-order Teles of the period were finished in sunburst.

The production of these early special-colour guitars was certainly casual. The first sign of a rather more commercial footing had come in the company's sales literature of 1956 when 'player's choice' coloured guitars were noted as an option, at five percent extra cost. In the following year these Du Pont paint finishes were described in Fender's catalogue as Custom Colors (a name that has stuck ever since) and in the pricelist as "custom Du Pont Duco finishes", still at five percent on top of regular prices.

Fender also announced early in 1957 a Strat in see-through blond finish and gold-plated hardware. Randall said the gold plating was his idea. "The White Falcon had come out from Gretsch, and we couldn't be outdone. Wasn't a very good move, actually. It was very hard to keep the gold to stay on. We found ourselves having to apologise and do it over."[51] George Fullerton also recalled the difficulties such luxury caused. "Whatever was on your hands – sweat, dirt, acid, alcohol – had a tendency to eat through the gold-plating pretty fast. Wasn't long before it looked bad. So we didn't feel that was a good advertisement for the musician or the company or anybody else, and we resisted somewhat making gold finish instruments."[52]

That gold-hardware blond Strat was in effect Fender's first official Custom Color

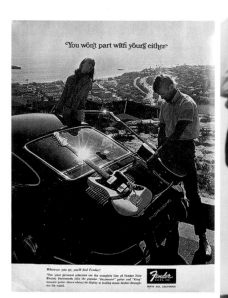

■ First appearing in 1958, the Jazzmaster became Fender's top-of-the-line model. It featured an enlarged headstock design and had a distinctive body with an offset waist, the subject of one of Fender's growing pile of patents. Other 'Fender firsts' on the Jazzmaster included a separate rhythm circuit, floating vibrato unit, and the original appearance of the company's new separate rosewood fingerboard.

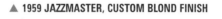

▲ 1959 JAZZMASTER, CUSTOM BLOND FINISH

▲ 1959 JAZZMASTER

■ The Ventures were famous for their early-60s U.S. instro hits 'Perfidia' and 'Walk – Don't Run'. Among guitar fans they may be better known for their use of Mosrite guitars but were keen Fender players too. This promo shot (above left) has them posing with a brace of Jazzmasters and a Precision Bass.

■ As with the Stratocaster, the regular look for Fender's brand new Jazzmaster guitar was sunburst, but some, like the blond example pictured here, came with custom finishes. The 1960 Fender pricelist pitched a sunburst Jazzmaster at $349.50, while a Custom Color, including blond, would set you back $366.97.

■ Fender began a stylish and (for guitar companies) innovative series of ads in the 1950s with a couple of taglines: the better-known "You Won't Part With Yours Either" and also 'Wherever You Go You'll Find Fender". Each pictured a Fender guitar in an unlikely situation, and the three Jazzmaster examples here illustrate the imaginative power of ad exec Bob Perine and his team. That's skydiver Roy Fryman (above, for now) who free-fell 5,000 feet with a Fender over California for the shot. Strap-locks essential.

guitar – although the term has always been more popularly applied since to solid-colour varieties. (This particular scheme on a Strat later became known as the Mary Kaye style, thanks to musician Kaye appearing with a mid-50s blond-body/gold-hardware Strat for a series of photos that ran for some time in Fender publicity material. Kaye never played the guitar: Fender loaned it for the shoot and then took it back.)

Fender eventually came up with a defined list of the officially available Custom Colors, and in the early 1960s, when many more Custom Color Fenders were being made, the company issued colour charts to publicise and help select the various shades. Of the first three charts, the original, in 1961, featured Black, Burgundy Mist Metallic, Dakota Red, Daphne Blue, Fiesta Red, Foam Green, Inca Silver Metallic, Lake Placid Blue Metallic, Olympic White, Shell Pink, Sherwood Green Metallic, Shoreline Gold Metallic, Sonic Blue, and Surf Green.

The second, in 1963, had lost Shell Pink and gained Candy Apple Red Metallic. The third, in 1965, lost Burgundy Mist Metallic, Daphne Blue, Inca Silver Metallic, Sherwood Green Metallic, Shoreline Gold Metallic, and Surf Green, and gained – all Metallics – Blue Ice, Charcoal Frost, Firemist Gold, Firemist Silver, Ocean Turquoise, and Teal Green.

The automobile industry clearly had a profound effect on American guitar manufacturers in the 1950s, not least in this ability to enhance the look of an already stylish object with a rich, sparkling paint job. The Gretsch company in New York had been the first guitar maker to adopt colourful car paints as standard colours for guitar models, creating new-look electric instruments such as the Country Club in Cadillac Green and the Streamliner in Jaguar Tan, both during 1954.

Du Pont was the biggest supplier of paint to the car factories, notably General Motors. Fender used paints from Du Pont's Duco nitro-cellulose lines, such as Fiesta Red or Foam Green, as well as the more colour-retentive Lucite acrylics like Lake Placid Blue Metallic or Burgundy Mist Metallic. Custom Color researcher Clay Harrell has established that the names Fender gave to the colours usually came from the original car makers' terms: Fiesta Red, for example, was first used in 1956 on a Ford Thunderbird, while Lake Placid Blue originally appeared on a 1958 Cadillac Brougham. Candy Apple Red, however, was unusual in that it was a Fender original and not a car colour.

George Fullerton remembered going out to a local paint store around 1957, buying a Fiesta Red mix, and then going back to the factory and applying it to a guitar body. He said this experiment was what started Fender's defined Custom Color line. "That first one became Fiesta Red," recalled Fullerton. "The Du Pont company made that colour and you could buy it right across the counter. That should have been a patent, that colour, but who knows at the time you do a thing? Meanwhile, the sales office and Don Randall laughed at it, said who in hell wants a coloured guitar, specially a red one."[53]

Randall had a different recollection of the genesis of Fender's Custom Color line. "Gretsch had their Country Club which was green, the White Falcon which was white, and there were others. So it was just my idea to diversify and get another product on the market. They didn't sell as well as the traditional sunburst and blond colours."[54]

Whatever the origins of Fender's Custom Colors, decades later the guitars bearing these original Fiesta Reds, Sonic Blues, Burgundy Mists and the like have become prime collectables, and many collectors rate a Custom Color Fender, especially an early one, as an essential catch.

The colours didn't add much to the price, originally. In 1961, for example, a Custom Color would add just $17.47 extra on top of a regular $349.50 Jazzmaster and $14.47 extra to a $289.50 Stratocaster. Telecasters and Esquires were far less often seen in non-standard colours and were rarely listed as such in Fender literature. In today's collector market, the price differential between an original regular guitar and one finished in a genuine Custom Color is of course much greater, despite the prevalence of 're-finished' guitars. These have become so accurate that even alleged experts can be fooled into declaring a fake finish as original. Just how much is a coat of paint worth?

In the late 1950s Fender made a few cosmetic and production adjustments to their electric guitars. As we've seen, the Jazzmaster had been their first with a rosewood fingerboard, and this was adopted for other Fenders around 1959. The company also altered the look of their sunburst finish at the time, adding red to give a yellow-to-red-to-black three-tone effect. Four new factory buildings and a warehouse were added to the South Raymond site in 1958, and by the following year the number of employees topped the 100 mark.

DOUBLE-NECK COPY?

A guitar style that Fender didn't produce at the time was the double-neck. These large instruments, combining two guitars on one big body, were always something of a compromise between convenience and comfort. The idea was relatively new: the first one was custom-made by Paul Bigsby in 1952 (and the concept would have been obvious to him, because he also made pedal-steel guitars, on which multiple necks are common). Gibson followed six years later with their EDS and EMS double-neck models.

In a later interview, Freddie Tavares offered an intriguing postscript on Fender's involvement in the double-neck story. "Guys in groups were always dropping by at the factory and seeing stuff lying on the workbench," he said. "Next thing you know, there would be rumours of some new Fender development. A case in point was my double-neck. I built it purely to test the pickups. It was almost impossible to build two guitars that sound exactly the same. So I built a big one with two necks to compare pickups. Next thing I know, everyone's talking about a new double-neck that Fender are developing. Soon after, competitors of ours were producing them. It was just a useful

▶ **1958 STRATOCASTER, BLOND**

■ More grabby ads were pouring from the Fender promo machine in the latter half of the 1950s, including the trio of tasty Tele teasers here and opposite. About the only place they didn't manage an ad shoot was underwater, but of course that could have encouraged very dangerous activity. Not nearly so bad as taking a Fender on an open-top plane ride. Meanwhile, Custom Color guitars were still relatively rare, although a Strat in this combination (right) of blond body and gold hardware was announced in 1957. It became known as the 'Mary Kaye' after Ms. Kaye appeared in a number of Fender catalogues posing with just such a guitar.

▲ **1963 CUSTOM TELECASTER**

"You won't part with yours either"

Wherever you go, you'll find Fender!
For your personal selection see the complete line of Fender fine electric instruments (like the Telecaster Guitar shown above) on display at leading music dealers throughout the world.

Fender MUSICAL INSTRUMENTS

SANTA ANA, CALIFORNIA

◀ 1960 TELECASTER, FIESTA RED

■ The Custom Telecaster (main guitar) appeared in 1959 alongside a similar Esquire and only differed from the regular model by virtue of the bound-edge body – a deluxe feature then for a Fender. Remarkably, the Tele version lasted in the line until the early 1970s, the Esquire until 1969. Apparently even rarer than coloured-finish Strats and Jazzmasters at the time was a Custom Color Telecaster, and this one (right) is a luscious Fiesta Red piece. Fiesta Red was one of the first Fender colours, and like many of these finishes it was originally devised by Du Pont for car manufacturers. Fiesta Red had first been an option on Ford's 1956 Thunderbird.

idea I came up with and we had no intention of manufacturing them. I had unwittingly started a craze."[55]

The last 'new' Fender electrics of the 1950s were the bound-body Custom versions of the Esquire and Telecaster, launched in 1959 at the NAMM show in New York City. Forrest White acquired some valuable advice on the process of binding from Fred Martin, head of the leading American flat-top acoustic guitar manufacturer Martin. "I said Fred, I'd like to put binding around a Telecaster but I don't know a darned thing about it. He showed me how they cut the binding material, bought in sheets and cut it into strips, and what kind of adhesive to use."[56] The Esquire Custom listed at $194.50 and the Telecaster Custom at $229.50, each $30 more than the regular unbound version.

As Fender entered the 1960s, the company boasted apparently ever-extending lines of products in addition to their electric guitars. By July 1961, the pricelist included 13 amplifiers (Bandmaster, Bassman, Champ, Concert, Deluxe, Harvard, Princeton, Pro Amp, Super, Tremolux, Twin Amp, Vibrasonic, Vibrolux), five steel guitars (Champ, Deluxe, Dual, Stringmaster, Studio Deluxe), two pedal steel guitars (400, 1000), and two bass guitars (Jazz, Precision).

Fender hadn't give up on the idea of a high-end electric. Now they decided to give it another try and introduced a new top-of-the-line model in 1962, the Jaguar. (In sunburst it listed at $379.50; a similar-finish Jazzmaster was by then pegged at $349.50, and a sunburst Strat with vibrato cost $289.50.) Like the Jazzmaster, the Jaguar was an offset-waist multi-control instrument. It had a separate bridge and vibrato unit, but added a spring-loaded 'string mute' at the bridge. Fender rather optimistically believed that players would prefer a mechanical string mute to the natural edge-of-the-hand method. Some did; most did not. Feel-related playing techniques simply cannot be replaced by an on-or-off gadget.

There were a number of notable differences between the Jaguar and Jazzmaster. Visually, the Jag had distinctive chromed control panels, and was the first Fender with 22 frets, not 21 like the rest. Its 24-inch scale-length ("faster, more comfortable" said Fender) was shorter than the Fender standard of 25.5 inches and closer to Gibson's 24.75. It meant an easier playing feel for the Jag compared to other Fenders.

The model was offered from the start in four different neck widths, one a size narrower and two wider than normal (coded A, B, C or D, from narrowest to widest, with 'normal' B the most common). These neck options were also offered from 1962 on the Jazzmaster and Stratocaster.

The Jag's pickups looked much like Strat units but had metal shielding added at the base and sides, probably in response to the criticisms of the Jazzmaster's tendency to noisiness. The controls were yet more complex than the Jazzmaster's, using the same rhythm circuit but adding a trio of lead-circuit switches to select the pickups or a 'strangle' low-end filter.

The company's new model was the first regular electric to carry the new Fender logo on the headstock. Around 1960, Fender's print ads had started to feature a chunky new logo drawn up by Bob Perine, the man responsible for the stylish look of Fender's advertising from the late 1950s to the end of the 1960s. Fender gradually applied the new logo to headstock decals, too. It's since become known to collectors as the transition logo because it leads from the original thin 'spaghetti' style to the bolder black one brought in at the end of the 1960s. In 1965, Fender began to stamp the modernised 'F' of the new logo on to neckplates and, shortly after, on to their new-design tuners.

Like the Jazzmaster, the Jaguar enjoyed a small burst of popularity soon after it was introduced. Carl Wilson of The Beach Boys was one of the most prominent Jaguar players in the 1960s, influencing lesser outfits to pick up a Jag – such as The Trashmen, whose 'Surfin' Bird' was a big US hit. But this new top-of-the-line guitar, "one of the finest solidbody electric guitars that has ever been offered to the public" in Fender's original sales hype, never enjoyed sustained success, and again like the Jazzmaster has been marked down by many players since as a Fender also-ran.

The Jazzmaster and Jaguar could not have been in greater contrast to the still gloriously simple Telecaster and Esquire. And these straightforward guitars were finding a true voice in the hands of similarly uncomplicated yet accomplished musicians. In the Stax studio in Memphis, cool-hand Steve Cropper translated the good ol' Telecaster's simple design into music as his lean lines graced the 1962 Booker T & the MGs hit 'Green Onions'. Cropper popularised a new classic Tele look as he opted for the more recent style of blond body, white 'guard, and rosewood neck.

A new sound emerging in the early 1960s became known as Bakersfield (that was the California city, 100 miles north of Los Angeles, where it started). The key guitarist in this danceable music based on deep, driving electric guitars was Telecaster man Don Rich. He played with Buck Owens & The Buckaroos, first on fiddle and from 1962 on guitar. Listen to his bassy rhythm and chicken-pickin' breaks on Owens hits like 1963's 'Act Naturally' (soon covered by The Beatles, who were big fans of guitar twang). Two of the most famous Telecasters of the time were the sparkle-finish models custom-made for Rich and Owens. Rich died at the age of just 32 in 1974, following a motorcycle accident.

The Strat had its fans too, of course. Guitar-based pop groups were multiplying at a rate that must have satisfied Fender Sales, with instrumental outfits becoming particularly popular. Dick Dale headed one faction when he became known as the 'king of the surf guitar'. Left-hander Dale and his distinctive Strat poured out surging, staccato lines, borrowing scales from his East European heritage, all played on heavy-gauge strings and set adrift in a sea of reverb. His big hit was 1961's 'Let's Go Trippin'' – but surf music wouldn't last much beyond the British invasion a few years later.

Over in Britain itself there was a different king of the Strat. He wore Buddy Holly-

■ Fender's 1958/59 catalogue (right) had the most striking cover yet and was the first in full-colour, impressively designed to represent the complete Fender line. It's also the first to show a Custom Color guitar: that Stratocaster in Fiesta Red with gold hardware, third from the right, just above the groovy guy's head.

▲ SHADOWS' 1959 STRATOCASTER

The Shadows (above) hold a prized new possession in 1959: one of the first Stratocasters (many argue the very first) to go into Britain. At the time, the U.K. was just about to end a decade-long importation ban on American instruments. The Shads and their boss, Cliff Richard, pored over a '58/59 Fender brochure (opposite) and concluded that their hero, U.S. picker James Burton, naturally must play the best guitar on the cover, a Fiesta Red Strat. In fact, he was a confirmed Tele fan. But the oblivious Brits went ahead and ordered their Strat. The group's lead guitarist, bespectacled Hank Marvin, played it proudly on many a Shadows hit. Much debate has ensued since about the colour of the original instrument, with some claiming it was pink, but it certainly looks red in our period shot. The guitar is pictured opposite in its current refinished state.

Wow! Now here's a real beauty: this '58 Strat is in Custom Color finish and has gold-plated hardware. Soon this particular colour would be known officially as Shoreline Gold, but at the time that this instrument came off the line at Fender, the company had still not formally announced its list of colours.

▲ **1958 STRATOCASTER, CUSTOM GOLD FINISH**

style specs and his name was Hank Marvin. Guitarists in the UK had been unable officially to buy any US-made guitars since 1951 when a government ban on importing American merchandise was imposed.

Singer Cliff Richard and his guitarists Hank Marvin and Bruce Welch loved the American records featuring James Burton, and were pretty sure that Burton played a Fender. They wrote to Fender in California for a brochure and drooled over the 58/59 catalogue they received, especially that luscious red Strat with gold hardware and maple neck on the cover. They guessed that Burton himself must play this most luxurious looking Fender, and the generous Mr. Richard ordered one. Only later did they discover that Burton was, of course, a confirmed Telecaster man.

So Hank Marvin found himself early in 1959 playing a red Stratocaster with gold hardware. It may have been the first Strat in the UK; it was certainly the most visible. Hank and his group The Shadows displayed it to thousands of adoring fans as Cliff and the quartet began their rise to fame. The Shads alone scored a string of instrumental Number 1 hits in Britain between 1960 and '63 – 'Apache', 'Kon-Tiki', 'Wonderful Land', 'Dance On', 'Foot Tapper' – and Marvin's clean, spare Strat is at the heart of them all. (During 1959, the import ban was lifted, and once again US guitars could be legally sold in Britain.)

MUSTANG SAVVY

In 1964, Fender introduced a model at the Chicago NAMM show for the lower end of the pricelist. The new Mustang was effectively a Duo-Sonic with vibrato. This time, the vibrato was a simplified unit with semi-'rocker' bridge adjustable for height and length. "The new 'Floating Bridge'," said Fender's press release, "works in conjunction with the [vibrato] and contains a master bridge channel with new 'barrel-type' individual bridges for each string." Two three-position switches controlled each pickup, offering on/off/reverse-phase, and there was an overall knob each for volume and tone.

At first the Mustang shared the slab body of the Duo-Sonic, but Fender gradually introduced a contoured body to all of its 'student' models of the time: the one-pickup Musicmaster, two-pickup Duo-Sonic, and vibrato-equipped Mustang. While the existing Duo-Sonic and Musicmaster had previously been available only with a short 22.5-inch scale, from 1964 they were also offered in optional 24-inch versions. The new Mustang too was offered in either scale-length.

Fender's distinctive "You Won't Part With Yours" ads were boosted in the mid 1960s with a fresh series, and the company detailed the making of one of the most spectacular in *Fender Facts* magazine in late 1964. The ads had begun in 1957 and were based on the idea that your Fender guitar was so important to you, you'd take it anywhere. One of the new set featured a skydiver in full flight – with a Jazzmaster strapped to his body.

The team met up at Skylark airport near Lake Elsinore, California, less than an hour's drive from the Fullerton factory. The two veteran skydivers employed for the Fender shoot were Roy Fryman and Bud Kiesow. *Fender Facts* reported: "On an 8,000-foot drop from *Yellow Jacket*, a Cessna monoplane with doors removed, Roy carried the guitar, grinned like a true Fender owner, and free-fell 5,000 feet along with Bud, who snapped away with a Japanese serial camera. After 30 seconds of these shenanigans, they returned to the serious business of opening the chutes for a safe terra firma landing."[57]

Down on the ground, Fender now found themselves in the midst of the rock'n'roll revolution. They were happy to ensure that players had a good supply of affordable guitars available in large numbers. In a relatively short period the brilliantly inventive quartet of Stratocaster, Telecaster, Precision, and Jazz Bass had combined to establish in the minds of musicians and guitar-makers the idea of the solidbody electric guitar as a viable modern instrument. What is remarkable is that in these circumstances Fender got so much right, and very often the first time. In short, they had become remarkably successful.

Exporting was important to Fender's success and had started in 1960 when Don Randall first visited the leading European trade show in Frankfurt, Germany. "Our products were known over there because of the GIs playing our guitars," he recalled, "and they were very much prized. So we started doing business in Europe."[58]

In 1960, Jennings became the first official British distributor of Fender gear, joined by Selmer in 1962. A Jennings pricelist from 1961 pitches the Musicmaster at £64/7/4 (£64.36, about $180 at the time), the Duo-Sonic at £80/14/7 (£80.73, $225), Esquire £88/12/1 (£88.60, $250), Telecaster £107/9/7 (£107.48, $300), Stratocaster £147/17/6 (£147.88, $415), and Jazzmaster £177/10/0 (£177.50, $500). By August 1965, both Selmer and Jennings had been replaced as the British Fender distributor by Arbiter, who would continue for many years as the brand's sole UK agent.

"Fender was the biggest musical instrument exporter in the United States," said Randall. "In fact I think we exported more US-made musical products than all the other companies combined. We had it to ourselves for maybe three or four years."[59] Western Europe was the biggest export market, but Fender also did well in Scandinavia, South Africa, Rhodesia (now Zimbabwe), Japan, Australia, Canada, and elsewhere.

Fender commanded a big chunk of the new market. Many buildings had been added to cope with increased manufacturing, and by 1964 the operation employed some 600 people (500 in manufacturing) spread over 29 buildings. Forrest White said his guitar production staff were making 1,500 instruments a week at the end of 1964, compared to the 40 a week when he joined the company ten years earlier. As well as electric guitars, Fender's pricelist in 1964 offered amplifiers, steel guitars, electric basses, acoustic guitars, effects units, a host of related accessories, and Fender-Rhodes electric pianos, added to the line the previous year.

▼ 1961 STRATOCASTER, BURGUNDY MIST

■ Fender gradually began to make more Custom Color guitars and as a result issued special charts to publicise their availability and help customers select from the options. The one shown here (right) is from the first year of issue, 1961, and includes Burgundy Mist (like this Strat, main guitar) and Black (like the Jazzmaster below).

CUSTOM FINISHES FOR *Fender* FINE ELECTRIC INSTRUMENTS

These 14 Colors, plus Blond, Available at 5% Additional cost
Sunburst Finishes Standard at no Extra cost

→ LAKE PLACID BLUE METALLIC	SHERWOOD GREEN METALLIC ←
LUCITE 2870-L	DUCO 2576-H
→ DAPHNE BLUE	FOAM GREEN →
DUCO 2601	DUCO 2253
→ SONIC BLUE	
DUCO 2295	
→ SHORELINE GOLD METALLIC	SURF GREEN →
LUCITE 2935-L	DUCO 2461
→ OLYMPIC WHITE	INCA SILVER METALLIC →
LUCITE 2816-L	LUCITE 2436-L
	FIESTA RED →
	DUCO 2219-H
→ BURGUNDY MIST METALLIC	DAKOTA RED →
LUCITE 2936-L	DUCO 2590 H
→ BLACK	SHELL PINK →
DUCO 1711-X	DUCO 2371

Not Available for DuoSonic and Music master
Colors Subject to Change Without Notice

▲ 1960 JAZZMASTER, BLACK

■ During 1959, Fender altered the look of the sunburst finish that was used on many guitar bodies. Until then, they created the look with just two colours, yellow and black, starting with a yellow centre and radiating to darker tones toward the edge of the instrument's body. This '64 Strat (right) shows how the new-for-1959 sunburst looked quite different. Notice that there is now a third colour in the mix, with a distinct red layer between the centre and the edge of the sunburst. This became known as the three-tone sunburst, and it provides a broad visual clue to a particular (original) guitar being from the 1950s or the 1960s.

◄ 1964 STRATOCASTER

You won't part with yours either.

Wherever you go, you'll find Fender!
*For your personal selection see the complete line of Fender fine electric instruments (like the Stratocaster Guitar shown above) on display at leading music dealers throughout the world.
FREE CATALOG / Write Fender Musical Instruments, Dept. DB-8, 1402 East Chestnut, Santa Ana, California

Fender
MUSICAL INSTRUMENTS
SANTA ANA, CALIFORNIA

Don Randall remembered writing a million dollars' worth of sales during his first year in the 1950s, which rose to some ten million dollars' worth in the mid 1960s, translating to about $40 million of retail sales. By now the beat boom, triggered by The Beatles and the so-called British Invasion of pop groups, was taking the United States by storm. Electric guitars were at a peak of popularity, and Fender were among the biggest and most successful producers.

Then, in January 1965, the Fender companies were sold to the mighty Columbia Broadcasting System Inc, better known as CBS. *The Music Trades* magazine reported in shocked tones: "The purchase price of $13 million is by far the highest ever offered in the history of the [musical instrument] industry for any single manufacturer, and was about two million dollars more than CBS paid recently for the New York Yankees baseball team. The acquisition, a sterling proof of the music industry's growth potential, marks the first time that one of the nation's largest corporations has entered our field. With sales volume in excess of half a billion dollars annually, CBS currently does more business than the entire [musical instrument] industry does at retail. Actual purchase of Fender was made by the Columbia Records Distribution Division of CBS whose outstanding recent feats have included the production of *My Fair Lady*."

Economic analysts were advising the big corporations of the time to diversify and acquire companies from a variety of different businesses. They were doubtless told that all they had to do was finance and expand the new acquisitions and rich pickings would follow. Columbia Records boss Goddard Lieberson said of Fender: "This is a fast growing business tied into the expanding leisure time market. We expect this industry to grow by 23 per cent in the next two years."[60]

Leo Fender was by all accounts a hypochondriac, and his acute health worries prompted the sale of Fender. His main concern was the staph infection in his sinuses that had troubled him since the mid 1950s. And he was nervous about financing expansion. He recalled later: "I thought I was going to have to retire. I had been suffering for years with a virus infection of the sinuses and it made my life a misery. I felt that I wasn't going to be in the health to carry on."[61]

Don Randall handled the sale of Fender to CBS. He said that Leo had earlier offered him the company for a million-and-a-half dollars but he didn't feel he was ready for that kind of career move. Instead he suggested to Leo that he might see what he could get from an outside buyer. Leo agreed, and Randall's first tentative discussions took place in early 1964 with the Baldwin Piano & Organ Co of Ohio. Randall also contacted an investment banker, who at first suggested that Fender go public, which neither Leo nor Randall wanted to do. The bankers then came up with CBS as a potential purchaser.

"Now we had two companies up there," Randall remembered, "but Baldwin's attitude to purchasing turned out to be totally unsatisfactory for our purposes. So finally we got down to the nitty gritty with [CBS], and I made about half a dozen trips back and forth to New York: jam sessions with attorneys and financial people.

"The guys at CBS came in with a really low price at first," Randall continued, "but eventually we came to a fairly agreeable price, and I called Leo and said, how does that suit you? He said, oh Don, I can't believe it, are you trying to pull my leg? And I said, no – does that sound like a satisfactory deal we can close on? 'Well, anything you say Don, that's fine, you just go ahead and do it,' he said. And so the rest is history. We went on and sold it to CBS after a lot of investigation. They did a big study on us – people came in to justify the sale and the price paid – and we consummated the deal. Leo wouldn't even go back to New York for the signing, for the pay-off or anything. 'You get the money and you bring it out to me,' he said."[62]

In the year following their $13m acquisition, CBS published a survey that estimated the number of guitar players in the USA at nine million and placed total American retail sales of guitars during 1965 at $185 million, up from $24 million in 1958. CBS were clearly enthusiastic about the potential for music and went on to buy more instrument companies, including Rogers (drums), Steinway (pianos), and Leslie (organ loudspeakers).

Over the years, the sale of Fender to CBS provoked much retrospective anger among guitar players and collectors, some of whom consider so-called 'pre-CBS' instruments – in other words those made prior to the beginning of 1965 – as superior to those made after that date. This is a meaningless generalisation, but there can be little doubt that over a period of time after the sale, CBS did introduce changes to the production methods of Fender guitars, and that a number of these changes were detrimental to the quality of some instruments.

According to some insiders, the problem with CBS at this time was that they seemed to believe that it was enough simply to pour a great deal of money into Fender. And certainly Fender's sales did increase and profits did go up – Randall recalled income almost doubling in the first year that CBS owned Fender. Profit became paramount, said Forrest White, who remained as manager of electric guitar and amplifier production. "CBS had a vice president for everything. I think they had a vice president for cleaning the toilets. You name it, whatever it was, it had a vice president."[63]

Here was a significant clash of cultures. The new CBS men, often trained engineers with college degrees, believed in high-volume production. Fender's old guard were long-serving craft workers without formal qualifications. A job ad in the *Los Angeles Times* in March 1966 summed up the changes. It was for a Systems Analyst to oversee a computer feasibility study at Fender for a proposed "management information system" covering "sales order processing, material control, manufacturing systems, and accounting systems". It's not hard to imagine the rumours that this probably set in motion among the old team. Now they want to run the place with computers! Whatever next!

▼ **1964 JAGUAR, CANDY APPLE RED**

■ Launched in 1962, the Jaguar superseded the Jazzmaster at the top of the Fender pricelist. It was based on the Jazz but with a shorter neck and more complex controls, and it was the first Fender with 22 frets rather than the usual 20, which combined with the shorter neck made for an easier playing feel.

■ Pictured above is the instrument that could well be described as the first custom Fender guitar – long before the idea of a proper custom shop had occurred to the company. It's a highly decorated black and gold Jaguar, built to order by Fender for a ludicrous 1963 movie, *Bye Bye Birdie*. In the film, a rock'n'roll star briefly strums this luscious black Jag, which features his name, Conrad Birdie, on the front (left) and a B for Birdie insignia on the back (right).

■ Fenders continued to appear in unlikely settings for ads, and Jaguars made their mark in the series soon after launch: poised on the ski slopes (opposite) and perched on a motorcyclist's back (above)

■ Carl Wilson of The Beach Boys (right) was a prominent Jaguar player in the 1960s, with the California group a natural co-promotion for local firm Fender. Wilson may have influenced others to try a Jag, including The Trashmen (opposite) whose 'Surfin' Bird' was a big U.S. hit at the end of '63.

Opinions seem divided among the original Fender men who talked later about the effect of the CBS takeover on Fender's guitars. George Fullerton said that management were first alerted to criticisms when complaints started to filter back from the stores through the sales reps. "They'd say the guitars don't play like they used to, they aren't adjusted like they used to be," Fullerton recalled.[64]

Salesman Dale Hyatt reckoned that the quality stayed relatively stable until around 1968, and then quality-control declined. "It got to the point where I did not enjoy going to any store anywhere, because every time I walked in I found myself defending some poor piece of workmanship," said Hyatt. "They got very sloppy with the finish, with far too many bad spots, and the neck sockets were being cut way over size. They blamed that on the new three-bolt neck, but it wasn't that – put six bolts in it and it still would have moved. And they created their own competition, letting the door wide open for everybody else, including the Japanese."[65]

Randall, who under the new owners became vice president and general manager of Fender Musical Instruments and Fender Sales (both soon part of the new CBS Musical Instruments Division), thought the supposition that quality deteriorated when CBS took over a fallacy. "I will say this for CBS, they were just as interested in quality as we were," said Randall. "They spared no amount of time or effort to ensure the quality was there. There's always this suspicion when a big company takes over that they're going to make a lousy product and sell it for a higher price, and that's not true here. But the other problems that existed were multiple."[66]

Leo too said many years later that he didn't think the changes made by CBS had lowered Fender quality. "They weren't trying to cheapen the instrument. Maybe they tried to accelerate production, but it was natural for them to do that, because on one instrument alone – I think it was the Mustang – we were back-ordered something like 150,000 units. On a back-order of that size, and there were others too, you can't just sit around," he said.[67]

Leo's services were retained as "special consultant in research and development". CBS's confidential pre-sale report into the Fender operation had concluded that Leo, unlike Randall, was not essential to running the business, and that while "a competent chief engineer" could easily keep products moving forward in the contemporary marketplace, it would be "highly desirable, at least for a period of four or five years, to maintain the active interest and creativity of Mr Fender".[68] In other words, CBS didn't want Leo taking his ideas elsewhere – but didn't particularly want him getting in the way of the newly efficient Fender business machine. So he was set up away from the Fender buildings and allowed to tinker as much as he liked – with very little effect on the product. A 1965 CBS brochure showing the key personnel at Fender listed Leo way down in 18th place among the 28 management posts.

A couple of years after the sale to CBS, Leo changed doctors and was given a massive dose of antibiotics that cured his sinus complaint. He completed a few projects for CBS and left when his five-year contract expired in 1970. He went on to make instruments for his Music Man company (originally set up in 1972 and named Music Man in 1974) and his later G&L operation, where the ASAT model was more or less a Telecaster with a different name.

Leo had not been the first of the old guard to leave CBS. Forrest White departed in 1967 "because I wouldn't build some products – the solid state amps – that I thought were unworthy of Leo's name".[69] He went on to work with Leo at Music Man, as well as for CMI (which owned Gibson) and Rickenbacker. White died in November 1994.

Don Randall resigned from CBS in April 1969, disenchanted with corporate life, and formed Randall Electric Instruments, which he sold in 1987. George Fullerton left CBS in 1970, worked at Ernie Ball for a while, and with Leo formed the G&L company in 1979, although Fullerton sold his interest in 1986. (G&L at first stood for "George & Leo", later "Guitars by Leo".) Dale Hyatt, who resigned from CBS in 1972, also joined the G&L set-up. G&L were sold to BBE Sound Inc after Leo Fender's death in March 1991 at the age of 82.

THE DEEP-TONE TWELVE

Back at Fender Musical Instruments, the Electric XII – a guitar that had been on the drawing board when the CBS sale took place – finally hit the music stores in the summer of 1965. Electric 12-strings had recently been popularised by The Beatles and The Byrds, who both used Rickenbacker instruments, so Fender joined in the battle with their own rather belated version. There were no surprises in the guitar's body – it was that familiar offset-waist design again (and at $349.50 the 12-string was pitched at the same price as a sunburst Jazzmaster). The Electric XII had a long headstock, necessary to carry the extra machine heads, finishing in a distinctive curved end that has earned it the nickname 'hockey-stick'.

The guitar's four-position switch, said Fender's press release, "allows the player to select either of the two pickups; both; or a 'deep-tone' effect". An innovation was the 12-saddle bridge that allowed for precise adjustments of individual string heights and intonation, a luxury hitherto unknown on any 12-string guitar. But the 12-string craze of the 1960s was almost over and the Electric XII proved shortlived, lasting in the line until 1968.

One of Fender's first CBS-era pricelists, dated April 1965, reveals a burgeoning line of products in addition to the company's 11 electric guitar models (Duo-Sonic, Electric XII, Esquire, Esquire Custom, Jaguar, Jazzmaster, Musicmaster, Mustang, Stratocaster, Telecaster, and Telecaster Custom). The other lines included three bass guitars (Jazz, Precision, VI), six flat-top acoustic guitars (Classic, Concert, King, Malibu, Palomino, Newporter), and 15 amplifiers (Bandmaster, Bassman, Champ, Deluxe, Deluxe Reverb, Dual Showman, Princeton, Princeton Reverb, Pro Reverb, Showman, Super Reverb, Tremolux, Twin Reverb, Vibro Champ, Vibrolux Reverb), as well as various Fender-

■ Fender was sold to CBS at the very start of 1965 and became part of CBS Musical Instruments (logo below). For many Fender fans this would come to mark a cut-off point after which for some time things would never be the same again. At first the prospects seemed good as the new owner pumped money and enthusiasm into their impressive new purchase, but in years to come the relationship did indeed sour.

CBS Musical Instruments
A DIVISION OF COLUMBIA BROADCASTING SYSTEM, INC.
1402 East Chestnut, Santa Ana, California 92701

■ After The Beatles and The Byrds popularised the electric 12-string in the mid 1960s, many guitar makers jumped on the bandwagon and adapted an existing six-string by adding a new neck and more tuners. Not so Fender, who went to more trouble, notably devising a unique 12-way bridge, a relatively complex piece of engineering that suggests the involvement of Leo Fender. Although Leo was sidelined after the sale to CBS, the XII had been on the drawing board before the sale, even if it was launched after the new buyers took control. The main guitar pictured here is from that first year and finished in Candy Apple Red.

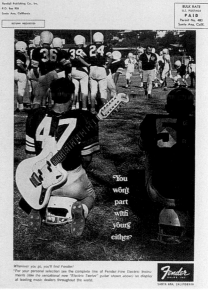

▲ 1965 ELECTRIC XII, FIREMIST GOLD

▲ 1966 ELECTRIC XII, CANDY APPLE RED

■ A notable visual feature of the XII (seen at planning stage in Fender's R&D department, opposite) was its so-called 'hockey stick' headstock, extended and curved to accommodate the increased number of tuners. (This Firemist Gold XII has had its original pickup switch replaced with a different knob).

Rhodes keyboards, steel and pedal steel guitars, the solidbody electric mandolin, and reverb and echo units.

Uniquely for Fender, a guitar appeared in the 1965/66 literature that never made it into production. Naturally, a company prepares many designs and prototypes that do not make it to commercial release, but for an instrument to get as far as printed sales material and then be withdrawn implies a serious error of judgement somewhere along the line. The guitar was the Marauder, and its obvious distinction was summed up by Fender as follows in their hapless catalogue entry: "It appears as though there are no pickups. There are, in reality, however, four newly created pickups mounted underneath the pickguard."

The design had been offered to Fender by one Quilla H. Freeman, who had a patent for his idea of hiding powerful pickups under a guitar's pickguard. Forrest White remembered that there were nonetheless problems with weak signals from the pickups, and George Fullerton recalled that there may have been a dispute between Freeman and CBS concerning the patent. Freeman later took the hidden-pickups idea to Rickenbacker, who got no further than prototypes.

Gene Fields worked on a second proposed version of the Marauder in 1966. Fields had worked in the factory at Fender since 1961 and was taken on in R&D after the CBS sale. He recalled years later that eight prototypes were built, this time with three conventional, visible pickups plus complex associated control switching. According to Fields, four prototypes bore slanted frets. "We never got any real excitement when we field-tested it," he recalled. Thus the Marauders finally died.

In 1966, CBS completed the construction of a new $1.3 million Fender factory, which had been planned before they purchased the company. It was situated next to Fender's existing buildings on the South Raymond site. The new owners were well set for a big push on production. CBS didn't have much cause for concern in terms of demand. Pop music was, of course, flourishing in the 1960s – and Fenders were everywhere.

Mike Bloomfield turned up with a Telecaster for an apparently casual Bob Dylan performance at the Newport folk festival in July 1965, introducing an audience used to acoustic guitars to the capabilities of a turned-up Tele. Dylan himself strummed a Strat. A month earlier, Bloomfield had played his Tele on the recording of 'Like A Rolling Stone'. The following year Robbie Robertson too toted a Tele when he and his band backed Dylan for a series of now legendary live shows that further staked out the ground for electric folk-rock. This time, Bob too opted for a Tele.

In Britain, despite strong competition for Fender during this heady decade from the Gibson Les Paul, the Telecaster in particular held its own among pro players. An early boost came with Mick Green in Johnny Kidd & The Pirates, notably on hits such as 'I'll Never Get Over You' (1963) where Green's deft mix of chords and single-line work benefited from the Tele's cutting sound.

As psychedelia loomed, Syd Barrett of Pink Floyd was setting the controls of his Fender Esquire for a series of long, experimental work-outs. Barrett exploited the Esquire's potential for noise and sound effects as well as its more customary sonic values. He used a typical rosewood-board Esquire of the time, probably bought new around 1964. Barrett had his guitar refinished several times but its most famous finish came when he covered it in plastic sheeting and silver discs.

Jeff Beck played a Tele and an Esquire to devastating effect when he replaced Eric Clapton in The Yardbirds in February 1965. Beck made a great series of Yardbirds recordings, each one an object lesson in the inventive, experimental use of electric guitar on bluesy-pop records: 'Heart Full Of Soul' was the Tele; 'Shapes Of Things' the Esquire. When he left The Yardbirds at the end of 1966, Beck passed on the Telecaster to Jimmy Page, by now the group's other guitar player. Page would use the same guitar in Led Zeppelin early in the next decade for his solo-to-end-all-solos on 'Stairway to Heaven'.

Meanwhile, back at Fender HQ in California, some cosmetic changes were made to various models. In 1965, the Stratocaster gained a broader headstock to match that of the Jazzmaster and Jaguar. Also that year, the fingerboards of the Electric XII, Jaguar, and Jazzmaster gained binding at their edges, while in 1966 the same trio were given block-shaped fingerboard inlays rather than the previous dot markers. Generally, CBS seemed to be fiddling for fiddling's sake.

A firm innovation – for Fender, at least – came in the shape of a new line of hollow-body electrics. These were the first electric-acoustics from Fender who were clearly identified in the player's mind as the prime maker of solidbody guitars. Evidently the strong success of Gibson's ES line of electric-acoustics and models by Gretsch and others must have tempted CBS and their search for wider markets.

Leo Fender brought Roger Rossmeisl into the company in 1962 to design acoustic guitars, and Rossmeisl was also responsible for the new electric-acoustics. They were all manufactured at Fender's separate acoustic guitar plant on Missile Way in Fullerton. Rossmeisl, the son of a German guitar-maker, had come to the States in the 1950s and at first worked for Gibson in Michigan, soon moving to Rickenbacker in California where he made a number of one-off custom guitars and designed production models, including the classic 330/360 instruments. Rossmeisl's work influenced other makers, notably Mosrite of California.

Rossmeisl's Coronado thinline guitars were launched in 1966, the first of his electric designs for Fender. Despite their conventional equal-cutaway bound bodies with large stylised f-holes, they stubbornly employed the standard Fender bolt-on neck and headstock design. Options included a new vibrato tailpiece, and there was a 12-string version that borrowed the Electric XII's 'hockey-stick' headstock.

Virgilio 'Babe' Simoni remembered a particular problem with the Coronados. Simoni had worked for Fender since joining the company at the age of 16 in 1953, and

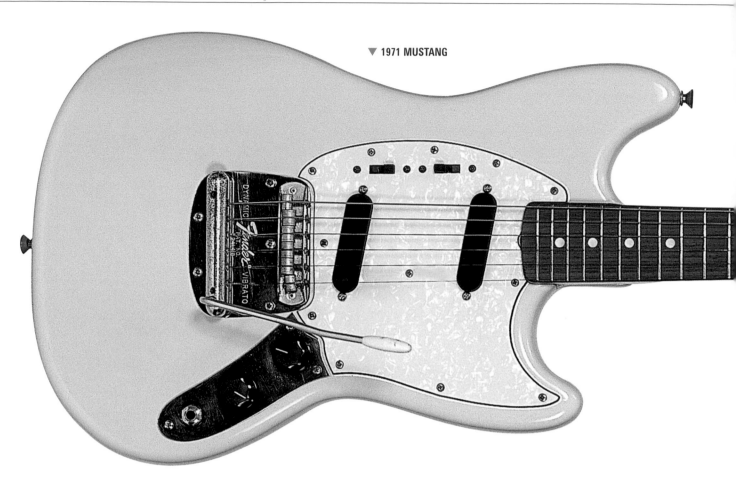

▼ **1971 MUSTANG**

■ Launched in 1964, the Mustang (main guitar) seemed to bridge the gap between Fender's 'student' models and the higher-end guitars. It was offered in two scale-lengths and, echoing the theme of the earlier Duo-Sonic, had two pickups, but with more versatile circuitry. In reciprocal fashion, the Duo-Sonic itself received an updated pickup layout and circuitry in 1964 to match the new model. The added attraction for the Mustang was a new-design vibrato tailpiece. The guitar pictured probably started life in blue finish, but its lacquer coat has yellowed over time to make it green. The Fender Marauder began its tragic life as a hidden-pickups guitar in the 65/66 catalogue that never reached production. Further prototypes (below) of a multi-switch version with angled frets and conventional pickups also failed to reach the music store.

▲ **1966 MARAUDER**

■ Bob Perine, who transformed the look of Fender's advertising at this time, was responsible for the striking paintings that illustrate the covers of some Fender catalogues of the period, like this 1965/66 example (right). Meanwhile, when Bob Dylan controversially went electric in the mid 1960s, he chose a Telecaster to deliver the message (seen on the '66 tour, below).

by the mid 1960s he was product manager of stringed instruments. "We couldn't get the binding material to stick to the Coronados," he said later. "We'd bind them at night and come back in the morning and the thing would be popped loose. The company that supplied the binding material told us we were using the wrong material. [So we had to] re-bind them several times, and the veneer is very thin on them."[70] In order to cover up the burn marks caused by this re-binding, the team had no choice but to devise a special white-to-brown shaded finish, which they called Antigua, to salvage the scorched Coronados.

In 1967, Fender introduced more unusual coloured versions of the Coronado models, this time called Wildwood. As pop culture immersed itself in the dazzling, drug-influenced art of psychedelia, so Fender predictably announced the Coronado Wildwoods as "truly a happening in sight and sound" with "exciting rainbow hues of greens, blues, and golds". They certainly did look different.

The Wildwood effect was achieved by injecting dyes into beech trees during growth, which produced in the cut wood a unique coloured pattern that followed the grain. "They were beautiful guitars," remembered Don Randall, "but they never went any place. Never caught on."[71] Which was true of the feedback-prone Coronados in general. Fender's first foray into thinline electric-acoustics was not a success, and the various versions were all dropped from the line by 1971.

Rossmeisl, assisted by Simoni, came up with a lightweight version of the Tele in 1968. The Thinline Telecaster had three hollowed-out cavities inside the body, offering a different tonality, and the modified pickguard was shaped to accommodate the single, token f-hole. Fender's press release of the time said: "[The] famous Telecaster guitar is now available in a semi-acoustic model with a choice of two natural wood finishes, mahogany or ash. The lightweight hollow-body guitar incorporates Fender's distinctive f-hole design and new styled pickguard. The polyester-finished maple neck comes equipped with special lightweight strings for fast playing action." The new Telecaster Thinline at first came in what a Fender ad called "groovy natural" finishes – in ash or mahogany – and the model lasted in the line until 1971.

It was around this time that two members of The Byrds, guitarist Clarence White and drummer Gene Parsons, came up with their B-string-pull device, ingeniously controlled by a lever fitted inside a hacked Tele body and attached to the strap button on the top. If the player pulled down on the neck, the strap button would move, shifting the lever and some springs and rods inside, raising the pitch of the B-string. Presto! String-bends within chords to emulate pedal steel-type sounds. After a hiccup with Leo and the CBS management, Parsons and White applied for a patent themselves for their B-Bender, or StringBender, in October 1968, granted 17 months later. Parsons began custom-building and retro-fitting the devices into Teles around 1973. (After a long wait, the Fender connection did come good, with the Custom Shop offering a couple of B-Bender Tele models starting in the late 1990s.)

Fender reacted further to the psychedelic style of the late 1960s when they applied paisley or floral-pattern self-adhesive wallpaper to some Telecasters in order to give them flower-power appeal. The best known player of the model was James Burton, who used a Paisley Red throughout his time with Elvis Presley in the 1970s. But despite such prominence, Fender's dazzling wallpaper experiment with the Paisley Red and Blue Flower Telecasters did not last long.

In 1967, Fender launched another of their 'student' solid electrics, the $150 Bronco with single pickup and simple vibrato, sold as a set with the Bronco amp. The following year Roger Rossmeisl was let loose with a couple more guitar designs – and these were even less like the normal run of Fenders than the Coronado models. Roger's speciality was the German carve taught to him by his father, Wenzel. It gives a distinctive indented lip around the top edge of the body, following its outline. Rossmeisl adopted this feature for the new hollow-body archtop electric Montego and LTD models, all eminently traditional but still obstinately using Fender's customary bolt-on neck. Evidence suggests very few of these were made, and one insider suggested that some of those that did manage to reach music stores were subsequently recalled to the factory.

Rossmeisl did not last much longer at Fender. "He had a drinking problem," said Forrest White, "and finally we had to let him go because of it."[72] George Fullerton echoed a general feeling when he said: "Roger was a marvellous designer and didn't become the person he should have been. I think he was his own worst enemy. Such a waste."[73] Rossmeisl died in Germany in 1979 at the age of 52.

Toward the end of the 1960s came firm evidence of CBS wringing every last drop of potential income from unused factory stock that would otherwise have been written off. Two shortlived guitars, the Custom and the Swinger, were assembled from leftovers, as Babe Simoni recalled later. "Production was way down, and we had a bunch of Electric XII necks and bodies. They asked if anyone had any ideas on what to do with them before they scrapped them out. That's when I converted them to six-strings and carved the bodies into a different design." This was the Custom, also called the Maverick (examples exist with either name on the headstock). "First we made those from scrap material," said Simoni. "Then someone in engineering got the bright idea to make hard tooling for it: they did tool up and actually produce Customs."[74]

Dale Hyatt remembered the headache which the Maverick/Custom concoction caused him and his fellow salesmen. "It was an abortion. Everybody knew what it was: a way to get rid of stuff. But people out there in the field are smarter than that. The dealers are smarter; they know. The musicians know better. But CBS didn't care, they made 'em and said here, you go sell 'em."[75]

The Swinger was the other bitser, made from unused Musicmaster or Bass V bodies mated with unpopular short-scale Mustang necks. Simoni: "Instead of using the Mustang headstock design, I made it more rounded, like an acoustic's. Then somebody came along and cut the end of it off – made it look like a spear. And the

▼ 1966 JAZZMASTER, BLUE ICE

■ Fender made some cosmetic changes to some of its models in 1965, giving the Strat a broader headstock and adding edge binding to the fingerboards of the Electric XII, Jaguar, and Jazzmaster (main guitar). The following year the same trio added block-shaped fingerboard inlays rather than the previous dot markers. The Jazzmaster pictured is finished in Blue Ice, one of Du Pont's Lucite acrylic paints, which Fender called metallic finishes.

► 1968 WILDWOOD CORONADO XII

◄ 1968 CORONADO XII, TEAL GREEN

■ This Coronado XII in Teal Green (right) is from Fender's first electric-acoustic line, launched in 1966 and intended as competition for the various models made by arch-rivals Gibson such as the popular ES-335. They were designed by Roger Rossmeisl, who had worked for Gibson as well as Rickenbacker. The Coronados appeared to be conventional semis but stubbornly employed Fender's standard bolt-on neck as well as the distinctive Fender head shape, in this case the 12-string 'hockey stick' style of the earlier XII. Some Coronados also appeared in shaded Antigua finish (second left in catalogue above).

■ An optional line of Coronados came in Wildwood, like this XII. The effect was achieved by injecting dye into beech trees, which in the resulting timber produced a unique coloured pattern following the grain. But the feedback-prone Coronados never caught on and were dropped from the line by 1971.

body was chopped up and changed a little bit. We never tooled up for them like we did with the Custom."[76] Both the Maverick/Custom and the Swinger were made in necessarily limited numbers. The Swinger never featured in Fender's literature, while the Custom made the 1970 catalogue and pricelist at $299.50.

Fender offered a new finish option for the Mustang in 1968 when it released the Competition Mustang. "Three diagonal competition stripes race across the body," declared the press release, "big, bold, bright. Fender's Mustang is available in three wild colours: burgundy with light blue stripes, yellow with orange stripes, and candy apple red with gray stripes." These striking Mustang variants lasted until 1973.

As the close of the 1960s loomed, Strats took a boost when an inspired guitarist by the name of Jimi Hendrix applied the guitar's sensuous curves and glorious tone to his live cavorting and studio experiments. Salesman Dale Hyatt: "When guys like that came along, we couldn't build enough of them. As a matter of fact I think Jimi Hendrix caused more Stratocasters to be sold than all the Fender salesmen put together."[77]

JAMES FLIPS HIS STRAT

Hendrix got his first Strat in 1966 – he'd already tried Duo-Sonics and a Jazzmaster – and almost instantly made it his own. He may have been influenced in his choice by a hero, Curtis Mayfield, who played a Strat. In the final period of his life, between 1968 and 1970, Jimi mainly played two Strats. Both were new '68 maple-board models, one black and one white. Before that he'd generally played new sunburst rosewood-board models. All were regular guitars that Hendrix would flip over and re-string to accommodate his left-handedness. He probably made more players aware of the Strat's tonal and musical possibilities than any other individual before or since.

Hendrix died shockingly young in 1970, and his stone monument that stands at Greenwood Memorial Park in Renton, Washington, has an appropriate motto upon it: "Forever in our hearts." Alongside that and his dates is the depiction of an electric guitar, unmistakeably and proudly a Fender Stratocaster.

We cannot leave the 1960s without considering The Beatles. Concertgoers knew George Harrison and John Lennon primarily as players of Gretsch and Rickenbacker guitars, but they each acquired a Stratocaster in 1965 for studio use. They're clearly heard dueting on them during the solo in 'Nowhere Man' from *Rubber Soul*. Paul McCartney, increasingly confident with six rather than four strings, got himself an Esquire two years later, using it for his soaring, concise solo on *Sgt Pepper*'s 'Good Morning, Good Morning'.

Nonetheless, the public face of the band remained distinctly Fender-less. This led Fender's Don Randall to try to persuade manager Brian Epstein to get his boys more visibly into the brand. "It was the only time we ever tried to buy somebody off," Randall recalled. "I sent a member of my staff to try and buy Brian Epstein off. But no, it was a pittance."

In summer 1968, Randall managed to secure a meeting with Lennon and McCartney at the band's Apple headquarters in London. "I was still kind of interested in getting them to use our products. So we went up there and had quite a long conversation with Paul. He had some great ideas, a real animated guy. Finally John and Yoko came in, and we all sat down at this big conference table."[78] The results were the band's Fender-Rhodes pianos, a VI six-string bass, a Jazz Bass, a number of amps including a PA system, and Harrison's Rosewood Telecaster. From this point Fender's U.K. agent, Arbiter, supplied the group with more or less whatever they wanted.

The Beatles famously played their last ever 'concert' on the rooftop of their Apple HQ in London in January 1969. It featured in the following year's *Let It Be* movie, which effectively charted their break-up. On the roof and at other points during the making of the film and the accompanying album, Harrison played his Rosewood Telecaster, an unusual and shortlived model. Fender had sent one of the prototypes to Harrison in December 1968. They made two prototypes of the Telecaster and two of a Rosewood Stratocaster, one of the latter intended for but never reaching Jimi Hendrix.

The Rosewood Tele went into production later in 1969 and lasted a couple of years in the line. It had a body constructed from a thin layer of maple sandwiched between a solid rosewood top and back. This made for a striking yet heavy instrument. Fender attempted to lighten the load by moving to a two-piece construction with hollowed chambers inside, but the weight and unusual tonality meant it was never a popular instrument.

Meanwhile, the Jazzmaster had remained near the top of the Fender pricelist. American guitar dealer George Gruhn later wrote an intriguing postscript to the model and its place among the devious excursions of guitar fashion. "In about 1970, Eric Clapton began buying and playing vintage Strats, and their popularity consequently grew," said Gruhn. "Clapton bought quite a few Strats from me during this period, and when he asked one day that I find a good Jazzmaster for him I had hopes that his use of the model would do comparable things for its collectability. However, circumstances intervened, Clapton decided he didn't want a Jazzmaster after all, and nothing further developed."[79]

It's interesting to speculate that perhaps the Jazzmaster's status might have taken a needed boost had god's dice rolled another way. Of course, we know now that, following Clapton's adoption of the Stratocaster, he's made a firm impression on its popularity ever since. He acquired a '56 Strat, nicknamed Brownie, for his first solo album in the early months of 1970, switching from the various Gibsons that had served him well until then. He also played it on the *Layla* sessions that year. Towards the end of 1970 he bought some more '50s Strats, picking the best bits from three of them to make Blackie – which became his favourite guitar from then until the mid 1980s.

As far as the Telecaster was concerned, the 1970s might well be described as the

■ The Custom (below) was part of an ill-advised series of instruments added to the line in the late 1960s derived from leftover parts – in this case a mix of Electric XII and Mustang bits. The unusual styling did not prove popular and production of this curious model was limited. More attractive to some musicians were two flower power Fenders (right). These were Telecasters finished in Paisley Red and Blue Flower, the effect achieved by attaching self-adhesive wallpaper to the normally mild-mannered Tele. Visibility of the lurid patterns was ensured with a clear plastic pickguard.

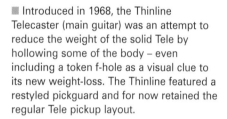

▼ 1969 CUSTOM

■ Introduced in 1968, the Thinline Telecaster (main guitar) was an attempt to reduce the weight of the solid Tele by hollowing some of the body – even including a token f-hole as a visual clue to its new weight-loss. The Thinline featured a restyled pickguard and for now retained the regular Tele pickup layout.

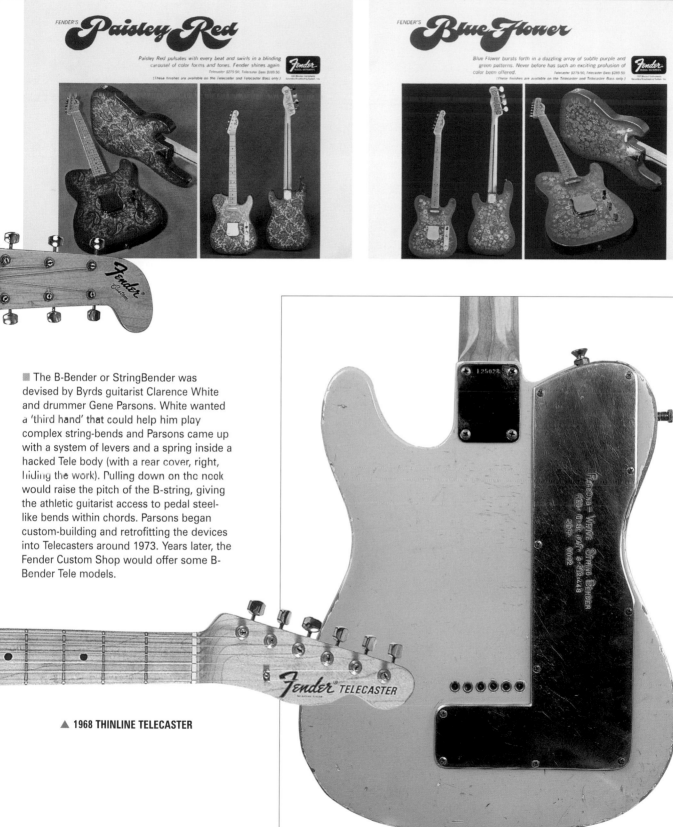

FENDER'S Paisley Red

Paisley Red pulsates with every beat and swirls in a blinding carousel of color forms and tones. Fender shines again. Telecaster $279.50, Telecaster Bass $289.50. (These finishes are available on the Telecaster and Telecaster Bass only.)

FENDER'S Blue Flower

Blue Flower bursts forth in a dazzling array of subtle purple and green patterns. Never before has such an exciting profusion of color been offered. Telecaster $279.50, Telecaster Bass $289.50. (These finishes are available on the Telecaster and Telecaster Bass only.)

■ The B-Bender or StringBender was devised by Byrds guitarist Clarence White and drummer Gene Parsons. White wanted a 'third hand' that could help him play complex string-bends and Parsons came up with a system of levers and a spring inside a hacked Tele body (with a rear cover, right, hiding the work). Pulling down on the neck would raise the pitch of the B-string, giving the athletic guitarist access to pedal steel-like bends within chords. Parsons began custom-building and retrofitting the devices into Telecasters around 1973. Years later, the Fender Custom Shop would offer some B-Bender Tele models.

▲ 1968 THINLINE TELECASTER

decade of the humbucker. Part of Fender's distinction had come from using bright-sounding single-coil pickups; the warmer, fatter-sounding humbucking types were always seen then as a Gibson mainstay. Humbucking pickups had two coils wired in such a way that the noise often associated with single-coil pickups was cancelled.

The bridge pickup on a Telecaster (or an Esquire) is the heart of its sound, but the neck pickup has often been seen as the guitar's weak link. Some players simply didn't use it. Others took the matter into their own hands, or at least passed the problem on to their repairman. A popular choice was to replace the mellow neck pickup with a ballsier humbucker, often lifted from a Gibson.

Keith Richards was the most visible user of a modified humbucker'd Tele. He was playing Teles regularly on stage with the Stones from early in the 1970s. His most famous is a black-'guard 1950s Tele, nicknamed Micawber, complete with added Gibson humbucker. Many other players at the time whacked 'buckers on their Teles in various combinations: Denny Dias in Steely Dan; Andy Summers in The Police; Jeff Beck with his 'Tele-Gib' hybrid.

Fender reacted to the humbucker trend. The existing Telecaster Thinline model was modified in 1971 with two new Fender humbuckers. The guitar was presumably designed to send a signal that Fender was invading Gibson territory and recognised that players had pre-empted the move. Fender said in a press release: "The humbucking pickups not only help eliminate feedback, they also add a gutty mid-range and bass sound." It was about as close as Fender would come to saying, "This Fender is like a Gibson."

Fender had enticed Seth Lover to California in 1967, away from the Gibson company in Michigan where he had famously invented Gibson's humbucking pickup in the 1950s. Warm, powerful humbuckers had given a distinctive edge to dozens of Gibson models, not least the Les Paul electrics that had come back into vogue during the late 1960s.

BRILLIANT HUMBUCKERS

Lover explained what his new employers were after. "The Fender sales force wanted a copy of a Gibson humbucking pickup, wanted it to sound exactly like that," he said. "The patent had not quite run out, so I designed them a pickup that looked a little different. Also, I used cunife magnets [an alloy of copper-nickel-iron], not Gibson's alnico [aluminium-nickel-cobalt]. I hesitated in making it sound exactly like the Gibson – I figured Fender was known for a brilliant type sound, so I kept a little more brilliance in the Fender pickup than there was in the Gibson."[80] Lover made it look different, too, staggering the polepieces, with the three bass ones to the front of the cover and the three treble ones to the rear.

Fender reconsidered the double-humbucker layout on that revised Thinline model and in 1972 came up with a more restrained arrangement for the new Telecaster

Custom. This time the classic Tele lead pickup stayed put, and just the neck pickup was changed to a humbucker. Fender's Dave Gupton combined hype with prescience in his press statement about the new instrument. "Musicians looking for sound versatility will be able to do just about anything with the new Telecaster Custom," he boasted in typical ad-speak. But then he got real. "By incorporating the latest humbucking-design Fender pickup along with the unique world-renowned Telecaster lead pickup, a whole new spectrum of sounds is created." Fender were back to twin humbuckers for the Telecaster Deluxe of 1973. It was a cross between the big-headstock neck of the contemporary Stratocaster (some even had Strat-style vibratos), the body of a Telecaster, and the pickups and controls of a Gibson.

None of the humbucker'd Teles were very successful at the time, with potential customers generally confused and staying away. The humbucker-equipped Telecaster Deluxe and Custom models would both disappear from the pricelist by 1981, the Thinline two years earlier. But they would become fashionable years later as some players discovered the potent combination of Tele playability and humbucker raunch.

Like many Fenders of the period, the humbucker'd Teles were fitted with a bullet truss-rod adjuster and a neck-tilt system. (The 'bullet' term described the appearance of the truss-rod adjustment nut at the headstock; the neck-tilt system was a Fender device of the time at the neck-to-body joint that allowed easier adjustment of neck pitch, or angle.) Fenders from the early 1970s also came with the company's new high-gloss 'thick skin' finish, achieved by spraying more than a dozen coats of polyester on to the unfortunate instrument, and today reviled by some for its plastic appearance and giveaway period vibe.

Fender's marketing director, Dave Gupton, announced that 1972 was a record year for the company, with unit production and dollar sales figures both higher than ever before. He was in little doubt that 1973 would yield still higher figures and that the trend would continue upward. A major expansion program was on at the Fullerton plant to boost output still further. Completed in summer 1974, it provided the Fender operation with a new total of 289,600 square feet of production, warehouse, and shipping space.

This is precisely why CBS had purchased Fender back in 1965: to make more instruments and widen the market. But the increase in the number of guitars leaving the factory inevitably affected quality. A feeling was beginning to set in that Fenders were not made like they used to be. A number of top musicians were regularly to be seen playing older guitars, which were beginning to be described as 'vintage' instruments. It all added to the growing impression that numbers might be more important to Fender than quality. Some guitarists were becoming convinced that older instruments were somehow more playable and sounded better than new guitars. Some players and collectors, then and now, believe that the 1970s offered the poorest instruments in Fender's production history. Others who got their first

▼ **1972 THINLINE TELECASTER**

■ Changes to the Fender line in the 1970s included a big vote for humbucking pickups, which were added to some Telecaster models. The earlier f-hole Thinline model was altered in 1971 to incorporate two of Fender's new humbuckers (and, necessarily, a separate six-saddle bridge). The humbucker trend for Fender showed that the company was by no means finished with the idea of a guitar that strayed into Gibson territory – the guitar-making rival had always been associated in players' minds with the ballsier raunch of the humbucker.

▲ 1969 ROSEWOOD TELECASTER

■ This exotic Telecaster (main guitar) in rosewood makes for a striking but heavy guitar. Fender sent a prototype to George Harrison in December 1968. They made two prototypes of the Telecaster and two of a Rosewood Stratocaster, one of which was intended for but never reached Jimi Hendrix.

■ Curtis Mayfield is pictured (above) recording with his band The Impressions. Mayfield was a key influence on Jimi Hendrix, who in turn became one of the major influences in the years following his rise to fame in the late 1960s and early death in 1970. Both Mayfield and Hendrix favoured Stratocasters.

instruments then have fonder memories, and dealers have in recent years been pushing up prices and demand for period examples – no doubt in part because they've run out of earlier guitars to sell us.

But it's easy to get all this vintage business out of proportion. It's impossible to generalise and say if pre-1965 or pre-1985 (or even pre-2008) Fenders are superior to the rest, but the more you look at the idea the more irrelevant it seems today. Many guitarists get on well with contemporary Fenders; others cherish their older guitars. There is only one rule: pick up an instrument – new, old, or somewhere in between – and see if you like it. What anyone else says about the importance of particular periods or what they might pay for this or that instrument has nothing to do with it.

During the 1970s, CBS management cut back on the existing Fender product lines and offered hardly any new models. The last Esquires and Duo-Sonics of the period were made in 1969. The Jaguar disappeared around 1975, and by 1980 the Bronco, Jazzmaster, Musicmaster, and Thinline Tele would all be phased out of production. The humbucker-equipped Telecaster Deluxe and Custom models had both gone by 1981, the same time that the Mustang went. Most were later reissued, but back in the day it made for a bare catalogue. The original acoustic flat-tops had all gone by 1971, and ten years later the steels and pedal steels would all disappear, with only amplifiers (some 14 models) offering anything like Fender's early coverage of the market.

Most of the original Custom Colors had been discontinued in the late 1960s and early 1970s. The December 1974 pricelist revealed the $490 Jaguar and $460 Jazzmaster in sunburst only. By now, the Stratocaster came in just six finishes: standard sunburst ($405), or natural, blond, black, white, or walnut ($425 each). The Telecaster too was offered in only six finishes: standard blond ($315), or natural, sunburst, black, white, or walnut ($330 each). The basic two-humbucker Tele Deluxe in walnut was $440 and the single-humbucker Custom in sunburst $345. All the regular models had the rosewood fingerboard of the period, but a maple board was also offered (as were left-handers, plus a Bigsby-equipped Telecaster and a vibrato-less option for the Strats).

The search for old guitars and the notion that they were mysteriously and inherently better grew steadily among some players. Norman's Rare Guitars, established in California during the middle of the 1970s, was one of the newer dealers specialising in the 'vintage' requirements of rock players. Proprietor Norman Harris was in no doubt why so many guitarists were taking up older instruments – like those he offered for sale. "You simply cannot compare what I have to offer with what the big companies are mass producing today," he boasted.[81] The first published attempt to acknowledge this interest and list the various old Fenders and their dates of manufacture came in Tom Wheeler's *The Guitar Book* in 1974, later expanded and corrected in other books as further information was revealed.

CBS may have been making fewer models, but they were manufacturing in much greater numbers. They were selling 40,000 Fender instruments a year by the end of the 1970s. A further sign of this vastly increased production was the end of the tradition for putting a date on an instrument's neck. Since the earliest days of the first Fender models, workers had almost always pencilled and later rubber-stamped dates on the body-end of necks. It remains about the most reliable way to date a Fender (leaving aside the question of fakes). But from 1973 to the early 1980s, Fender stopped doing it. Presumably they were simply too busy.

The company made another attempt at electric-acoustics with the ill-fated Starcaster in 1976, again aimed at competing with Gibson's ever-popular ES line. Designer Gene Fields recalled: "When I started with the Starcaster it was to use up the old Coronado parts ... but during the field test reports somebody said it's a great guitar — and we see you've finally found a way to use up your old scrap. So Dave Gupton said forget it, start over and get me a new design. ... Then when Mudge Miller got in as vice president, Teles and Strats were real hot, and he closed the Starcaster down because he didn't want the production time wasted on it."[82] The $850 Starcaster had left the Fender list by 1980.

Throughout the 1970s there was hardly a leading guitarist who did not at some time play a Fender. At the start of the decade this had been in large part due to the continuing influence of Hendrix and now Clapton, but notable among other Fender players of the time were Ritchie Blackmore, foregrounding his Strat with metallic merchants Deep Purple, and James Burton, whose paisley Tele graced many Elvis and Emmylou Harris sessions. And near the end of the 1970s, as punk and synthesisers seemed set to devalue and even eclipse electric guitars in pop, Mark Knopfler's clean melodic tone within Dire Straits once more underlined the apparently timeless appeal of the Stratocaster.

In Britain, punk was — depending on your viewpoint — giving a welcome opportunity to fresh young hopefuls or wiping out the idea of good musicianship. There was some good Tele action amongst it all, most visibly by Clash mainman Joe Strummer with his bashed-up black Tele covered in stickers.

Dr Feelgood straddled the stylistic gap between pub-rock and punk, mixing old-style R&B with a thoroughly modern brutality supplied by manic Telecaster-wielding guitarist Wilko Johnson. Punks in almost everything but name and sartorial style, the Feelgoods hit hard in October 1976 when their third album, the live *Stupidity*, topped the British album charts. Johnson generally used one of his pair of '63 Teles for a brittle, seat-of-the-pants sound that harked back to the lead-and-rhythm-all-at-once style of his chief influence, Mick Green of The Pirates.

Boardroom doubts in California that led to the dropping of the Jaguar and Jazzmaster from the line coincided with a new popularity of those models among punk and new-wave guitarists. This was partly due to the punk ethic, where it was essential to show off that you had little money (at least in theory). Jazzes and Jags

■ We've illustrated many examples of stylish and thoughtful Fender advertising, much of it devised and developed by Bob Perine. Perine stopped working for Fender in the late 1960s, and in the 1970s the company's promo material came in for some changes. Shown here are three examples that continue the old idea of a tagline unifying the ads: in this case 'The world's favorite … machine'. On the left is a Stratocaster ad, 'The world's favorite flying machine,' which sees a Strat suitably airborne and frightening a startled bird. In the centre is the bass ad of the series, apparently the 'favorite road machine', with a gig no doubt just beyond that sunset. The Telecaster (right) is plugged as the 'recording machine' in an almost Disney-like fantasy that suggests an ad team ingesting at the very least some high-octane coffee.

▼ 1976 TELECASTER DELUXE

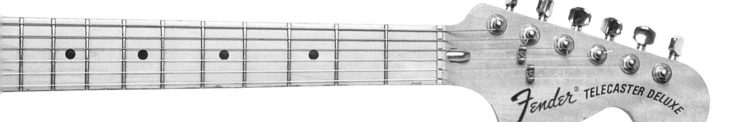

■ Fender's new series of Telecasters fitted with humbucking pickups – the earlier Thinline and now the Deluxe (main guitar) and Custom –acknowledged one of the most popular modifications that guitarists made to the instrument: replacing at least the 'weak' single-coil neck pickup of the regular Tele, and sometimes both pickups, with a more powerful humbucker. At the time, Keith Richards often used an old Telecaster on stage to which he'd added the favoured neck 'bucker (pictured opposite). This Tele proved to be a favourite, and Richards lovingly nicknamed the guitar Micawber.

were relatively unloved and therefore relatively cheap on the secondhand market compared to the burgeoning prices of what were now being tagged 'vintage' Strats and Teles.

One of the best of the new breed of so-called punks was Tom Verlaine in the New York group Television. Verlaine played a Jazzmaster and showed its versatility on 1977's classic *Marquee Moon* album. In Britain there was Robert Smith in The Cure and Elvis Costello fronting his Attractions, and both selected a Jazzmaster as their six-string of choice.

Fender began a shortlived revival in 1977 of the Antigua finish, offered as an option on various Strats, Teles, and Mustangs. This light-to-dark shaded colour had first been offered as an option during the late 1960s on some Coronado models as an emergency measure to disguise manufacturing flaws. This time around it was deployed purely for its aesthetic appeal. The new Antigua style, now with more of a graduated tone, was matched to similarly finished pickguards. The Antigua guitars also featured the new black hardware that Fender had started to use from 1975. All the plasticware – knobs, pickup covers, switch caps and all – was now black, and this certainly enhanced the overall look of the Antigua-finish instruments.

By 1976 Fender had a five-acre facility under one roof in Fullerton and employed over 750 workers. John Page, who would go on to run Fender's Custom Shop from the mid 1980s, started working for Fender in 1978, spending some months on the production line before moving to R&D. He described the chaos of Fender in the late 1970s. "You couldn't even tell Purchasing what part you wanted or where you wanted it from. All you could tell them was the spec of the part you wanted," Page said. "It was so compartmentalised, and virtually no one got to know anyone else in any of the other departments. There was no communication."

Page recalled his horror when he discovered one of the CBS executives at the time cheerfully disposing of Fender's history. "This guy came through our office, and he was putting green dots on all our guitars. I asked what he was doing. 'Oh well, I got this great programme, I'm gonna give these away to dealers, yes sir.' What! And before we were able to stop it he had given away about 80 percent of our original prototypes and samples."

One of Page's colleagues in R&D at the time was Gregg Wilson, who designed a pair of new 'student' models to replace the Musicmaster, Bronco, Duo-Sonic, and Mustang. These were the Lead I and Lead II guitars of 1979, simple double-cutaway solids, though not especially cheap at $399. Page himself designed a later variation, the Lead III, but none of them lasted beyond 1982. Wilson remembered a joke heard around Fender at the time: "We don't build them like we used to, and we never did."

In 1979, an anniversary edition of the Stratocaster was issued to celebrate the guitar's first 25 years, a silver-finish guitar with an uninspiring birthday logo on the body's upper horn. The earliest examples were in a new white finish that unfortunately tended to crack spectacularly. Many were recalled and the main production was changed to the more appropriate silver finish. "The quantity, naturally, is limited," announced Fender – who proceeded to make stacks of 25th Anniversary Stratocasters during 1979 and 1980. "They went fast in '54. They'll go fast now," ran the insistent blurb.

Fender's September 1979 pricelist listed 11 basic electric models: Bronco ($300); Jazzmaster ($740); Lead I ($399 inc case); Lead II ($399 inc case); Musicmaster ($280); Mustang ($415); Starcaster ($850); Stratocaster ($640); Telecaster ($535); Telecaster Custom ($580); and Telecaster Deluxe ($685). Some were offered with maple board and left-handed options.

BUDGET WITH A BULLET

John Page's next project was a fresh stab at budget-price solids with the single-cutaway Bullet series. The Bullets began production in 1981, but Fender decided for the first time in its history to shift manufacturing outside the United States, to lower costs. Joining a general trend in the early 1980s among many guitar companies both Western and Eastern, Fender decided to try Korean manufacture. Page remembered the early samples. "In comes this guitar with half-inch action and yes, it's like that because we got it real cheap. So back they went."

Fender decided not to have the Bullets made entirely in Korea, and so at first the instruments were assembled in the States using Korean-manufactured parts. But even this method did not produce guitars of a high enough standard. By late 1981, the Bullets were back to full American production, and Fender's first experience of oriental manufacturing was over. The Bullets lasted until 1983, in which year various shortlived double-cutaway versions were also produced.

Another Gregg Wilson design from this period was the Strat – an official use, at last, of the common abbreviation. The Strat combined standard Stratocaster visuals with updated circuitry (contributed by guitar-maker Dan Armstrong) and fashionable heavy-duty brass hardware. The intention was also to re-introduce the old-style narrow headstock of the original Stratocasters, but unfortunately worn-out tooling was used that delivered a not entirely accurate re-creation.

Colour schemes were brightened somewhat during the 1980s, with the shortlived International Colors in 1981 and the Custom Colors and Stratobursts of '82. Some of the new hues were distinctly lurid, such as Capri Orange, Aztec Gold, or Bronze Stratoburst, and they were not much liked at the time. In 1983 there were short runs of marble 'bowling ball' finishes for some Strats and Teles, in red, blue, or yellow. At least the idea of a decent selection of Custom Colors seemed to be back in place.

With generally trimmed model lines and a massive output from the factories, it was hard to resist the feeling as the 1980s got underway that the newly-important calculations of the balance sheet had become firmly established at Fender and taken precedence over the company's former creativity.

the fender story

■ Fender's second attempt to crack the semi-acoustic market came in 1976 with the Starcaster (main guitar), with an offset-waist body that alluded to the solidbody Jaguar plus an unusual variant on the Fender headstock shape. Despite the instrument's quality it was not widely accepted and marked another failure to compete effectively with Gibson's still-popular ES models. The ad department meanwhile went fairytale crazy (left), here with Snow White and the Witch getting down to a Starcaster-led groove.

◀ **1978 STARCASTER**

■ The late 1970s meant punk, and Fender was represented in the versions that grew up on both sides of the Atlantic. Television in New York featured the inventive Jazzmaster rambles of Tom Verlaine (opposite). Over the water, The Clash's Joe Strummer (below) played a stickered Tele that became a punk icon during the band's rise from pubs to stadiums.

THE FENDER ELECTRIC GUITAR BOOK

At the start of the decade, CBS management decided that they needed new blood to help reverse a decline in Fender's fortunes. During 1981, they recruited key personnel from the American musical instrument division of Yamaha, the giant Japanese company. John McLaren was hired as head of CBS Musical Instruments overall, and among the other newcomers from Yamaha were Bill Schultz and Dan Smith. Schultz was hired as Fender president and, a few months later, Smith as director of marketing electric guitars.

Smith said: "We were brought in to turn the reputation of Fender around and to get it so it was making money again. It was starting to lose money, and at that point in time everybody hated Fender. We thought we knew how bad it was. We took it for granted that they could make Stratocasters and Telecasters the way they used to make them. But we were wrong. So many things had been changed in the plant."[83]

Schultz was given the go-ahead by CBS to try to improve matters. One of the first changes Smith made on his arrival was to revise the overall spec of the Stratocaster, reverting to what was generally felt to be the more stable four-bolt neck-body joint (as used from 1954 to 1971, when CBS brought in the three-bolt joint). "We also changed it to the right headstock," said Smith, referring to the revamped Strat's approximation of the pre-'65 head shape. "We had a lot of stock to use up, and we couldn't release the four-bolt until the three-bolt was gone." The four-bolt Standard Strat started to leave Fender's Fullerton plant toward the end of 1981.

Smith recalled an early shock as he toured the factory, before the four-bolt Strats had come on-stream. "I remember looking at the body contours. People were complaining about contours, and here's a rack of 2,000 guitars. Every one of them had a different edge contour! We also went and pulled guitars out of the warehouse and did general re-inspections on them, 800-and-something guitars, and out of those I think only about 15 passed the existing criteria. So we sat down and re-wrote the criteria."[84]

Schultz recommended a large investment package, primarily aimed at modernising the factory. This had the immediate effect of virtually stopping production while new machinery was brought in and staff were re-trained. Another recommendation that Schultz had been working on was to start alternative production of Fenders in Japan. The reason was relatively straightforward: Fender's sales were being hammered by the onslaught of copies made in the orient. These Japanese copyists made their biggest profits in their own domestic market, so the best place to hit back at them was in Japan – by making and selling guitars there.

When the Japanese had started emulating classic American guitars in the early 1970s, most Western makers didn't see much to worry about. Gradually the quality of the Japanese instruments improved, but some American makers kept their heads stuck firmly in the sand. Dave Gupton, vice president of Fender in 1978, said: "Fender is not adversely affected by the Japanese copies as perhaps some of the other major manufacturers, because we have been able to keep our costs pretty much in line."[85]

That casual attitude changed dramatically in a few short years. By the start of the 1980s, the dollar had soared in value relative to the yen. Coupled with the high quality of many Japanese guitars, this meant that instruments built in the orient were making a real impact on the international guitar market. Many were copies of Fender and Gibson models, and especially the Fender Stratocaster, which was enjoying renewed popularity. "We had to stop this plethora of copies," said Smith. "A lot of these companies basically told Bill Schultz and me that they were going to bury us. They were ripping us off, and what we really needed to do was to get these guys where it hurt – back in their own marketplace."[86]

With the blessing of CBS, negotiations began with two Japanese distributors, Kanda Shokai and Yamano Music, to establish the Fender Japan company. The joint venture was officially established in March 1982 combining the forces of Fender, Kanda, and Yamano. Fender US licensed Fender Japan the right to have Fender guitars built within Japan for the Japanese market. Kanda and Yamano would sell the Japanese-made Fenders in Japan; Yamano would also sell US-made guitars there. This set-up would last until early 2005.

After discussions with Tokai, Kawai, and others, the factory finally chosen to build guitars for Fender Japan was Fujigen, based in Matsumoto, some 130 miles north-west of Tokyo. Fujigen were best known in the West for the excellence of their Ibanez-brand instruments. Fujigen had been making Greco copies of Fender and Kanda Shokai had been selling them, so they were well prepared to make and sell Fender guitars.

Meanwhile in the States, the new management team were working on a strategy to return Fender to their former glory. The plan was, quite simply, for Fender to copy themselves, by recreating the guitars that – as we've seen – many players and collectors were spending large sums of money to acquire: the 'vintage' Fender guitars made during the company's glory years in the 1950s and 1960s.

Freddie Tavares, still a consultant to Fender R&D, began work around 1980 on a Vintage Telecaster, planned as a re-creation of a 1952 model. It was to be the first modern reissue of a vintage-style Fender guitar. At the July NAMM music-trade show in 1981, Fender showed a prototype. Dan Smith arrived at the company a month later. "This supposed '52 Telecaster had polyester finish, the wrong body shape, a whole bunch of stuff wrong with it," said Smith. "I told them we can't ship that. So we shut down the vintage reissue series. We brought in Ted Greene, a great guitar player here in Southern California, who had I think 13 or 14 old Broadcasters and Nocasters and Telecasters. We spent a lot of time with him and his Teles, making sure we had all the details right."[87]

The new team needed more information to assist in their proposed re-creations of other vintage instruments. So R&D man John Page travelled with Smith to vintage guitar dealer Ax In Hand in Illinois, where they took further measurements and photographs and paint-tests from the relevant old Fenders. "And we left having

► **1982 BULLET, RED**

■ The next generation of Fender's 'student' models appeared in 1981 with the single-cutaway Bullet (right). It marked the first time that Fender tried overseas manufacturing, although for now the idea did not succeed. Early experiments at full Korean manufacture and at Korean parts being assembled in America failed, and by late '81 the instruments were back to Fender's regular all-U.S. production. The Bullets themselves were shortlived too, lasting until 1983, when a number of double-cut versions were made.

▼ **1979 25TH ANNIVERSARY STRATOCASTER**

■ Another crack at providing a successful new 'student' model for Fender came with the Lead models of 1979 (1981 ad for Lead III, right). They were intended to replace Fender's original budget trio, the Mustang, Bronco, and Musicmaster, at the evidently tricky position at the bottom of the company's pricelist. The Lead I and II were designed by Gregg Wilson and the III by John Page. They were simple double-cut solids – "they're cutting into rock music history like a hot knife in butter" insisted Fender in some shameless publicity – but they ended up not especially cheap at around $400. None of the Leads lasted beyond 1982.

■ Commemorating the launch of the Strat in 1954, the so-called limited edition 25th Anniversary Stratocaster (main guitar) bore little evident relationship to that original and iconic instrument. Today we might expect a nit-picking replica, but not so in 1979. OK, there was a fretted maple neck and body-end truss-rod adjustment. But otherwise, what you got in your surprise birthday package was a '79 Strat with a unique silver paint job, a cheesy Anniversary logo on the upper horn, a neck-plate with special serial number, and locking tuners. Many unhappy returns?

bought perfect examples of each era," said Smith. "We spent $5,600 on a '57 Precision, '60 Jazz Bass, and a '61 Strat. Which for Fender at the time was ludicrous. We went out and bought back our own product!"[88]

Such industry resulted in the Vintage reissue series, begun in 1982. The guitars consisted of a maple-neck '57 and rosewood-fingerboard '62 Strat, as well as the '52 Tele. Production of the Vintage reissues was planned to start in 1982 at Fender US (Fullerton) and at Fender Japan (Fujigen) but the changes being instituted at the American factory meant that the US versions did not come on-stream until early 1983, and the factory there was not up to full speed until the start of '84.

Dan Smith and his colleagues at Fender USA received samples of the Japanese-made Vintage reissues before American production started, and he remembered their reaction to the high quality of these oriental Fender re-creations. "Everybody came up to inspect them and the guys almost cried, because the Japanese product was so good. It was what we were having a hell of a time trying to do."[89]

TODAY IS YESTERDAY'S TOMORROW

The vintage years allocated to the Strat reissues were chosen, said Smith, "because in the US 1957 is the classic year for automobiles" and, rather more Fender-related, because 1962 was the transition year for a change in fingerboard construction. "We knew that the vintage guys liked the slab board, so we felt that if we had neck problems we could always go to the curved fretboard and still call it a '62 without scrapping our pricelists and catalogues."[90] Smith said they also took into consideration the fact that, unlike other years close by, 1962 has no collective bad memories for most Americans.

The July 1983 pricelist pitched the '52 Telecaster reissue at $785 and the Vintage Stratocaster at $885 (each $345 more than the regular model). That same month, Guitar Trader, a dealer based in New Jersey and specialising in vintage instruments, offered a 1954 Telecaster and a 1957 Stratocaster, each for sale at $3,000. These were the most expensive guitars in their inventory apart from a few 1950s Les Paul Standards and a Flying V. The Tele was blond with maple neck, black pickguard, and level-polepiece lead pickup. It was, said Guitar Trader, "fully intact and supplied with original formfit hardcase" and "the most sought-after style of Telecaster produced". The Strat was in sunburst with vibrato, had a "maple v-neck construction" neck, and was an "exceptionally fine collectable specimen".[91]

Fender's new Vintage reproductions were not exact enough for some die-hard Fender collectors, but the idea seemed sound enough. If there was a growing and lucrative market for old guitars, then why not for guitars that looked like the old ones? But guitarists knew that the instruments had to feel and play right, too – the very attributes that made the older Strats and Teles so appealing. Clearly, Fender had more work to do. But they were definitely onto something.

Fender Japan's guitars were being made only for the internal Japanese market, but Fender's European agents were putting pressure on the Fullerton management to provide a budget-price Fender to compete with the multitude of exported models being sold in Europe and elsewhere by other Japanese manufacturers. So in 1982, Fender Japan made some less costly versions of the Vintage Strat and Tele reissues for European distribution. These were distinguished at first by the addition of a small 'Squier Series' logo on the tip of the headstock, soon changed to a large 'Squier' that replaced the Fender logo. The Squier guitar brand had been born.

The name came from a string-making company, V.C. Squier of Michigan, that Fender had acquired in 1965. Victor Carroll Squier was born in 19th-century Boston, the son of an English immigrant, and became a violin maker, moving to Battle Creek, Michigan, where he founded his string-making firm with Gus Crawford in 1890. The company operated at the same Battle Creek building from 1927 to 1972, when CBS relocated the operation within the town.

Towards the end of 1983, with the US Fender factory still not producing as much as the new team wanted, Schultz and Smith decided to have Fender Japan build an instrument for the US market. A Japanese-made Squier-brand '70s-style Telecaster and Strat, together with the earlier Squier Vintage Teles and Strats, saw the start of the sale of Fender Japan products around the world, and the move by Fender to become an international manufacturer of guitars.

"It taught us, contrary to what the guys believed at Fender six or seven years before, that people would buy Fender guitars with 'made in Japan' on them," Smith said. "In fact I really believe that our introduction of those instruments, worldwide and in the USA, was what legitimised buying Japanese guitars."[92] Certainly there had been a resistance by many musicians to the cheap image associated with Japanese-made guitars, but the rise in the quality of instruments from brands such as Ibanez, Yamaha, Fernandes, Aria, Tokai – and now Fender and Squier – wiped away a good deal of this prejudice and gave oriental guitars a new popularity and respectability.

At the US factory in 1983, cost-cutting changes were made to the Standard Stratocaster and Telecaster. This was done because of the dollar's strength and the consequent difficulty in selling US-made products overseas, where they were becoming increasingly expensive. Savings had to be made, so the Strat lost a tone control and its distinctive jack plate, while the Tele was deprived of its tone-enhancing through-body stringing. These were ill-conceived changes, and many onlookers who had applauded the improvements made since '81 groaned at the familiar signs of economics again apparently taking precedence over playability and sound. Fortunately, these mutant varieties of Fender's key models were gone by the end of 1984.

Another shortlived pair from the same time was the Elite Stratocaster and Telecaster, intended as radical new high-end versions of the old faithfuls.

▼ 1988 '57 STRATOCASTER, SURF GREEN

■ A reorganised and apparently revitalised Fender company launched a vintage reissue series in 1982 among the continuing popularity of old Strats and Teles. Included in the first batch of models was a maple-neck '57 Stratocaster (main guitar), a rosewood-fingerboard '62 Stratocaster, and a '52 Telecaster (right). The idea turned out to be a masterstroke, allowing Fender to capitalise on its own increasingly valuable history. The reissue models amounted to an attempt to re-create the originals as authentically as possible. Given modern production methods, some compromises had to be made, but these new oldies have proved to be a successful move for Fender and a line that has seen a programme of advances and improvements, still in development at the company's HQ today.

VINTAGE TELECASTER

■ This page from a 1982 catalogue (right) introduces the reissued '52 Telecaster as the 'Vintage Telecaster', the very first model to be given attention in Fender's new reissue programme of the early 1980s. The idea was to make close replicas of the old guitars – by then almost always called 'vintage' rather than simply 'secondhand' or 'old'. Many musicians were beginning to think that key vintage instruments had special qualities which newer instruments did not seem to possess.

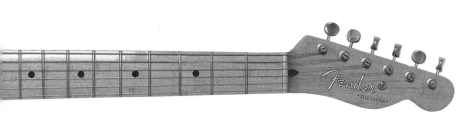

▲ 1982 SQUIER SERIES STRATOCASTER

■ Fender began guitar production in Japan in the early 1980s, and some of the earliest models from that source were branded Squier, advertised (below) as "brilliant executions of classic instruments". The Squier name came from a string company that Fender had acquired years earlier. At first, the guitars had a small Squier Series logo on the tip of the headstock (as with this Strat, left), but soon a large Squier logo replaced 'Fender' as the main brand.

▲ 1984 '52 TELECASTER

THERE'S MAGIC IN THE BREED

Unfortunately, the vibrato-equipped Elite Strat came saddled with a terrible bridge, which is what most players recall when the Elites are mentioned. In-fighting at Fender had led to last-minute modifications to the vibrato design, and the result was an unwieldy, unworkable piece of hardware. The Elite Strat featured three pushbuttons for pickup selection, which were not to the taste of players brought up on the classic Fender switch. There were good points – the new pickups, the effective active circuitry, and an improved truss-rod design – but they tended to be overlooked. The Elites too were dropped by the end of '84.

Three new-design Fender lines were introduced in 1984, made by Fender Japan, that were intended to compete with Gibson. The overall name for the new instruments was the Master Series and they included electric archtop D'Aquisto models, with design input from American luthier Jimmy D'Aquisto, and semi-solid Esprit and Flame guitars. Significantly, they were the first Fender Japan products with the Fender rather than Squier headstock logo to be sold officially outside Japan, and the first Fenders with Gibson-style glued-in 'set' necks.

Their overtly Gibson image was to be their undoing, as Dan Smith admitted. "They were made real well, they sounded good and everything else – but they weren't 'Fender'. Also, Fujigen had manufacturing problems, and we didn't get any for over a year. So we introduced them to all this excitement – and nothing came out for a year. And then CBS pulled the plug."[93]

For a variety of reasons, CBS decided during 1984 that they had finally had enough of the music business and wanted to sell Fender Musical Instruments. A newspaper report in January 1985 detailed the reasons. Essentially, CBS blamed Japanese competition for Fender's recent losses. "The Fullerton-based firm's last domestic guitar-manufacturing unit, which employs 60 senior craftsmen who build top-of-the-line instruments for professional musicians, is scheduled to be shut down February 1st," wrote the reporter. "Company officials say tentative plans call for the continued manufacture of electric pianos until the end of February at the plant in this Orange County community 25 miles southeast of Los Angeles. The future of the company's famed product lines – the guitars pioneered by Leo Fender, pianos by Harold Rhodes, Rogers drums, and Squier guitar strings – will depend on Fender's new owner, who must decide which ones to continue and which, if any, will be made in the United States."

The story went on to explain that the Fender name and business were being sold separately from the large manufacturing plant. "There are a lot of broken hearts around Fullerton," said former CBS musical instruments division president John McLaren. The paper pointed out that McLaren, Schultz, and their team had tried to turn the company around between 1981 and 1983. McLaren had left Fender a year ago. One estimate put sales of Fender guitars down 50 percent in the last three years. "CBS does not report financial statistics for its division separately but attributed an

$8.3 million Columbia Group operating loss for the third quarter of 1984 in part to 'continued losses in the musical instruments business'."

The report speculated that the US guitar industry's problems were not due solely to the Japanese. It suggested that the baby boom generation was past the prime instrument-buying age and, in a still familiar phrase, that "today's young people seem to be more interested in video games and computers than guitars". The newspaper reckoned that some fault lay also with the corporate giants who began snapping up the best instrument manufacturers during the 1960s but were "ill-suited to running businesses in which success depended so much on craftsmanship and personal service".[94]

CBS invited offers for Fender. Interested parties included International Music Co (IMC), which marketed Hondo and Jackson guitars among others, and the Kaman Music Corp, best known for Ovation guitars. Smith recalled: "In mid to late November of 1984, CBS finally said, look, we're not going to have any success selling this for what we want. We're getting all these low-ball offers. We'd like to offer it to you guys. If you can raise the capital, we'll sell you the company, as long as your offer is better than liquidation.

"To be honest," said Smith, "if nobody had come up with an offer better than liquidation, Fender would have gone under. That would have been it. Over. Done."[95] It's worth considering that remark again. Just imagine: the company was just an executive's signature away from closing in 1984. Such a devastating move would have marked the end for one of the most important guitar makers ever. Fortunately, the team at Fender had other ideas.

At the end of January 1985, almost exactly 20 years since they had acquired it, CBS announced they would sell Fender to "an investor group led by William Schultz, president of Fender Musical Instruments". The contract was formalised in February and the sale completed in March for $12.5 million. Alert readers will recall the $13 million that CBS originally paid for the company back in 1965.

With the hectic months of negotiations and financing behind them, Schultz and his team could now run Fender for themselves (and a number of investment banks, of course). They faced many problems, but probably the most immediate was the fact that the Fullerton buildings were not included in the deal (CBS sold the factories separately). So US production of Fenders stopped in February 1985 – although the new team had been stockpiling bodies and necks and had acquired some existing inventory of completed guitars as well as production machinery. The company went from employing over 800 people in early 1984 down to just over 100 in early 1985. "Scary but exciting" is how Dan Smith described it at the time. "We're not going to be in the position to be able to make any mistakes," he said. "There'll be nobody behind us with a big cheque-book if we have a bad month."[96]

Administration headquarters were established in Brea, California, not far from

▲ **1983 GOLD ELITE TELECASTER, EMERALD GREEN**

■ The Elite Telecaster (main guitar) and Stratocaster (below) were shortlived high-end versions of the old faithfuls. The Tele had two new humbucking pickups linked to active circuitry, providing a wide array of tones, only a few of which would be familiar to traditional Tele players.

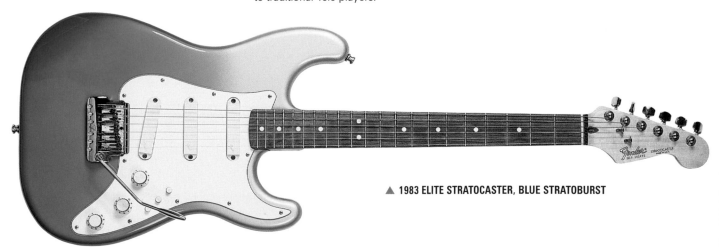

▲ **1983 ELITE STRATOCASTER, BLUE STRATOBURST**

■ The Standard Stratocaster (right) was revised in 1983 after a relatively respectable first version had been introduced two years earlier with some sensible and welcome modifications. Now, however, costs were cut and the amended Standard lost the traditional recessed jack socket as well as the second tone control and the regular vibrato system – all of which were features that had remained intact since the very first Strat had been launched almost 30 years earlier. The changes were unwise and proved unpopular, and the Standard was with good reason withdrawn in 1984.

Fender Elite: Where Tomorrow's Music Is Headed.

■ The Stratocaster Elite was the less popular of the two new Fender Elites. Players were particularly disturbed by the ill designed vibrato, highlighted by this close-up (above) in the 1983 catalogue. The Freeflyte vibrato, as it was known, was an operational disaster. Along with the replacement of the traditional pickup-selector with three pushbuttons, it was a major contributor to the model's failure. The example pictured (opposite) is in blue Stratoburst finish, also offered in black or bronze.

▶ 1983 STANDARD STRATOCASTER

Fullerton. Six years later, Fender would move admin from Brea to Scottsdale, Arizona, where it remains today. A new factory also had to be found, of course, but in the meantime Schultz and Smith considered using existing production sources further afield. Among the potential sources examined was the Godin factory in Canada, but the various options proved unworkable and Fender began searching for a factory site in the familiar Orange County area of Los Angeles.

Fender had been working on a couple of radical guitar designs before the sale campaign started, and these became victims of the crossfire. One was a John Page design, the Performer, which started life intended for US production. But with nowhere to build it in the States, Fender had it manufactured at the Fujigen factory in Japan.

The Performer had a distinctive body shape, two angled pickups, 24 frets, and an arrow-shape headstock quite different from the usual Fender Strat derivative. The headstock was in fact based on the 1969 Swinger head, to avoid the need for a new trademark, and was a reaction to the newly popular so-called superstrat design popularised by Jackson and Kramer. The visual signature of these instruments was a much-emulated drooping, pointed headstock. All in all, Fender's Performer was a brave and thoroughly modern instrument with few nods to the company's illustrious past.

"We had players lining up to play the Performer," remembered Smith, "but they wanted an American-made product. We had a great response at the New Orleans trade show, but right after that was when CBS pulled the plug. I think it was a great guitar, but it just got caught up in the midst of the sale. The same thing happened with the Master series. We just started to get some players, we just started to do some advertising – and the word came down that it was over. We basically had to kill all those projects."[97]

The Performer did manage to stay on Fender's books until 1986, but it now seems a pity that such a relatively innovative move should have been dropped for reasons largely unconnected with the instrument itself. Of less interest was the Katana, a response to the fashion for odd body-shapes among guitar makers at the time. Key dealers pressured Fender to come up with their own weird shape. Once again, players resisted the styling and the imposed Japanese origin of the Katana, and this guitar too limped on only until 1986. The Japanese operation now became Fender's lifeline, providing much-needed product to the company, which still had no US factory.

All the guitars in Fender's 1985 catalogue were made in Japan, including the new Contemporary Stratocasters and Telecasters, the first Fenders with the increasingly fashionable heavy-duty vibrato units and string-clamps. Production in Japan was based on a handshake agreement that Fujigen would continue to supply Fender with guitars after CBS pulled the plug. One estimate put as much as 80 percent of the guitars that Fender US sold from around the end of 1984 to the middle of 1986 as made in Japan.

The story of Fender's oriental production is slightly complicated at this stage by the fact that Fujigen were not able to make as many guitars as Fender needed. So around 1985 the Moridaira Musical Instrument Co of Tokyo began to make some models (they already supplied acoustic guitars to Fender). In the midst of this activity, the dollar had started to weaken against other currencies and Fender again had trouble competing on price. So they looked to another of their offshore acoustic guitar producers, the Young Chang Akki Co of Seoul, South Korea, to make electric guitars.

Company insiders remember that Fender's first truly Korean guitars were pretty good: these were the Squier Standard Strats and Teles, which began to appear in 1985 and lasted around three years. A number of Squier models are still made in Korean factories today (and some Fender-brand guitars too), while at the time of writing the lowest-price Squiers are usually made in China, Indonesia, or India.

Back in the United States, Fender had finally established their new factory at Corona, about 15 miles east of the defunct Fullerton site. Production started on a very limited scale towards the end of 1985, when they were building only about five guitars per day for the Vintage reissue series. But Dan Smith and his colleagues wanted to re-establish the US side of Fender's production with some good, basic Strats and Teles (and of course a Precision Bass and Jazz Bass), instruments that they wanted players to recognise as continuations of the best of Fender's American traditions. That plan translated into the American Standard models.

CREATING AN AMERICAN STANDARD

The new Fender operation had little money in the bank, and they decided their first efforts must centre on making a basic, straightahead Strat. The team had learned from mistakes such as the Elite vibrato that the focus had to be on simplicity. The result of their efforts appeared in 1986, the $589.99 American Standard Stratocaster, an efficacious piece of re-interpretation. It drew from the best of the original Stratocaster but was updated with a flatter-camber 22-fret neck and a revised vibrato unit using two stud pivot points. Once the Corona plant's production lines reached full speed, the American Standard Strat proved extremely successful for the revitalised Fender company – and soon the guitar would become a bestseller. The American Standard Telecaster was updated with a 22-fret neck and a six-saddle bridge and was launched (along with the two basses) in 1988 at $599.99, two years after the Strat.

For a year or two, the American Standard Strat was offered in a Deluxe version, fitted with Fender's special Lace Sensor pickups. Don Lace, an expert in magnetics, had tried to interest Fender in his designs before the CBS sale. Discussions reopened afterwards. Lace's original idea was for a bass pickup, but Fender said that their main requirement was for a new guitar pickup. They wanted to continue in the direction started with the Elite pickups, aiming for the ideal of a low-noise unit with low magnetic attraction that still delivered the classic single-coil sound.

These requirements resulted in the Lace Sensor pickups. While not to every player's

▼ 1984 TELECASTER STANDARD, BOWLING BALL GOLD

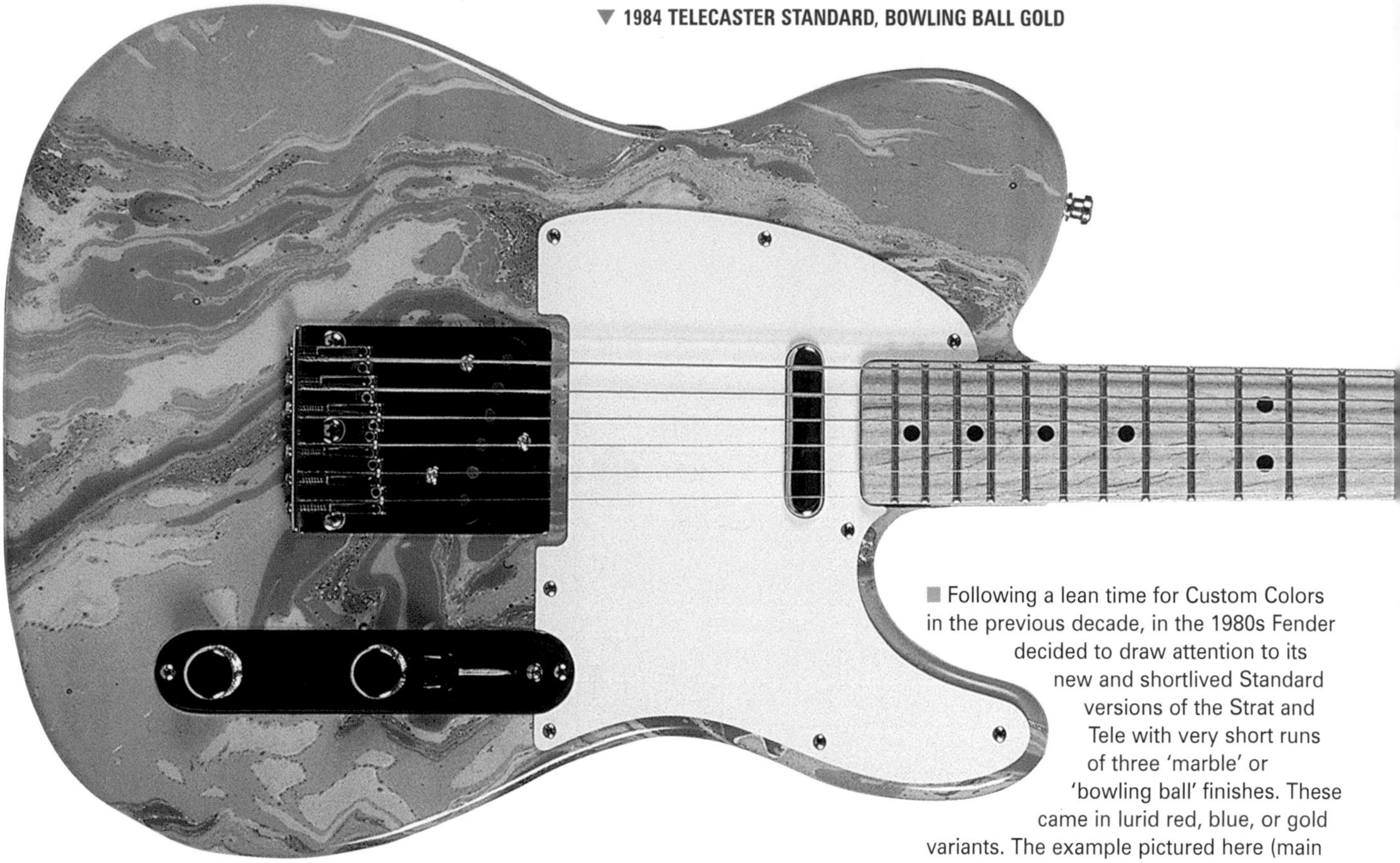

■ Following a lean time for Custom Colors in the previous decade, in the 1980s Fender decided to draw attention to its new and shortlived Standard versions of the Strat and Tele with very short runs of three 'marble' or 'bowling ball' finishes. These came in lurid red, blue, or gold variants. The example pictured here (main guitar) is of the gold finish on a Telecaster Standard; note this model's lack of through-body stringing.

▼ 1986 PERFORMER, EMERALD MIST

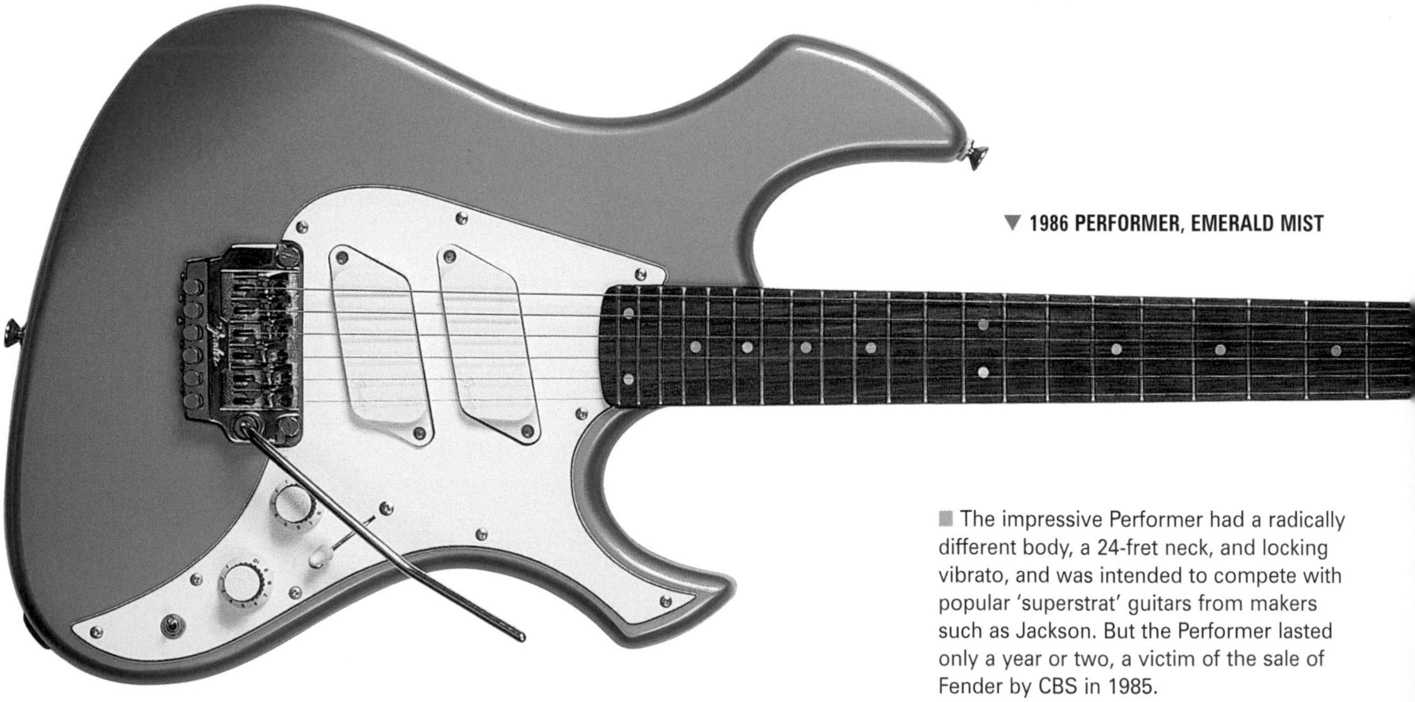

■ The impressive Performer had a radically different body, a 24-fret neck, and locking vibrato, and was intended to compete with popular 'superstrat' guitars from makers such as Jackson. But the Performer lasted only a year or two, a victim of the sale of Fender by CBS in 1985.

**Flamé: Bold In Concept,
Brilliant In Execution**

**Esprit: Homage To The Past,
An eye To The Future**

▼ **1985 KATANA, BLACK**

■ Aside from superstrats, Fender also had a go at the metal-inclined odd-shapes brigade. The shortlived Katana (above) was the result, clearly a contender for ugliest Fender ever. In contrast, the Master Series included semi-solid Flame and Esprit models (ads, above) and the archtop

D'Aquisto. Renowned guitar-maker Jimmy D'Aquisto began his collaboration with Fender at this time and at first the D'Aquistos were made in Japan. Later, following D'Aquisto's untimely death in 1995, further models appeared (right) made at the Custom Shop.

▶ **1997 D'AQUISTO DELUXE**

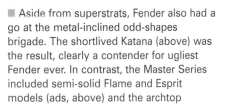

■ The Performer's pointed headstock was an unusual touch for Fender, but was part of the move toward the looks and playability of 1980s 'superstrats', which had exaggerated pointed heads. In fact, the Performer's head was derived from an old and obscure Fender model, the Swinger from 1969.

taste, they are a viable alternative to Fender's standard pickup designs, and have been offered on various models since the Strat Plus became the first Fender to carry Lace Sensors in 1987. More pickups of various kinds have been offered since on some Fender guitars, either supplied by the better-known pickup brands or coming from the company's own production lines. Recent developments include two stacked single-coil pickup types, the SCN (Samarium Cobalt Noiseless), designed with the help of pickup legend Bill Lawrence, and the Vintage Noiseless pickups, designed by ex-EMG man Bill Turner. Both aim for the pickup designer's dream combination – vintage sound and low noise – but tackle the various problems using different technical solutions.

Fender's business and production headaches didn't help them in the 1980s, and new competing styles of solidbody electric guitars were appearing, notably the 'superstrat' style popularised by Jackson and Charvel. But the Telecaster could still be seen and heard in some engaging company. Albert Lee was the Tele player's Tele player, notably working with Sonny Curtis's Crickets, Emmylou Harris, and Eric Clapton, but he made solo albums too, and included amongst them was the 1979 track 'Country Boy' that defined his deft picking, full of tumbling arpeggios.

Jerry Donahue was another Tele player who'd worked widely with others – as a member of Fotheringay and Fairport Convention, and with Joan Armatrading, Gerry Rafferty, Chris Rea, and many others in the studio and on the road. In 1986, Donahue released a firm solo statement of his guitar preference, the *Telecasting* album. When someone like Tele maestro Danny Gatton called him "the string-bending king of the planet", any players who hadn't already grasped Donahue's importance were sure to take notice.

Prominent Strat men of the 1980s ranged from guitarist's guitarist Eric Johnson to shred king Yngwie Malmsteen. David Gilmour had been playing Strats to great effect in Pink Floyd for some time – 1975's *Wish You Were Here* had underlined that – but his solo on 'Comfortably Numb' from *The Wall*, and especially his live version on top of the bricks during the early-1980s *Wall* shows, remains for many a definitively sublime Strat moment.

Stevie Ray Vaughan brought the Stratocaster's capabilities spectacularly to notice in 1983 when the Texan blues-rocker made a surprisingly effective pairing with David Bowie on Bowie's *Let's Dance* album. Vaughan's own *Texas Flood* of the same year went on to reveal more of his abilities, including some inspired Hendrix-flavoured outings. Vaughan died prematurely in a helicopter crash in 1990, but not before he defined contemporary blues-rock guitar playing, mostly performed on his distinctively careworn '63-body/'62-neck Strat.

Fender established a Custom Shop in the mid 1980s at the Corona factory. It began so that they could build one-offs and special orders for players who had the money and the inclination. "We were only going to make ten Vintage pieces a day," said Dan Smith, "so we were going to start a Custom Shop to build special projects for artists, to make certain that the prestige was still there for the company."[98] This role remains – customers have included everyone from Bob Dylan and Pops Staples to David Bowie and Kurt Cobain – but today the Shop plays a much wider and more visible part in Fender's expanding business.

Guitar builder George Blanda was originally recruited in 1985 to make the artist guitars, but a year later, as shifting exchange rates began to favour exports, demand for US-made product increased dramatically. Fender needed an R&D specialist to come up with new models and the job fell to Blanda. He had the perfect combination of an engineering capability and a love of guitars. Blanda's move left the Custom Shop position vacant.

Fender discussed the idea with guitar makers Michael Stevens and John Carruthers, and also with former Fender R&D man John Page, who had left the company a year earlier to concentrate on his music. The result was that Stevens and Page joined Fender to start the Custom Shop in January 1987. Their first official job was to make a left-handed Foam Green Telecaster Thinline for Elliot Easton of The Cars. The order was placed at the end of February 1987, and Page completed the instrument on August 10th.

The expansion of the Custom Shop's business prompted a move in 1993 to new buildings – still close to the Corona factory – providing extra space and improved efficiency. When Fender's new plant was unveiled five years later, the Custom Shop was at last shifted into the factory. At the start of the 1990s, the Shop was building about 2,500 guitars a year, and by 1996 that figure had risen to some 7,000 instruments. Fender will not discuss current numbers, but it's safe to assume that they have climbed dramatically.

Dan Smith said that the long-running Strat Plus, introduced in 1987, followed on logically from the new company's important early developments – the vintage-style Fenders, the US-made American Standard models, and the establishment of Fender Japan. "The Strat Plus was a real modern guitar that addressed a lot of needs that modern players had, but retaining the integrity of the Stratocaster. That applied to the whole Plus series."[99]

The Tele Plus of 1990 offered an especially wide choice of pickup tones by combining three of Fender's low-noise/no-string-pull Lace Sensor single-coil units, with two grouped at the bridge that could be switched in together as a humbucker. A shortlived later version opted for the Burton-type layout with three single-coils arranged Strat-style. The Plus guitars established the notion of modern-style Fender models and would evolve into later instruments with the same underlying idea, such as the American Deluxe models.

An early job for the Custom Shop was to make a yellow Vintage reissue Stratocaster

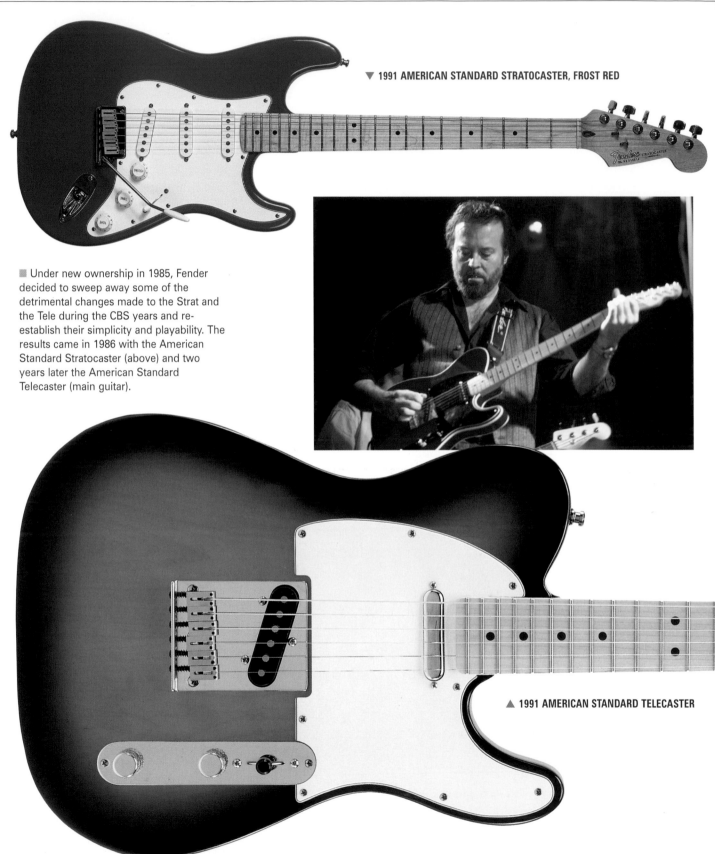

▼ 1991 AMERICAN STANDARD STRATOCASTER, FROST RED

■ Under new ownership in 1985, Fender decided to sweep away some of the detrimental changes made to the Strat and the Tele during the CBS years and re-establish their simplicity and playability. The results came in 1986 with the American Standard Stratocaster (above) and two years later the American Standard Telecaster (main guitar).

▲ 1991 AMERICAN STANDARD TELECASTER

Behind the better-known pop names and all the rest who line up to play Fenders at any given time in guitar history, there usually resides a more select bunch of guitarists. These players are revered among their fellow musicians and known only to the more inquisitive general music fan. Two fine examples leap out from this period: Texan Strat man Eric Johnson (above), whose pure tone and dextrous fretwork make him an obvious choice for the guitarist's guitarist award, and New York-born Tele maestro Jerry Donahue (opposite), memorably described by another pickers' role-model, Danny Gatton, as "the string-bending king of the planet".

▲ **1989 BLUE FLOWER STRATOCASTER**

After Fender Japan was officially established in 1982, the operation made instruments for the home market as well as for export to the USA and elsewhere. The Japanese were especially keen on vintage-style Fenders and a stream of older-flavoured models appeared from the appointed Fujigen factory. One example was this revived Blue Flower finish on a Stratocaster (left), which in fact had only appeared originally on a Telecaster.

for Jeff Beck. At this stage Beck vetoed Fender's wish to produce a Jeff Beck signature edition Strat, and the design originally intended for that purpose evolved into the Strat Plus. A Jeff Beck signature Strat, not dissimilar to the Plus, finally appeared in 1991. In fact, the first musician with whom Fender informally discussed the possibility of a signature model had been James Burton, back in 1981, but Burton too had to wait (until 1990) for his signature Telecaster to appear on the market.

The first signature guitar produced by Fender was the Eric Clapton Stratocaster. Clapton had asked Fender to make him a Strat with the distinct v-profile neck of his favourite 1930s Martin acoustic guitar as well as what he described to Dan Smith as a "compressed" pickup sound. George Blanda built various prototypes, and the final design eventually went on sale to the public in 1988. Lace Sensor pickups and an active circuit delivered the sound Clapton was after, and the production model even offers a blocked-off vintage-style vibrato unit, carefully duplicating that feature of Clapton's original. New versions appeared in 2001, with Noiseless pickups, and from the Custom Shop in 2004, without the active circuit.

A number of Fender signature models have followed – some made in the Custom Shop, others from Corona or further afield – and each one is generally endowed with features favoured by the named artist. They have ranged from the posthumous and long-running Stevie Ray Vaughan Stratocaster model to the Waylon Jennings 'Tribute Series' Telecaster, the Dick Dale surfing Strat to the Danny Gatton Tele-player's-Tele-player Telecaster, and from John Lowery's J5 Triple Tele Deluxe with three split-polepiece pickups and a Strat vibrato to the one-humbucker/one-knob Tom Delonge Stratocaster.

Fender's 1988 pricelist included a case with everything and showed 13 Stratocasters: three signatures (Eric Clapton $1,299; Yngwie Malmsteen $1,299; Alex Gregory seven-string "to be announced"), two $999.99 Vintage models ('57 and '62), the US Strat Plus ($849.99), the American Standard ($649.99), Japanese Paisley ($579.99), Blue Flower ($579.99), and '68 ($509.99), the HM Strat (in three varieties, $589.99-$669.99), the Standard ($619.99), and the Stratocaster XII ($719.99). There were four Telecasters, also all including case: the US-made Vintage '52 ($999.99) and American Standard ($649.99), and the Japanese '62 Custom ($579.99) and Blue Flower ($549.99).

Floyd Rose, a guitar hardware designer best known for his heavy-duty locking vibrato system, joined forces with Fender towards the end of 1991. Fender acquired the exclusive rights to Floyd Rose products bearing his name. Other makers could still buy licensed hardware, but Fender seemed to be more interested in gaining access to Rose's undoubted design skills as well as the assistance that his name brought to sell guitars to metal players.

To such musicians, 'Floyd Rose' was almost synonymous with the heavy-duty double-locking vibrato systems that were so closely associated with the fast, intense, and highly-technical style of playing that reached a peak of popularity in the early

1990s. But by the middle of the decade the locking vibrato had slipped in the fashion stakes, and instead there was a marked return to simplicity amid moves to earlier retro designs and modern interpretations – all of which could hardly have been hindered by Fender's own emphasis on vintage-style vibratos. Fender's deal with Floyd Rose came to an amicable end in 2001.

Aside from the shortlived Esprit and Flame guitars of 1984, Fender have not strayed much from their customary bolt-on-neck construction. Three Set Neck Teles and three Strats in the 1990s offered the glued joint, enabling a smooth, heel-less junction where neck meets body (which some players find more comfortable and usefully playable). They were replaced by Fender's super-est superstrats yet, the set-neck carved-top Showmaster models, the first of which appeared in 1998.

A shortlived new design in 1991, the Prodigy, was a further attempt to compete with superstrats from Ibanez, Charvel, and others. It had an offset-waist body with sharper horns than a Strat, two single-coils and a humbucker, and an optional locking vibrato. Significantly, it was among the first Fender models to receive attention at the company's new factory in Ensenada, Mexico, which had been established in 1987. Ensenada is some 180 miles south of Los Angeles, just across the California/Mexico border, about a three-hour drive from the Corona factory. Fender amps started to appear from the Mexico plant in 1989, with guitars following soon after.

By early 1992, the Mexican factory at Ensenada was producing around 175 Fender Standard Stratocasters per day. Following a devastating fire in February 1994, the plant was rebuilt. In the absence of official current figures from Fender, our own estimate is that today Mexico is capable of producing over 100,000 guitars a year, the same number that Corona can produce. Again, Fender will not discuss how many employees they have, but our own estimate is that there are around 1,200 workers at Ensenada and about 800 at Corona.

Following the success of the Vintage reissue series, introduced in 1982, Fender Japan marketed more models that re-created many of the guitars from Fender's past, including reproductions of the Paisley, Blue Flower, Rosewood, and Thinline Telecasters, the Jaguar and Jazzmaster, the Mustang, and of course a plethora of Strats recalling various periods. Many of these are sold only in Japan; some also appear from time to time in the US, Europe, and elsewhere. Fender effectively wiped out copy guitars by establishing the Japanese company and producing good lower-priced versions of their best-known models. In recent years the company have also actively defended their trademarks for model names and headstock shapes, and now make a point of claiming trademarks for body shapes too.

Fender made some changes to its management structure in 1995. Company president Bill Schultz became CEO and Bill Mendello was made the new president, with Kurt Hemrich promoted to senior executive vice president. Mendello had joined CBS corporate in 1971 as a financial graduate and held various positions in that

When you're cooking, use the best ingredients.

Robert Cray

Fender
We Make
History

Signature models are guitars endowed with features favoured by the named artist and sold to anyone who cares for the connection. For Fender, this line began in 1988 with the Eric Clapton Stratocaster model (see God with said instrument, opposite). Many more have followed that debut, including Strats named for Robert Cray (ad, left), Richie Sambora, Bonnie Raitt, and Robin Trower, and Telecasters for Muddy Waters, Francis Rossi, Will Ray, and Danny Gatton.

Jeff Beck was a natural for a Fender signature model, and his Strat (right) appeared in 1991. It is similar to the earlier Strat Plus with extra bridge pickup, locking tuners, and roller nut. A revised version in 2001 had Noiseless pickups replacing the Lace Sensors, and a Custom Shop edition was launched in 2004.

◄ 1991 JEFF BECK STRATOCASTER, SEAFOAM GREEN

▼ 1990 STRAT PLUS, GRAFFITI YELLOW

The Strat Plus (main guitar) was intended as a modern Strat upgrade that would appeal to pro players of the day while retaining the Strat's integrity. It had the fashionable roller nut and locking tuners to assist extreme vibrato work and was the first Fender with the new Lace Sensor pickups, which aimed for low noise and classic sound.

company's publications, broadcasting, and recordings divisions before joining CBS Musical Instruments as Chief Financial Officer in 1977. He'd joined the new team at Fender in Fullerton in 1981 and four years later worked alongside Bill Schultz to buy the company from CBS.

MINT OR WITH DINGS, SIR?

Also in 1995, Dan Smith moved from his job as vice president of marketing electric guitars, at the firm's corporate HQ in Scottsdale, Arizona, to become vice president of guitar R&D, based at Corona. Much of Fender's research and development (R&D) is done in-house, and the R&D department had been merged with the Custom Shop in 1990. John Page had moved from the Custom Shop to set up the Fender Museum of Music & The Arts Foundation. He left Fender in January 2003, moving to Oregon where he now builds furniture and guitars. Schultz stepped down as Fender CEO in 2005, staying on as chairman of the board of directors, and Mendello became CEO, which he remains at the time of writing. Schultz died in September 2006.

Leo Fender had died in 1991. The Associated Press wire report for March 21st was stark: "Clarence Leo Fender, whose revolutionary Stratocaster was the guitar of choice for rock stars from Buddy Holly to Jimi Hendrix, died today. He was 82. Fender was found unconscious in his Fullerton home by his wife, Phyllis, and died on the way to hospital. Fender had suffered Parkinson's disease for decades but continued to work on guitar designs." Leo had been at his bench at his G&L company just the day before, tinkering with yet another guitar improvement.

He was honoured at a Rock & Roll Hall Of Fame ceremony in January 1992, one of 12 music legends inducted into the Hall, alongside Jimi Hendrix, Johnny Cash, and others. Leo's second wife, Phyllis, was there for him. "When I accepted his award I said that Leo truly believed that musicians were special angels, special envoys from the Lord," said Mrs Fender. "He believed he was put here to make the very best instruments in the world, because these special angels would help us get through this life, would ease our pain and ease our sadness, and help us celebrate."[100]

Keith Richards also spoke on behalf of Leo, rather more prosaically. "He gave us the weapons," Richards told the Hall Of Fame gathering. He then left them with what he called the guitar players' prayer: "Caress it. Don't squeeze it."[101]

Richards was well aware of the power of Fender's past. A common request at the time from some artists was for the Custom Shop to make them a replica of a favourite old guitar, often because the original was too fragile or valuable to risk taking out on the road. The story according to a Fender insider was that Richards told the Shop that some replicas they had made for him for a Stones tour looked too new. "Bash 'em up a bit and I'll play 'em," he said. So the Shop began to include wear-and-tear distress marks to replicate the overall look of a battered old original. It was not a new idea but certainly an effective one.

Then J.W. Black, a Fender Master Builder who had been working with the Stones, came up with the idea of offering these aged replicas as regular Custom Shop catalogued items, called Relics. "It started almost as a tongue-in-cheek thing," admitted John Page, "like worn-in Levis or something. It would look cool: in the first three rows it'd look like you're playing an incredibly valuable Nocaster. But only you know that it's not really. That was how it started."

The Shop made two aged 1950s-era samples: a Nocaster (nickname for the transitional Broadcaster/Telecaster with no model name) and a 'Mary Kaye' Stratocaster (blond body, gold-plated parts). "We took them to the January 1995 NAMM trade show," said Page, "and put them under glass cases like they were pieces of art. Everyone came along and would say oh, that's really cool, you brought original ones as a tribute. And we were saying, er, yeah – how many do you want? People went nuts! It was amazing." Soon the Custom Shop was reacting to the demand, offering a line of three Relic Strats and a Relic Nocaster.

The line was expanded in 1998 by offering three strands of these 're-creations' in what is now known as the Time Machine series. There's the original Relic style, given 'aged' knocks and the look of heavy wear, as if the guitar has been out on the road for a generation or so; the Closet Classic, made to look as if it had been bought new way back when, played a few times, and then stuck in a closet; and N.O.S. ('New Old Stock'), as if an instrument had been bought brand new in the 1950s or 1960s and then put straight into a time machine that transported it to the present day. The kind of thing, in fact, that vintage guitar collectors and dealers regularly dream about, but which in real life rarely happens.

By 2007, the Custom Shop's Time Machine series included a '56, '60, '66, and '69 Stratocaster (the '66 and '69 with rosewood or maple board), a '59 Esquire, a '51 Nocaster, and a '63 and '67 Telecaster (maple or rosewood board). All were available in each of the three levels of aging – Relic, Closet Classic, or N.O.S. – with the list-price for most averaging around the $3,500 mark. This may seem a high price, but when you compare what you might have to pay today for good-condition originals – from about $7,500 for a '67 Tele, through maybe $15,000 for a '59 Esquire and a cool $65,000 for a '56 Strat, and upwards of $100,000 for a Nocaster – the attraction becomes clearer.

And even if you could find clean originals at those prices, there's always the worry with a vintage piece about the veracity of this paint finish or that pickguard screw or those solder joints. The Custom Shop's Time Machine guitars at least take away any niggling doubts about originality. They appeal to guitar fans keen to acquire a new Fender with the feel and perhaps even the playability of an oldie, and in the case of the Relics made to look as if decades of wear-and-tear have stained the fingerboard, scuffed the body, and tarnished the hardware. It's still not quite the look of a genuine oldie, but it's pretty damned close.

▼ 1992 SET NECK TELECASTER COUNTRY ARTIST, RED

■ Fender strayed from its regular paths during the late 1980s and into the new decade. The Set Neck models, such as this Telecaster (above), meant a rare move away from the company's customary bolt-on neck joint and into Gibson territory. Another wander came with a further attempt to compete with the Jackson-style superstrats so popular at the time: the Fender HM Strats included US guitars as well as the Japanese models in this catalogue (right) that featured one very Jackson-like head (far right).

■ John Frusciante (above) departed the Red Hot Chili Peppers in 1992 after spraying some inspired Strat-fuelled madness all over the band's *Mother's Milk* and *Blood Sugar Sex Magik* albums, the latter in particular featuring his fractured, jagged, and intensely personal style of playing. Replaced for a while by Dave Navarro, Frusciante was back among the Peppers in '98 to appear on their top-notch comeback album, *Californication*.

▲ 1991 PRODIGY II, LAKE PLACID BLUE

■ Yet another superstrat competitor was the Prodigy (main guitar), with an offset body and sharper horns than a Strat, the defining two single-coils and bridge humbucker layout, and an optional locking vibrato. The Prodigy was one of the first guitars to receive attention at Fender's new Mexican factory, located just across the California/Mexico border at Ensenada, although the model was officially US-made. The Mexican factory opened in 1989 to produce amps, with guitars following soon afterward. Fender's Prodigy, launched in 1991, was shortlived and had disappeared from the company's pricelists within two years.

For some reason, neither the Jaguar nor the Jazzmaster has ever had the honour of inclusion as one of these made-to-look-old instruments, or even a Custom Shop catalogue item. But one of the very first custom Fenders was a Jaguar, long before the notion of a proper custom shop. It was built by Fender for a ludicrous 1963 movie, *Bye Bye Birdie*. In it, a rock'n'roll star briefly strums a luscious black Jag with gold fittings and a decorated body that incorporates his (fictional) name, Conrad Birdie. Will we ever see a Conrad Birdie signature Jaguar?

GRUNGE GUITAR GUIDE

There was no shortage of good Stratocaster players during the 1990s – from Mike McCready of Pearl Jam to John Frusciante of The Red Hot Chili Peppers – while the Telecaster appealed to guitarists as diverse as Blur's Graham Coxon and Frank Black of The Pixies. Around the turn of the decade and into the 1990s it was grunge that emerged as the overarching style, and for some it defined this era of guitar playing. But as with punk before, it was never quite that simple. Talented players made their own marks within and around the fashionable label. Also like punk, the attraction of relatively cheap instruments – and of being seen *not* to play the old-school favourites – meant that Fender also-rans such as Jaguars, Jazzmasters, and Mustangs made a good showing among some of the leading fretmen of the time.

There was J. Mascis in Dinosaur Jr., an inventive guitarist who played various Jazzmasters (primarily a modified $300 '63), Thurston Moore in Sonic Youth, who favoured Jazzes but didn't say no to a Jag or his modified three-pickup Mustang, and Stone Gossard, who toted the occasional Jaguar in Pearl Jam. And that's not to forget a few cheers for notable Jag-man Brian Molko of Placebo as well as Steve Turner in Mudhoney with his Competition Mustang.

In Nirvana, Kurt Cobain played his favoured left-hand Fender Jaguar (a '65 sunburst with humbuckers added and some of the switches removed and taped over) as well as a Mustang. Probably early in 1993, he cut up some photos of his Fenders and stuck them together this way and that, trying out different combinations. Larry Brooks in Fender's Custom Shop was given the paste-ups and asked to create a design for a new instrument. "Kurt always enjoyed playing both guitars," said Brooks. "He took photographs of each, cut them in half, and put them together to see what they'd look like. It was his concept, and we detailed it and contoured it to give him balance and feel."[102]

Cobain received the resulting red custom guitar from Fender, although he never saw the second (blue) one. Following his untimely death in 1994, Cobain's family collaborated with Fender to release a Japanese-made production version of the instrument, by that time named the Fender Jag-Stang. The model, which Fender described as "a collision of contemporary features fused together to create a combination of Jaguar and Mustang", hit the market in 1996 at $619.99 but has been on international pricelists only intermittently since then.

If there was one word that defined the electric guitar industry during the 1990s it was retro. Toward the end of the decade more guitar makers than ever were busily looking back to the past in a search for fresh inspiration as the craze for retro flavours seemed to be everywhere – in fashion, in cars, in music. Fender were ideally positioned to benefit from this.

It's easy enough to understand the trend. Some makers felt that there was almost no more to be done to the electric guitar, that it had reached its ultimate incarnation and that the general design and construction and manufacturing processes – still largely defined by Fender and Gibson – were just about as perfect as they could get. Instead of going forward, why not absorb the best factors that made past instruments so distinctive and catch a bonus from the fashionable retro vibe?

Fender simply had to keep making Strats and Teles for their major contribution, of course, but retro fever led them to launch a couple of 'new' Mexico-made designs in 1998 with the vibe of older instruments. The $649.99 Toronado was not unlike their recent Squier Jagmaster, but had covered humbuckers and a Gibson-like two-volume two-tone control layout, while the $599.99 Cyclone was a Mustang derivative, with bridge humbucker plus single-coil and a Strat-like vibrato. In a couple more guises, including some US and Korean variations, they lasted to 2006.

A big event for Fender in November 1998 was the opening of a new factory, still in Corona, California. The company proudly described the impressive state-of-the-art plant as the world's most expensive and automated guitar factory. Since starting production at the original Corona factory back in 1985, Fender had grown to occupy a total of 115,000 square feet of space in ten buildings across the city. Such a rambling spread proved increasingly inefficient, and Fender began to plan a new centralised factory during the early 1990s. The new $20 million 177,000-square-feet plant affords a potentially growing production capacity for the future.

Some models were reorganised into new series in the late 1990s, with new high-end US-made 'modern' models grouped as American Deluxes and reissues brought together as American Vintages, including US-made Jazzmasters and Jaguars alongside the more expected oldies. Fender had recognised from what was going on elsewhere in the marketplace that they had to shift their quality up a notch, and the general upgrading led to the renaming of the American Standard series as the American Series in 2000, plus souped-up revisions to the Highway One series in 2006.

More anniversaries were lining up for celebration. In 2005 there was the 20th birthday of the revived Fender operation, while the following year marked the 60th anniversary of Leo's original Fender Manufacturing company. The modern Fender Musical Instruments Corporation (FMIC) took the opportunity to blow their own trumpet (or maybe that should be strum their own guitar). "Fender is now the single largest and most successful manufacturer of electric guitars, basses, and amplifiers in the world," they claimed in press material. "In addition to the Fender brandname,

▼ 1998 RELIC 60S STRATOCASTER, DAPHNE BLUE

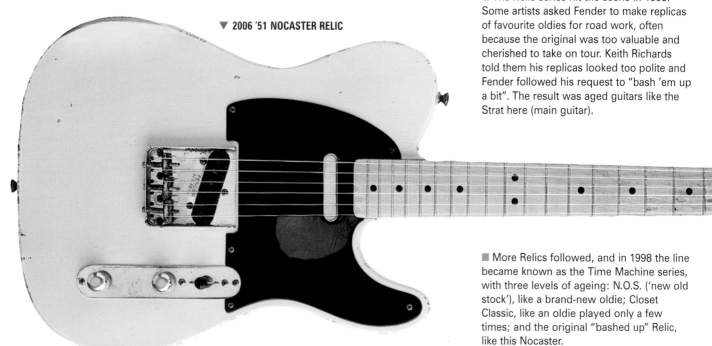

▼ 2006 '51 NOCASTER RELIC

■ The Relic series hit the scene in 1995. Some artists asked Fender to make replicas of favourite oldies for road work, often because the original was too valuable and cherished to take on tour. Keith Richards told them his replicas looked too polite and Fender followed his request to "bash 'em up a bit". The result was aged guitars like the Strat here (main guitar).

■ More Relics followed, and in 1998 the line became known as the Time Machine series, with three levels of ageing: N.O.S. ('new old stock'), like a brand-new oldie; Closet Classic, like an oldie played only a few times; and the original "bashed up" Relic, like this Nocaster.

Fender in the 1990s were enjoying the retro guitar trend, not only with the clever Relics and Time Machines, but also in their advertising. The two examples shown here hark back to the classic late-50s/early-60s 'You Won't Part With Yours Either' series, even adopting the full tagline for that Tele ad. Meanwhile, players were revelling in the retro fever, not least J. Mascis in Dinosaur Jr., seen (below) with his modified '63 Jazzmaster that he'd picked up for $300. Secondhand Jazzes and Jags and Mustangs were popular again as bargain-basement Fenders.

FMIC markets under the brandnames Squier, Guild, Jackson, Charvel, SWR, Tacoma, Olympia, Orpheum, Gretsch, and Rodriguez. The company operates directly in more than 12 countries around the globe ... and it maintains its own state-of-the-art manufacturing facilities in California, Washington, and Ensenada, Mexico."

Fender had acquired Guild in 1995 and made an alliance with Gretsch during 2002. With these two brands under the umbrella, they at last found a way to overcome their historically uncertain attempts to make decent and accepted flat-top acoustics and archtop electric-acoustics. A new Fender brand created as this book went to press was EVH, teaming the Custom Shop's master builders with guitar wizard Eddie Van Halen. They began in 2007 with a Tribute-style nit-picking re-creation of Eddie's famous striped 'Frankenstein' guitar.

Fender have reached the enviable point today where they dominate the world's electric guitar market. They've achieved their current successes in a variety of ways, not least by trying to provide a model or models that will appeal to every conceivable type of guitar player at every level of skill and affluence. Shrewd marketing, for sure. It's also one of the reasons that there are fewer copies of Fenders about these days. Why should we buy a copy when there's a guitar at that pricepoint with Fender on the head? But their attempt to fill every market niche also makes for an enormous line of what can appear to be only minimally different models.

At the time of writing, Fender's pricelist had no fewer than 56 different Fender-brand Stratocasters, plus 16 Squiers. There were 46 different Fender-brand Telecasters (including a few Esquires and Nocasters) plus nine Squiers, and 13 other electric models of various kinds. The list-prices ranged from a Squier Affinity Stratocaster at $248.99 to a Merle Haggard Signature Telecaster at $6,570.

Fender defended this vast array of variations in a recent catalogue. "So, why do we make so many models of Fender electric guitars? Because there are so many different styles of music, and even more individual artists playing them!" Dan Smith too offered some explanation for the size of the list. "Fender is more than just '57 Stratocasters," he said. "In order for the company to remain a force in the music business, it needs to work on a big scale. It never was a boutique product. When Leo sold it to CBS in 1965, it was one of the larger guitar companies in the world. You can't take that and suddenly decide it's going to be a boutique brand. The kind of growth the company has had was essential for Fender to be Fender. It has no choice but to be a big player."[103]

But with this huge catalogue – and often with nothing more on the guitar than the Fender logo and 'Stratocaster', 'Telecaster' or some other imprecise model name – it can be tricky to know for sure what you're looking at. For example, you might be buying a secondhand guitar, an occasion when people have been known to blur the truth. We've done our best to assist you in identifying the various models in the reference section at the back of this book, but it really is about time that Fender themselves recognised the value of their guitars to owners beyond the original purchaser. They ought to mark the instruments in some way with a precise model name.

By 2007, Fender organised their line of factory-made electric guitars into 11 series: American; American Deluxe; American Vintage; Artist; Classic; Classic Player; Deluxe; Highway One; Special Editions; Standard; and Vintage Hot Rod. Justin Norvell, senior marketing manager of Fender Electrics, described how they are divided. "The American series guitars are the modern interpretations of the Strat, Tele, Precision, and Jazz Bass, but in more of a regular package. They have modern fingerboard radiuses and hardware, but with more of a traditional nod than its older brother the Deluxe."

The American Deluxe models, said Norvell, are intended for the contemporary player – modern instruments featuring roller nuts (on some), SCN (Samarium Cobalt Noiseless) pickups, S-1 switching (push-pull volume knob giving extra sound options), locking tuners, and flashier cosmetics. American Vintage and Artist are what you'd expect: US-made period-style guitars and star-specific models. The Classic series are Mexico-made vintage-style guitars, while the new-for-2006 Classic Player models are, said Norvell, "the Mexican Classic series upgraded and made over by specific Custom Shop Master Builders, which allows for cool unique instruments and Custom Shop mojo at an affordable price".

Deluxe models are heavily upgraded versions of Mexico's basic Standard series, often with high-end electronics, including boost circuits and Noiseless pickups. "The Highway Ones," said Norvell, "have been made over into upgraded, hot-rodded instruments featuring new pickups, narrower string spacing, jumbo frets, and a thin satin nitro-cellulose lacquer. True road dogs, they are built for modern performance in a low profile package. Throw them in the back of the car night after night! The last place this guitar should live is in a glass case above the fireplace." Special Editions cover various other models, at the time of writing coming mainly from Japan.

The new-for-2007 Vintage Hot Rod models are, Norvell concluded, "a little similar to the Classic Players in that they are vintage-based models with player-centric upgrades. These models, based on the US-made vintage reissues, offer thin-skin lacquer finishes, flatter radiuses, bigger frets, modern pickups, custom wiring, and more. Everyone likes the look and feel of a vintage Fender, but many want it to play like a modern instrument. Plus, many vintage guitar owners are hesitant to reduce the value by making the desired modifications, so here is a guitar that solves that problem outright".[104]

The Custom Shop's products today are also divided up, this time into three different areas. First, they produce small runs and limited releases: special and often numbered runs of anything from a handful to hundreds of a specific model. The first of these was the 40th Anniversary Telecaster back in 1988. (Careful readers will spot a contradiction there, but back in the 1980s most people, including Fender themselves,

■ The Fender company was 50 years old in 1996 and celebrated the birth of Leo's Fender Manufacturing in '46 with anniversary models and a birthday decal (right). Meanwhile, the Japanese operation continued to revive some models that did not have US production yet, such as the Jaguar and Jazzmaster (ads, right). Both models would eventually enjoy US status in the American Vintage series, launched in 1999.

▼ 1998 TORONADO, CANDY APPLE RED

■ Continuing retro fever led Fender to launch two 'new' Mexican guitars in 1998 with the vibe of older instruments. The Toronado (above) was not unlike the recent Squier Jagmaster but with covered humbuckers and a Gibson-like control layout, while the Cyclone was a Mustang derivative. In a couple more guises, including some US and Korean variations, they lasted to 2006.

■ Nirvana's Kurt Cobain often played a Mustang (as seen in the live pic opposite) or a Jaguar, both of which he'd modified with humbuckers and personalised to suit his own playing style. Soon after the recording of the band's 1993 *In Utero* LP, Kurt cut up some pictures of his guitars and stuck the top half of his Jag on to the bottom half of the Mustang. Then he took his handiwork to Fender's Custom Shop, where builder Larry Brooks considered the idea, smoothing a line or two, and came up with a special customised instrument. Left-handed Kurt played a red version on Nirvana's '93 tour but sadly never saw the second (blue) one. Following Cobain's untimely death in 1994, his family collaborated with Fender to make a production version, the Jag-Stang (main guitar), first sold in '96.

▼ **1997 JAG-STANG, FIESTA RED**

believed that the first Broadcaster/Telecaster had been produced in 1948, which explains what we now recognise as a release date two years early.)

More numbered runs have continued to appear from the Custom Shop. They also build special limited runs for retailers and distributors. Some US music-store chains are regular customers, and overseas agents too such as Yamano in Japan are often treated to special models. In fact, Yamano remains the single largest customer for Custom Shop guitars at the time of writing, although the domestic US market is catching up fast.

The second type of production by the Custom Shop today is a general line of catalogued models, which began in 1992. By 2007 the catalogue items had reached such a level that they too were divided into eight further series: Custom Artist; Custom Classic; Limited Edition; Limited Release; Showmaster; Special Edition; Time Machine; and Tribute Series.

Mike Eldred, Director of Sales and Marketing at Fender Custom Division, described Custom Artist guitars as "patterned after a specific artist's instrument," the Custom Shop equivalent of Signature models. Custom Classics are geared to the modern player and include "many new designs in pickups, hardware, and finishes," he said. Limited Editions are, as the name implies, limited in production, feature customised aspects, and come with special documentation and cases. They are offered only briefly and then retired. Limited Release instruments are usually prototype or market-test guitars, occasionally offered for sale.

The Showmaster line consists of set-neck guitars made from "multi-species woods" and, according to Eldred, are "always evolving. The Elite is the primary instrument now and features a figured maple top, pickups personally voiced by Seymour Duncan and the Custom Shop, and unique inlay designs".

Eldred described the Special Edition category as an opportunity for the Shop's customers to have a glimpse of some of the model-making or prototyping that goes on in the Fender Custom Shop – and to own one of the results. The Strat Pro of 2006 and Tele Pro of 2007 were the first examples. Eldred said: "These models have many features drawn from artist instruments as well as experimental pickup designs. They are only available for a short time and are then replaced with other models."

We met the aged and exacting Time Machine models – the Relics, N.O.S.s, and Closet Classics – earlier in the book. The Tribute Series is an "elite program" designed to offer the ultimate artist instrument. Each one is a very limited run (usually 100) of an ultra-exact copy of a renowned artist's guitar. Examples so far have included Rory Gallagher's battered Strat, Andy Summers's careworn Tele Custom, Jeff Beck's early-days Esquire, and Mary Kaye's gleaming blond-body/gold-hardware Strat.

CUSTOM SHOP FANTASIES

All of this is not to say that the Custom Shop has abandoned its true custom-building role. One-offs, or 'Master Built' guitars as the Shop calls them, are the third strand of their production. These are exactly what most people would understand as the work of a custom shop: instruments made by a single person – one of the Shop's Master Builders – with acute attention to detail and a price to match. "They are still extremely important to the Custom Shop," said Eldred. "This is where we get to push ourselves, and from these types of projects, newer designs emerge."

At the time of writing the Shop has fewer than ten Master Builders who individually make the one-off instruments. These guitars include items made on the whim of a customer – maybe a vintage reproduction with absolutely dead-on accuracy, enough to satisfy the most nit-picking Fender-obsessed collector. Or there's 'quasi-exact' reproductions of classic Fenders, with player-defined modifications on top of a vintage vibe.

Or, of course, there's the entirely exclusive fantasy guitar. Eldred remembered a good example. "There was a contest with a guitar magazine in which people were encouraged to design a Stratocaster guitar to be built at the Shop. Many designs were submitted, and the magazine chose one that had an aluminium body with plastic chambers that held multi-coloured liquid that moved when the guitar moved. It was the hardest guitar that the shop ever built." Other whacky ones have included luxuriously appointed Rolls-Royce versions of traditional guitars, eight-string Strats, and weirdoes like an electric banjo with pedal steel footpedals.

Such outlandishly peculiar orders are rare, however, and the truly bizarre one-offs now tend to come from the Master Builders' own imaginations, effectively creating a further sub-division of the one-offs, the Custom Shop's 'art guitars'. Master Builder Fred Stuart's Egyptian Telecaster, made in 1994, was the first Fender art guitar. It had pyramids, snakes, and runes hand-carved by George Amicay into a finish of Corian synthetic stone. Another was the 2005 Fender Memorabilia Set created by artist Dave Newman for a Strat (plus Blues Junior amp) made by Master Builder Chris Fleming, covered in a fascinating collage of vintage Fender catalogues and ads.

These are expensive items. The Shop apparently turned down $75,000 for an Aztec Telecaster and $50,000 for a Bird-o-Fire Strat some years ago. Meanwhile, Mike Eldred said the trend continues today. "We have worked with several artists to really make the 'art guitar' moniker more true. Shepard Fairey, Pamelina, Shag, and Crash are just some of the artists we continue to work with, offering them a new and unique palette. The artists now usually do a matching amp with the guitar, too."

You're probably wondering what you might get from a Master Builder guitar that's not there on a regular 'catalogue' Custom Shop guitar. "More personal attention to detail," said Eldred. "The Master Builder can adjust specs and electronics to *your* personal liking." And what do we get from a Custom Shop catalogue guitar that's not there on a regular Fender factory guitar? "Again, more personal attention to detail. The Custom Shop models are made differently, including body routing, neck construction and shape, pickup design and construction, and so on."

■ The Highway One Strats first appeared in 2002, but four years later they were upgraded, like this (main guitar) HSS version (the letters indicate a humbucker/single-coil/single-coil pickup layout) . The Highways are now intended as hot-rod guitars with narrower string spacing, jumbo frets, and a thin satin finish. The big news among many late-90s/early 21st century Tele players was the rediscovery of the humbucker'd models from the 1970s. Among the popular models was the Custom, which kept the classic Tele bridge pickup but replaced the neck unit with a humbucker, and Fender's Mexican reissue (opposite, bottom right) appeared in 1999. Fender also underlined past achievements with a series of tasteful ads in 1998 with the tagline 'The Sounds That Create Legends'. Shown here (above, left to right) are four key Strat-men: Stevie Ray Vaughan, Eric Clapton, Jeff Beck, and Jimi Hendrix.

▼ 2007 HIGHWAY ONE STRATOCASTER HSS

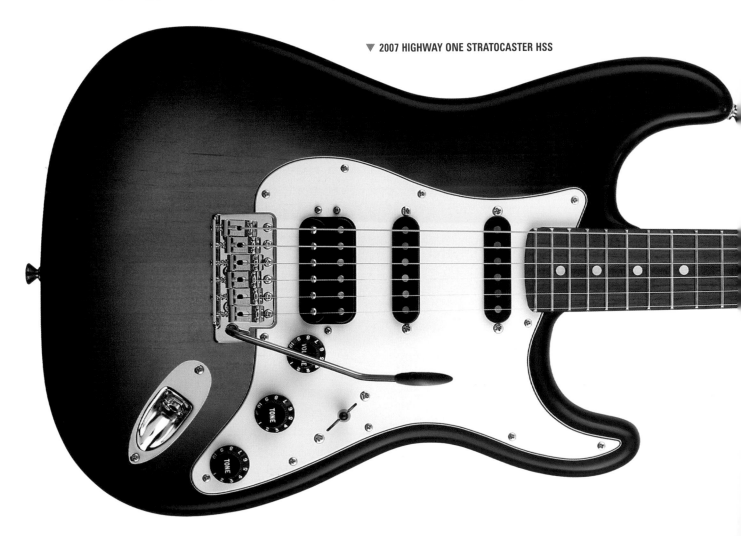

■ Many of us still opt for this Strat or that Tele, but a few braver souls check out the dustier corners of Fender history. They may even be encouraged by leafing through a copy of this very book. Perhaps Boyan Chowdhury (above) of the fabulous Zutons hesitated in the earlier pages to settle upon this Starcaster? Nice guitar, Boyan.

▲ 2006 CLASSIC '72 TELECASTER CUSTOM, BLACK

According to Eldred, the Custom Shop today sits at the pinnacle of the company. "The focus of the Fender Custom Shop is to assist in creating and developing new brands, designs, and techniques for all of our brands and facilities. We send builders to our Mexico, Tacoma [acoustic], and Japan facilities to teach as well as to learn. People do things differently all over the world, so why not look at those instances and possibly learn or develop something completely new? We maintain much of the original tooling, and we still use it to create some of the best instruments available. We offer a unique experience for the end user, whether that is John Mayer, Eric Clapton, Jeff Beck, or just a guy who likes a good guitar. They all have an opportunity to have a small team of builders make an instrument they have always dreamed of owning."[105]

Speaking of Eric Clapton, a special entry in the Tribute Series came late in 2006 with the Eric Clapton Blackie Stratocaster (not to be confused with the two regular signature models currently in the Fender catalogue). Blackie was the famous guitar that Clapton acquired towards the end of 1970, adapting parts from three '50s Strats to make what became his most cherished instrument until the mid 1980s. Guitar Center, the music-store chain, bought Blackie from Clapton at an auction at Christie's in New York City in June 2004 for a record-breaking $959,000 (plus buyer's premium), benefiting Clapton's Crossroads charity. The guitar's new owner allowed the Custom Shop access to it in October 2005, following an earlier session in 1998, so that Fender could spec the historic Strat for the exacting Tribute replicas.

Just 275 instruments were made, of which 185 were sold through Guitar Center (the rest went through Fender's international channels). Guitar Center sold all theirs in one day, November 24th 2006, and reported that the first 106 went within the first two minutes. The Blackie replicas had a suggested retail price of $24,000 each, with a portion of the proceeds donated to the Crossroads Centre in Antigua and a new Crossroads facility in Delray Beach, Florida.

Modelling was a new idea as guitarists entered the 21st century. The idea is to make available digital re-creations of classic guitar and amp sounds. California-based Line 6 were the leaders and their Vetta amps and Pod boxes showed what could be done. They launched a modelling guitar, the Variax, in 2003. Included on-board among the sounds were, of course, Fender imitations. Meanwhile, another California company was considering the implications of the new technology.

Ex-Steely Dan guitarist Jeff Baxter worked closely with Roland, the Japanese music technology pioneer, and he talked to Fender about making a guitar for him. Around 2003, Baxter went to Ikutaro Kakehashi, founder and chairman of Roland, and suggested a Fender–Roland modelling guitar – which became the American VG Stratocaster, launched in 2007 with a list price of $2,429 (about $1,100 more than a regular American Stratocaster).

It's an exciting development of Fender's relationship with Roland. Two

Fender–Roland Strats had appeared in the late 1990s, the shortlived American Standard Roland GR-Ready model and its 1998 replacement, the Mexico-made Standard Roland Ready Stratocaster. Both required an external synth of some sort to get new sounds, with Roland's VG-88 modelling module of 2000 a popular choice. Indeed, Roland's VG-8 box of 1995 was an early leader in the modelling-guitar world. Fender have made some respectable modelling amps of their own, including the 2001 Cyber-Twin.

WHEN IS A STRAT NOT A STRAT?

On the VG Strat, everything is done in the instrument: the only connection needed is through the regular jack to a regular amp. The modelling is done onboard. But the guitar can still play and sound exactly like the Strat it is, using the regular Strat magnetic pickups and controls. The bonus seems clear: a fall-back to Strat sounds and playability should you tire of that neat set of onboard modelled sounds (or if the batteries run out). Fender marketing manager Justin Norvell, who was involved in development of the instrument, emphasised that it was important to make the VG Strat simple and effective. "The temptation is to make it do a hundred things, but we pared it down to a five-way control, so it's intuitive and something you can really use in a professional setting."[106]

Two extra knobs control the new sounds, together with a small LED and a Roland GK bridge pickup. The Mode Control knob provides five sound settings: N for Normal (the regular Strat); S for modelled Stratocaster; T for modelled Telecaster; H for modelled Humbucking Pickups (what you and I might call the Les Paul mode); and A for modelled Acoustic. The Strat's five-way selector gives logical variations within each setting. Then there's the Tuning Control knob, which provides Normal (E-A-D-G-B-E) plus four alternative tunings – Drop D (D-A-D-G-B-E); Open G (D-G-D-G-B-D); D Modal (D-A-D-G-A-D); and Baritone (down a fourth) – and a simulated 12-string. The VG Stratocaster is a clever and exciting development for Fender, and it will be interesting to see how the instrument fares and where they go next with the idea.

Fender Japan was closed in early 2005 and a new company, Dyna Boeki, was formed to produce Fender's Japanese instruments. Fender said that this was a tidying-up of the business arrangements and that nothing about the physical production of the guitars has changed. At the same time, they simplified the distribution: now, all Japanese-made instruments are distributed in Japan by Kanda Shokai, while the rest of the Fender and Squier catalogue from the US and elsewhere is distributed there by Yamano Music.

Dan Smith retired in August 2006, but he had the opportunity at an emotional last meeting to give his thoughts on 25 remarkable years with Fender, including the crucial management buy-out from CBS in 1985 and the creative struggle through the years immediately following. "I said that in most people's lifetimes, you don't get the

▲ 2007 RORY GALLAGHER TRIBUTE
STRATOCASTER

■ The Custom Shop continues to build one-offs (above left) like this Strat with an aluminium body that has coloured plastic chambers with moving oil inside and two Teles, one a custom paint job (centre), the other covered in vintage Fender catalogues and ads.

▲ 2005 SHOWMASTER ELITE

■ The set-neck carved-top Showmasters are Fender's super-est superstrats yet. This Elite version (above) is the top of the line, with figured maple top and specially voiced pickups, plus some unusual fingerboard inlays. Meanwhile, modern players such as John Mayer (opposite) opt for the much more traditional Stratocaster, and Mayer has recently been honoured with a Fender signature model.

■ A relatively new part of the Custom Shop's business is the creation of very special Tribute Series instruments, described by Fender as an elite programme designed to offer the ultimate artist guitar. Each one is a very limited run (often 100 or fewer) of an ultra-exact copy of a renowned player's guitar. Examples so far have included Rory Gallagher's battered '61 Strat (main guitar), copied right down to the very, very worn sunburst alder body, maple neck, and rosewood fingerboard. Fender even matched the tuner layout precisely – five Sperzels and a Gotoh – and replaced the 12th-fret dot marker with white plastic instead of the original clay. It has three custom-wound single-coil pickups and aged chrome hardware. Other guitars in the Tribute Series have so far included Andy Summers's careworn Tele Custom, Jeff Beck's early-days Esquire, and Mary Kaye's gleaming blond-body/gold-hardware Strat.

opportunity to do something great. For all of us guys who are guitar players, to be part of resurrecting a legend is a pretty awesome thing to look back on. It's an opportunity that I feel very grateful to have had. In June 1984, CBS was ready to pull the plug. We couldn't let them throw Fender away! It meant too much to too many guitar players, myself included. If we hadn't been able to put together an offer that was better than liquidation, CBS would have shut Fender. And then, the most remarkable thing to me is that we were successful. We kept plugging away at it. There was blood, sweat, and tears. But the stars were in the right spot.

"Part of being able to retire," Smith concluded, "was that I knew we'd accomplished a lot. And the heart of the company is always the product. I could walk away proud, knowing that the company was so far ahead of where it had been, in terms of technology and training and people, and that it was going to continue and go way beyond that."[107]

The history of Fender and their electric guitars − which continues as you read these words − has been a remarkable mixture of inspiration and invention, of luck and mishap. The best of the resulting guitars will ensure that the Fender name lives on into the future, just as Smith predicts, and these instruments will no doubt help further generations of players to turn strings and frets and pickups into remarkable music. The key to the company's continuing success is a unique mix of historic substance and current power. Or as Fender Musical Instrument Corporation's present boss Bill Mendello put it: "Our culture, where we come from and who we were, is so important to where we want to be."[108]

Fashions for this or that model of electric guitar continue to come and go, just as they always have. At the time of writing, the Telecaster was the hip Fender, well ahead of the Strat. Specifically, it was the 1970s-style humbucker'd Teles, seen in the hands of everyone from Radiohead and Maroon 5 to Snow Patrol and Razorlight. Strats have taken something of a back seat, although John Mayer, Alex Turner (Arctic Monkeys), and Tom Morello (Audioslave) at least are assuring it some attention. At the same time, old or old-style Jaguars, Jazzmasters, and Mustangs still hold their appeal as the economic way into a little secondhand Fender magic. Boyan Chowdhury of The Zutons has even been brave enough to take out a Starcaster. But all of this will inevitably shift and change, and as you read this someone is concocting the sound of the future on the most unlikely instrument. Maybe it's you?

FOOTNOTES

1. *Washington Post* December 17th 1972
2. Author's interview February 6th 1992
3. *Guitar Player* October 1982
4. Author's interview February 10th 1992
5. *Bay Area Music* August 29th 1980
6. Author's interview with Karl Olmsted February 5th 1992
7. *Guitar Player* September 1971
8. Author's interview February 5th 1992
9. Author's interview February 8th 1992
10. Author's interview February 10th 1992
11. Author's interview with Forrest White February 5th 1992
12. Author's interview February 10th 1992
13. Author's interview February 5th 1992
14. *Daily News Tribune* November 8th 1949
15. *Bay Area Music* August 29th 1980
16. Author's interview with Bill Carson September 6th 1991
17. Author's interview February 8th 1992
18. Author's interview February 10th 1992
19. *Guitar Player* September 1971
20. *Washington Post* December 17th 1972
21. Author's interview February 8th 1992
22. Author's interview February 10th 1992
23. Author's interview February 10th 1992
24. *Guitar Player* December 1984
25. Author's interview February 10th 1992
26. Author's interview February 8th 1992
27. Author's interview February 8th 1992
28. Correspondence with author August 8th 2005
29. Author's interview February 8th 1992
30. *Guitar Player* May 1978
31. Author's interview February 6th 1992
32. Author's interview February 10th 1992
33. Author's interview with Dale Hyatt February 10th 1992
34. *Los Angeles Times* April 3rd 1955

35. *The Music Trades* June 1953
36. Author's interview February 5th 1992
37. Author's interview February 5th 1992
38. Author's interview February 5th 1992
39. Author's interview February 10th 1992
40. Author's interview February 10th 1992
41. Author's interview September 6th 1991
42. Author's interview February 8th 1992
43. *Guitar Player* October 1979
44. Author's interview February 8th 1992
45. Author's interview September 6th 1991
46. Author's interview February 10th 1992
47. Author's interview February 5th 1992
48. *Guitar Player* October 1979
49. Author's interview February 10th 1992
50. Author's interview February 5th 1992
51. Author's interview February 10th 1992
52. Author's interview February 8th 1992
53. Author's interview February 8th 1992
54. Author's interview February 10th 1992
55. *One Two Testing* January 1984
56. Author's interview February 5th 1992
57. *Fender Facts* November 1964
58. Author's interview February 10th 1992
59. Author's interview February 10th 1992
60. *The Music Trades* January 1965
61. *International Musician* August 1978
62. Author's interview February 10th 1992
63. Author's interview February 5th 1992
64. Author's interview February 8th 1992
65. Author's interview February 10th 1992
66. Author's interview February 10th 1992
67. *Guitar Player* May 1978
68. Smith *Fender: The Sound Heard 'Round The World*
69. Author's interview February 5th 1992
70. *Guitar Player* 1984
71. Author's interview February 10th 1992

72. Author's interview February 5th 1992
73. Author's interview February 8th 1992
74. *Guitar Player* 1984
75. Author's interview February 10th 1992
76. *Guitar Player* 1984
77. Author's interview February 10th 1992
78. Author's interview February 10th 1992
79. *Guitar Player* November 1985
80. Author's interview October 30th 1992
81. *Guitar Player* December 1976
82. *Guitar Player* March 1991
83. Author's interview February 5th 1992
84. Author's interview February 5th 1992
85. Author's interview February 4th 1992
86. Author's interview February 4th 1992
87. *Guitar Player* May 1978
88. Author's interview February 4th 1992
89. Author's interview June 2nd 2005
90. Author's interview February 4th 1992
91. Author's interview February 4th 1992
92. Author's interview February 4th 1992
93. *Guitar Trader Vintage Guitar Bulletin* Vol.2 No.7 July 1983
94. Author's interview February 4th 1992
95. Author's interview February 4th 1992
96. *San Francisco Chronicle* January 15th 1985
97. Author's interview February 4th 1992
98. Author's interview February 11th 1985
99. Author's interview February 4th 1992
100. Author's interview February 4th 1992
101. Author's interview March 30th 2007
102. Author's interview February 6th 1992
103. *New York Times* January 16th 1992
104. Author's interview December 2nd 1997
105. *Fender Frontline* Fall 1994
106. Author's interview March 30th 2007

▼ 2007 VINTAGE HOT ROD '52 TELE

■ The Vintage Hot Rod series was new for 2007, upgrades of the US-made vintage reissues with thin-skin lacquer finishes, flatter radiuses, bigger frets, modern pickups, and custom wiring. The Hot Rod '52 Tele (above) added a small humbucker at the bridge for an old vibe with a common mod already in place, saving you from grief with a chisel and a soldering iron.

▲ 2007 AMERICAN VG STRATOCASTER

■ The rear cover of Fender's 2007 catalogue (above) featured a Nocaster Closet Classic and a charming Fender Champion 600 amp, which recall the 1949–1951 period. Almost 60 years on from the first Fender electric solidbody guitars, those early designs continue to inspire new approaches. Who knows what tomorrow's musicians will do with the tools from this long and largely illustrious history? Just a couple of examples conclude our story: opposite are New York's Yeah Yeah Yeahs, with guitarist Nicolas Zinner digging into his Strat alongside vocalist Karen O; to the right is Jamie T from London, who broke his bass, moved to guitar, and removed the two higher strings of his Squier Strat to ease the conversion. Long may you run.

■ The American VG Stratocaster (main guitar) brings audio modelling to the Strat. Notice the Roland pickup at the bridge and the extra knob? Unlike earlier Fender–Roland Strats, this one makes all the sounds inside the guitar. It offers a host of flavours based on the five-way Mode knob: N for Normal (regular magnetic-pickup Strat); S for modelled Stratocaster; T for modelled Telecaster; H for modelled Humbucking Pickups; A for modelled Acoustic. The Strat five-way gives logical variations within each setting, and the Tuning knob selects regular EADGBE or one of four alternatives.

These 28 body shapes will help you to identify particular Fender models within this Reference Section. See the introduction opposite and then use the numbered shapes in conjunction with the reference listings (pages 142–186).

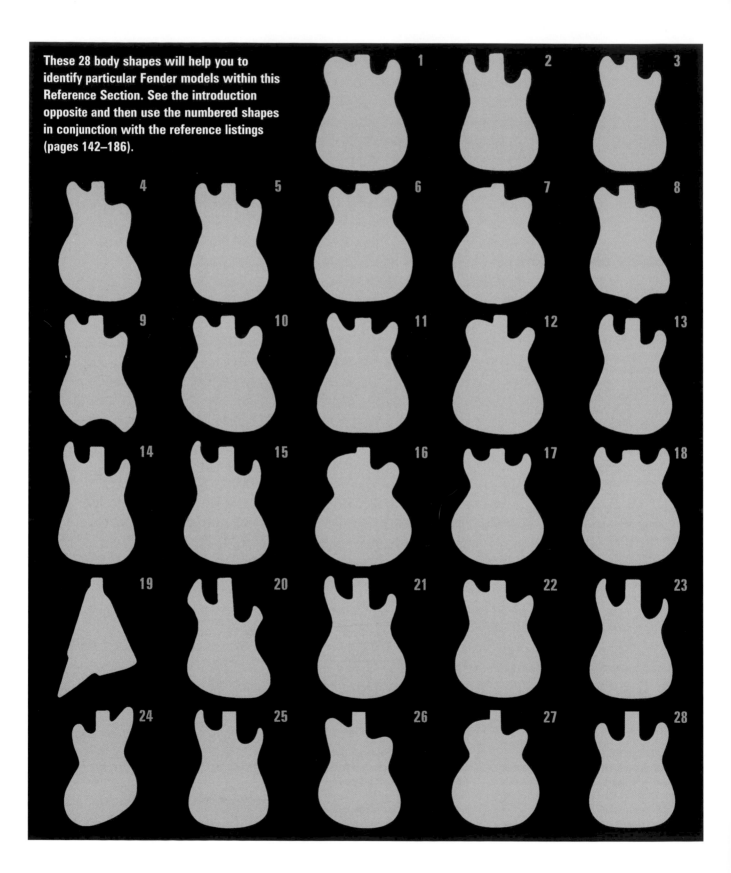

Reference Section

The rest of this book is taken up with the reference section. Following this introduction is the main Reference Listing of Fender models. It continues to page 186 and is analysed in detail below. Closing the reference section on pages 187–189 are explanations of the methods that can be used to try to date Fender guitars.

What's included

The main Reference Listing (pages 143–186) uses a simple, condensed format to convey a large amount of information about every Fender model, and the notes here are intended to ensure that you gain the most from this unique inventory.

The list covers all the production electric 'Spanish' models made by Fender US between April 1950 and early 2007, the output of Fender Mexico between 1991 and early 2007, the export models of Fender Japan issued since 1982, and the few Fender-brand models made in Korea since 1992. As in the rest of this book, there are no acoustic guitars, bass guitars, or complete listings of steel guitars.

The five main sections within the Reference Listing are: Fender US (pages 143–166); Fender Mexico (pages 166–172); Fender Japan (pages 172–180); Fender Korea (pages 180–182); and a brief round-up of other Fender-related brands (page 183). Following that is a chronology of models (pages 183–186).

What goes where

Within Fender US, Mexico, and Japan the models are grouped into Stratocasters, Telecasters, and Others, in that order. Within those groupings for US and Japan, Stratocasters and Telecasters are further divided into 'Regular', 'Replica', and 'Revised' models (meaning normal base models, reissues, and the rest).

Within these various subdivisions, each guitar is listed by the alphabetical order of its model name. Where a model name is also a person's name, the first word still supplies the alphabetical order. For example, the Bonnie Raitt Stratocaster is listed under B, not R. The main exception to alphabetical order is found under the 'Regular' Stratocaster and Telecaster groupings; these are listed in chronological order for ease of reference.

Reading the entries

At the head of each entry in the main listing is the model name in bold type, followed by a body shape reference number in brackets. The body shape numbers are explained on the opposite page for ease of reference. After the body shape number is a date or range of dates showing the production period of the instrument.

(It's worth stressing here that these dates are approximate. In many cases it's virtually impossible to pinpoint with total accuracy the period during which a model was in production at the factory. For example, Fender's dated promo material does not always reflect what was being made at that precise time. Naturally our extensive research has resulted in the most accurate dates possible – but please treat them as approximate, because that is all they can be.)

In italics – following the model name, body shape number, and production dates – is a brief one-sentence identification of the guitar in question, intended to help you recognise a specific model at a glance. To enable you to do this we have tried to note elements of the guitar's design that are unique to that particular model.

For some guitars, there may be a sentence below the body-shape panel reading "Similar to ... except:" which will refer to another model entry and then itemise any differences between the two.

Common features

To avoid repetition, we have considered a number of features to be common to all Fender models, and these are not shown in the main listings. You can always presume the following:

- Metal tuner buttons unless stated.
- Standard Fender headstock shapes unless stated.
- Four-screw neckplate unless stated.
- Bolt-on neck unless stated.
- 25.5-inch scale, 21 frets unless stated.
- Fingerboards with dot markers unless stated.
- Solid, contoured, offset-double-cutaway body unless stated.
- Single-coil pickups unless stated.
- Nickel- or chrome-plated hardware unless stated.

Specification points

In most guitar entries there follows a series of bulleted points. This list of specification points, separated into groups, provides details of the particular model's features. Of course, not every model will need all seven points. In the order listed the points refer to:

- Neck, fingerboard, headstock.
- Body.
- Pickups.
- Controls.
- Pickguard.
- Bridge.
- Hardware finish.

Some models were made in a number of variations, and where applicable these are listed (beginning *Also...*) after the specification points, in italics. Any other general comments are made in this position, and the Custom Shop's general production models are also identified here.

Some models have only a short listing, all in italics. This is often because the model is a 'replica' of an earlier guitar. The listing usually refers you to the entry for the original instrument.

All this information is designed to tell you more about your Fender guitar. By using the general information and illustrations earlier in this book combined with the knowledge obtained from this unique reference section you should be able to build up a very full picture of your instrument and its place in Fender history.

FENDER US

US-MADE STRATOCASTERS

US Stratocasters are divided into three sections: US Regular; US Replica; and US Revised.

US REGULAR STRATOCASTERS

Listed here in chronological order are the models we regard as the standard versions of the Stratocaster.

STRATOCASTER pre-CBS (2) 1954-65 *21 frets, small headstock, one string guide, four-screw neckplate, three controls.*
- Fretted maple neck (maple neck with rosewood fingerboard from 1959); truss-rod adjuster at body end; one string-guide.
- Body sunburst or colours.
- Three white six-polepiece pickups (bridge pickup angled).
- Three controls (volume, two tone) and three-way selector, all on pickguard; jack socket in body face.
- Eight-screw white plastic or anodised metal pickguard (11-screw white or tortoiseshell laminated plastic from 1959).
- Six-saddle bridge with through-body stringing or six-pivot bridge/vibrato unit.
Some examples with gold-plated hardware (when with blond body unofficially known as Mary Kaye model).

STRATOCASTER CBS Sixties (2) 1965-71 *21 frets, enlarged headstock, one string-guide, four-screw neckplate, three controls.*
- Maple neck with rosewood fingerboard (maple option 1967-69, replaced by fretted maple neck from 1969); truss-rod adjuster at body end; one string-guide; enlarged headstock.
- Body sunburst or colours.
- Three white six-polepiece pickups (bridge pickup angled).
- Three controls (volume, two tone) and three-way selector, all on pickguard; jack socket in body face.
- 11-screw white or tortoiseshell laminated plastic pickguard (only white from 1967).
- Six-saddle bridge with through-body stringing or six-pivot bridge/vibrato unit.
Early examples with STRATOCASTER PRE-CBS small headstock. Some examples with bound rosewood fingerboard.

STRATOCASTER CBS Seventies (2) 1971-81 *21 frets, enlarged headstock, two string-guides, three-screw neckplate, three controls.*
- Fretted maple neck, or maple neck with rosewood fingerboard; 'bullet' truss-rod adjuster at headstock end; two string-guides; enlarged headstock; three-screw neckplate.
- Body sunburst or colours.
- Three white (1971-75 and 1979-81) or black (1975-81) six-polepiece pickups (bridge pickup angled).
- Three controls (volume, two tone) and three-way selector (five-way from 1977), all on pickguard; jack socket in body face.
- 11-screw white (1971-75 and 1981) or black (1975-81) laminated pickguard.
- Six-saddle bridge with through-body stringing or six-pivot bridge/vibrato unit.
Some late examples with truss-rod adjuster at body end and four-screw neckplate.
Also ANTIGUA STRATOCASTER, with white/brown shaded body finish and matching-colour laminated plastic pickguard (1977-79).
Also INTERNATIONAL COLOR STRATOCASTER, with special colour finishes, white laminated plastic pickguard and black-plated pickguard screws (1981).

STRATOCASTER STANDARD first version (2) 1981-83 *21 frets, small headstock, two string-guides, four-screw neckplate, three controls.*
- Fretted maple neck, or maple neck with rosewood fingerboard; truss-rod adjuster at body end; two string-guides; small headstock.
- Body sunburst or colours.
- Three white six-polepiece pickups (bridge pickup angled).
- Three controls (volume, two tone) and five-way selector, all on pickguard; jack socket in body face.
- 11-screw white or black laminated plastic pickguard.
- Six-saddle bridge with through-body stringing or six-pivot bridge/vibrato unit.

STRATOCASTER STANDARD second version (2) 1983-84 *21 frets, small headstock, two string-guides, four-screw neckplate, two controls.*
- Fretted maple neck only; truss-rod adjuster at headstock end; two string-guides; small headstock.
- Body sunburst or colours.

- Three white six-polepiece pickups (bridge pickup angled).
- Two controls (volume, tone) and jack socket, all on pickguard.
- 12-screw white plastic pickguard.
- Re-designed six-saddle bridge/tailpiece or single-pivot bridge/vibrato unit.
Also in red, yellow or blue streaked finish, unofficially known as BOWLING BALL or MARBLE STRATOCASTER (1984).

AMERICAN STANDARD STRATOCASTER (2) 1986-2000 *22 frets, small headstock, two string-guides, four-screw neckplate, three controls.*
- Fretted maple neck, or maple neck with rosewood fingerboard; 22 frets; truss-rod adjuster at headstock end; two string-guides.
- Body sunburst or colours.
- Three white six-polepiece pickups (bridge pickup angled).
- Three controls (volume, two tone) and five-way selector, all on pickguard; jack socket in body face.
- 11-screw white laminated plastic pickguard.
- Two-pivot bridge/vibrato unit.
Also with 40th Anniversary medallion on headstock and commemorative neckplate (1994).
Also with anodised aluminium hollow-body option (1994-95).
Succeeded by AMERICAN STRATOCASTER (2000-current).

AMERICAN STANDARD STRATOCASTER HARD-TAIL (2) 1998-2000 *22 frets, small headstock, two string-guides, four-screw neckplate, three controls, six-saddle bridge with through-body stringing.*
Similar to AMERICAN STANDARD STRATOCASTER (see previous listing), except:
- Six-saddle bridge with through-body stringing.

AMERICAN STRATOCASTER (2) 2000-current *22 frets, small headstock, one string-guide, four-screw neckplate, three controls.*
- Fretted maple neck, or maple neck with rosewood fingerboard; 22 frets; truss-rod adjuster at headstock end; staggered height tuners; one string-guide.
- Body sunburst or colours.
- Three white six-polepiece pickups (bridge pickup angled).

- Three controls (volume, two tone) and five-way selector, all on pickguard; jack socket in body face.
- 11-screw white laminated plastic pickguard.
- Two-pivot bridge/vibrato unit.

AMERICAN STRATOCASTER HARD-TAIL (2) 2000-06 *22 frets, small headstock, one string-guide, four-screw neckplate, three controls, six-saddle bridge with through-body stringing.*
Similar to AMERICAN STRATOCASTER (see previous listing), except:
- Six-saddle small bridge with through-body stringing.

US REPLICA STRATOCASTERS
Listed here in alphabetical order are the models that replicate various standard-version US Regular Stratocasters.

AMERICAN VINTAGE '57 STRATOCASTER 1998-current *Replica of 1957-period original (see STRATOCASTER PRE-CBS listing in earlier US Regular Stratocasters section).*

AMERICAN VINTAGE '62 STRATOCASTER 1998-current *Replica of 1962-period original (see STRATOCASTER PRE-CBS listing in earlier US Regular Stratocasters section).*

AMERICAN VINTAGE 70s STRATOCASTER 2006-current *Replica of 1970s-period original (see STRATOCASTER CBS SEVENTIES listing in earlier US Regular Stratocasters section).*

N.O.S. STRAT 1998 *Replica of 1965-period original (see STRATOCASTER CBS SIXTIES listing in earlier US Regular Stratocasters section). Custom Shop production.*

RELIC 50s STRATOCASTER 1996-98 *Distressed finish replica of 1950s-period original (see STRATOCASTER PRE-CBS listing in earlier US Regular Stratocasters section). Gold-plated hardware option. Custom Shop production.*

RELIC 60s STRATOCASTER 1996-98 *Distressed finish replica of early 1960s-period original (see STRATOCASTER PRE-CBS listing in earlier US Regular Stratocasters section). Gold-plated hardware option. Custom Shop production.*

'54 STRATOCASTER 1992-98 *Replica of 1954-period original (see STRATOCASTER PRE-CBS listing in earlier US Regular Stratocasters section). Gold-plated hardware option. Custom Shop production.*

'56 STRATOCASTER 1999-current *Replica of 1956-period original (see STRATOCASTER PRE-CBS listing in earlier US Regular Stratocasters section). Available with three finish distress degrees: N.O.S., Closet Classic and Relic. Gold-plated hardware option. Custom Shop production.*

'57 STRATOCASTER 1983-85, 1986-98 *Replica of 1957-period original (see STRATOCASTER PRE-CBS in earlier US Regular Stratocasters section). Gold-plated hardware option.*

'58 STRATOCASTER 1996-98 *Replica of 1958-period original (see STRATOCASTER PRE-CBS listing in earlier US Regular Stratocasters section). Gold-plated hardware option. Custom Shop production.*

'60 STRATOCASTER first version 1992-98 *Replica of 1960-period original (see STRATOCASTER PRE-CBS listing in earlier US Regular Stratocasters section). Gold-plated hardware option. Custom Shop production.*

'60 STRATOCASTER second version 1999-current *Revised replica of 1960-period original (see STRATOCASTER PRE-CBS listing in earlier US Regular Stratocasters section). Available with three finish distress degrees: N.O.S., Closet Classic and Relic. Gold-plated hardware option. Custom Shop production.*

'62 STRATOCASTER 1983-85, 1986-98 *Replica of 1962-period original (see STRATOCASTER PRE-CBS in earlier US Regular Stratocasters section). Gold-plated hardware option.*

'65 STRATOCASTER 2003-06 *Replica of 1965-period original (see STRATOCASTER CBS SIXTIES listing in earlier US Regular Stratocasters section). Available with three finish distress degrees: N.O.S., Closet Classic and Relic. Custom Shop production.*

'66 STRATOCASTER 2004-current *Replica of 1966-period original (see STRATOCASTER CBS SIXTIES listing in earlier US Regular*

Stratocasters section). Available with three finish distress degrees: N.O.S., Closet Classic and Relic. Custom Shop production.

'69 STRATOCASTER first version 1996-98 *Replica of 1969-period original (see STRATOCASTER CBS SIXTIES listing in earlier US Regular Stratocasters section). Custom Shop production.*

'69 STRATOCASTER second version 1999-current *Revised replica of 1969-period original (see STRATOCASTER CBS SIXTIES listing in earlier US Regular Stratocasters section). Available with three finish distress degrees: N.O.S., Closet Classic and Relic. Custom Shop production.*

US REVISED STRATOCASTERS
Listed here in alphabetical order are the models we regard as revised and adapted versions of the standard-version US Regular Stratocasters.

ALUMINUM-BODY STRATOCASTER (2) 1994-95 *Anodised aluminium hollow-body option offered on AMERICAN STANDARD STRATOCASTER, STRAT PLUS, STRAT PLUS DELUXE and STRAT ULTRA (see relevant listings).*

AMERICAN CLASSIC STRATOCASTER (2) 1992-99 *Two-pivot vibrato, one string-guide.*
Similar to AMERICAN STANDARD STRATOCASTER (see listing in earlier US Regular Stratocasters section), except:
- One string-guide.
- 11-screw white pearl or tortoiseshell laminated plastic pickguard.
Gold-plated hardware option. Custom Shop production.

AMERICAN DELUXE ASH STRATOCASTER (2) 2004-current *Three white six-polepiece pickups, staggered height locking tuners, two-pivot vibrato, ash body.*
Similar to AMERICAN DELUXE STRATOCASTER second version (see later listing), except:
- Ash body.
- 11-screw white or black laminated plastic pickguard.

AMERICAN DELUXE FAT STRAT (2) 1998-2003 *Two Noiseless logo white pickups and one white humbucker, staggered height*

locking tuners, two-pivot vibrato.
Similar to AMERICAN DELUXE
STRATOCASTER first version (see later
listing), except:
- No string-guide; roller nut.
- Two Noiseless logo white six-polepiece pickups and one white coverless humbucker (at bridge).

AMERICAN DELUXE FAT STRAT/LOCKING TREM (2) 1998-2003 *Two Noiseless logo white pickups and one white humbucker, staggered height locking tuners, two-pivot locking vibrato.*

Similar to AMERICAN DELUXE
STRATOCASTER first version (see later
listing), except:
- No string-guide; roller nut.
- Two Noiseless logo white six-polepiece pickups and one white coverless humbucker (at bridge).
- Two-pivot locking bridge/vibrato unit.

AMERICAN DELUXE STRATOCASTER first version (2) 1998-2003 *Three Noiseless logo white pickups, staggered height locking tuners, two-pivot vibrato.*

- Fretted maple neck, or maple neck with rosewood fingerboard; 22 frets; truss-rod adjuster at headstock end; staggered height locking tuners; one string-guide.
- Body sunburst or colours.
- Three Noiseless logo white six-polepiece pickups (bridge pickup angled).
- Three controls (volume, two tone) and five-way selector, all on pickguard; jack socket in body face.
- 11-screw white laminated plastic pickguard.
- Two-pivot bridge/vibrato unit.

AMERICAN DELUXE STRATOCASTER second version (2) 2004-current *Three white or black six-polepiece pickups, staggered height locking tuners, two-pivot vibrato.*

Similar to AMERICAN DELUXE
STRATOCASTER first version (see previous
listing), except:
- Three white or black six-polepiece pickups (bridge pickup angled).
- Three controls (volume with push-switch, two tone) and five-way selector, all on pickguard.
- 11-screw white, tortoiseshell or black pearl laminated plastic pickguard, or gold plastic pickguard.

AMERICAN DELUXE STRATOCASTER FMT HSS (2) 2004-current *Figured-top body, no pickguard, two black six-polepiece pickups and one black humbucker.*

- Maple neck with ebony fingerboard; 22 frets; truss-rod adjuster at headstock end; staggered height locking tuners; roller nut.
- Body with figured top; sunburst or colours.
- Two black six-polepiece pickups and one black coverless humbucker (at bridge).
- Two controls (volume with push-switch, tone) and five-way selector, all on body; jack socket in body face.
- No pickguard.
- Two-pivot bridge/vibrato unit.

Also AMERICAN DELUXE STRATOCASTER QMT HSS, with figured-top body (2004-current).

AMERICAN DELUXE STRATOCASTER QMT HSS *See previous listing.*

AMERICAN DELUXE STRATOCASTER HSS (2) 2004-current *Two white or black six-polepiece pickups and one white or black humbucker, staggered height locking tuners, two-pivot vibrato.*

Similar to AMERICAN DELUXE
STRATOCASTER second version (see earlier
listing), except:
- No string-guide; roller nut.
- Two white or black six-polepiece pickups and one white or black coverless humbucker (at bridge).

AMERICAN DELUXE STRATOCASTER HSS LT (2) 2004-06 *Two white or black six-polepiece pickups and one white or black humbucker, staggered height locking tuners, two-pivot locking vibrato.*

Similar to AMERICAN DELUXE
STRATOCASTER second version (see earlier
listing), except:
- No string-guide; roller nut.
- Two white or black six-polepiece pickups and one white or black coverless humbucker (at bridge).
- Two-pivot locking bridge/vibrato unit

AMERICAN DELUXE STRATOCASTER 'V' NECK (2) 2004-current *Three white six-polepiece pickups, staggered height locking tuners, two-pivot vibrato, fretted maple neck with 'V' profile.*

Similar to AMERICAN DELUXE

STRATOCASTER second version (see
previous listing), except:
- Fretted maple neck only, 1950s-period 'V'-shaping.
- 11-screw white, gold or copper plastic pickguard.

Also 'Crew' neck and 'Polo' neck options.

AMERICAN DELUXE 50th ANNIVERSARY STRATOCASTER (2) 2004 *Commemorative neckplate, staggered-height locking tuners, gold-plated hardware.*

Similar to AMERICAN DELUXE
STRATOCASTER second version (see earlier
listing), except:
- Fretted maple neck only; commemorative neckplate.
- Body sunburst only.
- 11-screw white plastic pickguard.
- Gold-plated hardware.

AMERICAN DOUBLE FAT STRAT (2) 2000-03 *White pearl or tortoiseshell pickguard, two Seymour Duncan logo white humbuckers.*

Similar to AMERICAN STRATOCASTER (see
listing in earlier US Regular Stratocasters
section), except:
- Two Seymour Duncan logo white coverless humbuckers.
- 11-screw white pearl or tortoiseshell laminated plastic pickguard.

AMERICAN DOUBLE FAT STRAT HARD-TAIL (2) 2000-03 *One string-guide, white pearl or tortoiseshell pickguard, two Seymour Duncan logo white humbuckers, six-saddle bridge with through-body stringing.*

Similar to AMERICAN STRATOCASTER (see
listing in earlier US Regular Stratocasters
section), except:
- Two Seymour Duncan logo white coverless humbuckers.
- 11-screw white pearl or tortoiseshell laminated plastic pickguard.
- Six-saddle small bridge with through-body stringing.

AMERICAN FAT STRAT TEXAS SPECIAL (2) 2000-03 *White pearl or tortoiseshell pickguard, two white single-coils and one Seymour Duncan logo white humbucker.*

Similar to AMERICAN STRATOCASTER (see
listing in earlier US Regular Stratocasters
section), except:
- Two white six-polepiece pickups and one

Seymour Duncan logo white coverless humbucker (at bridge).
- 11-screw white pearl or tortoiseshell laminated plastic pickguard.

AMERICAN STANDARD DELUXE STRATOCASTER (2) 1989-90 *Two-pivot vibrato, two string-guides, three Lace Sensor pickups.*
Similar to AMERICAN STANDARD STRATOCASTER (see listing in earlier US Regular Stratocasters section), except:
- Three white plain top Lace Sensor pickups (bridge pickup angled).

AMERICAN STANDARD ROLAND GR-READY STRATOCASTER (2) 1995-98 *Two-pivot vibrato, two string-guides, extra slim white pickup at bridge.*
Similar to AMERICAN STANDARD STRATOCASTER (see listing in earlier US Regular Stratocasters section), except:
- Additional slim white plain-top Roland synthesiser pickup (at bridge)
- Three controls (volume, tone, synth volume), five-way selector, two pushbuttons and mini-switch, all on pickguard; jack socket in body face; side-mounted multi-pin synth output.

AMERICAN STRAT TEXAS SPECIAL (2) 2000-03 *White pearl or tortoiseshell pickguard, three white single-coils.*
Similar to AMERICAN STRATOCASTER (see listing in earlier US Regular Stratocasters section), except:
- 11-screw white pearl or tortoiseshell laminated plastic pickguard.
Fitted with different-specification visually similar pickups.

AMERICAN STRATOCASTER HH (2) 2003-06 *One string-guide, black pickguard, two black humbuckers.*
Similar to AMERICAN STRATOCASTER (see listing in earlier US Regular Stratocasters section), except:
- Two black coverless humbuckers.
- Three controls (volume with push switch, two tone) and five-way selector, all on pickguard.
- 11-screw black laminated plastic pickguard.

AMERICAN STRATOCASTER HH HARD-TAIL (2) 2003-05 *One string-guide, black pickguard, two black humbuckers, six-saddle bridge with through-body stringing.*

Similar to AMERICAN STRATOCASTER (see listing in earlier US Regular Stratocasters section), except:
- Two black coverless humbuckers.
- Three controls (volume with push switch, two tone) and five-way selector, all on pickguard.
- 11-screw black laminated plastic pickguard.
- Six-saddle small bridge with through-body stringing.

AMERICAN STRATOCASTER HSS (2) 2003-current *One string-guide, black pickguard, two black single-coils and one black humbucker.*
Similar to AMERICAN STRATOCASTER (see listing in earlier US Regular Stratocasters section), except:
- Two black six-polepiece pickups and one black coverless humbucker (at bridge).
- Three controls (volume with push switch, two tone) and five-way selector, all on pickguard.
- 11-screw black laminated plastic pickguard.

AMERICAN VG STRATOCASTER (2) 2007-current *Extra slim white pickup at bridge, two large and two small controls.*
Similar to AMERICAN STRATOCASTER (see listing in earlier US Regular Stratocasters section), except:
- Extra slim white plain-top Roland synthesiser pickup (at bridge).
- Four controls (two large: Volume, Tone; two small: M [Mode], T [Tuning]), five-way selector and LED, all on pickguard; jack socket in body face; side-mounted multi-pin synth output.

AMERICAN VINTAGE 1957 COMMEMORATIVE STRATOCASTER (2) 2007 Similar to American Vintage '57 Stratocaster (see listing in earlier US Replica Stratocasters section), except:
- Commemorative neckplate.
- Body white only.
- Gold-plated hardware.

AMERICAN 50th ANNIVERSARY STRATOCASTER (2) 2004 *Commemorative neckplate, locking tuners'*
Similar to AMERICAN STRATOCASTER (see listing in earlier US Regular Stratocasters section), except:
- Fretted maple neck only; commemorative neckplate.

AMERICAN 60th ANNIVERSARY STRATOCASTER (2) 2006 *Commemorative neckplate, maple neck with rosewood fingerboard.*
Similar to AMERICAN STRATOCASTER (see listing in earlier US Regular Stratocasters section), except:
- Maple neck with rosewood fingerboard only; commemorative headstock logo with jewel inlay; commemorative neckplate.

ANTIGUA STRATOCASTER *See STRATOCASTER CBS SEVENTIES listing in earlier US Regular Stratocasters section.*

BIG APPLE STRAT (2) 1997-2000 *Two-pivot vibrato, two string-guides, two white humbuckers.*
Similar to AMERICAN STANDARD STRATOCASTER (see listing in earlier US Regular Stratocasters section), except:
- Two white coverless humbuckers.
- 11-screw white pearl or tortoiseshell laminated plastic pickguard.

BIG APPLE STRAT HARD-TAIL (2) 1998-2000 *Two string-guides, two white humbuckers, six-saddle bridge with through-body stringing.*
Similar to BIG APPLE STRAT (see previous listing), except:
- Six-saddle small bridge with through-body stringing.

BONNIE RAITT STRATOCASTER (2) 1995-2001 *Signature on headstock.*
- Narrow maple neck with rosewood fingerboard; 22 frets; truss-rod adjuster at headstock end; one string-guide; Bonnie Raitt signature on large headstock.
- Body sunburst or blueburst.
- Three white six-polepiece pickups (bridge pickup angled).
- Three controls (volume, two tone) and five-way selector, all on pickguard; jack socket in body face.
- 11-screw white pearl laminated plastic pickguard.
- Six-pivot bridge/vibrato unit.
Also Custom Shop limited edition.

BOWLING BALL STRATOCASTER (also unofficially known as Marble Stratocaster) *See STRATOCASTER STANDARD SECOND VERSION listing in earlier US Regular Stratocasters section.*

BUDDY GUY STRATOCASTER (2) 1995-current *Signature on headstock.*
- Fretted maple neck; 22 frets; truss-rod adjuster at headstock end; one string-guide; Buddy Guy signature on headstock.
- Body sunburst or blond.
- Three white plain-top Lace Sensor pickups (bridge pickup angled).
- Three controls (volume, tone, boost), five-way selector and mini-switch, all on pickguard; jack socket in body face; active circuit.
- Eight-screw (11-screw from 2000) white pearl or tortoiseshell laminated plastic pickguard.
- Six-pivot bridge/vibrato unit.

CALIFORNIA FAT STRAT (2) 1997-98 *Six-pivot vibrato, 'California Series' on headstock, two singles-coils and one humbucker.*
- Fretted maple neck, or maple neck with rosewood fingerboard; truss-rod adjuster at headstock end; one string-guide; California Series on headstock.
- Body sunburst or colours.
- Two white six-polepiece pickups and one white coverless humbucker (at bridge).
- Three controls (volume, two tone) and five-way selector, all on pickguard; jack socket in body face.
- 11-screw white laminated plastic pickguard.
- Six-pivot bridge/vibrato unit.

CALIFORNIA STRAT (2) 1997-current *Six-pivot vibrato, 'California Series' on headstock, three single-coils.*
Similar to CALIFORNIA FAT STRAT, except:
- Three white six-polepiece pickups (bridge pickup angled).

CARVED TOP STRAT (2) 1995-98 *Two-pivot vibrato, no string-guides, two single-coils and one humbucker, figured carved-top body.*
- Fretted maple neck, or maple neck with rosewood fingerboard; 22 frets; truss-rod adjuster at headstock end; locking tuners; roller nut.
- Body with figured carved top; sunburst or colours.
- Two cream six-polepiece pickups and one black/cream coverless humbucker (at bridge).
- Two controls (volume, tone) and five-way selector, all on body; side-mounted jack socket.

- No pickguard.
- Two-pivot bridge/vibrato unit.
Known as CARVED TOP STRAT HSS (1998) Custom Shop production.

CARVED TOP STRAT HH (2) 1998 *Carved top, two metal-cover humbuckers.*
Similar to CARVED TOP STRAT (see earlier listing), except:
- Two metal-cover humbuckers.

CARVED TOP STRAT HSS *See earlier CARVED TOP STRAT listing.*

CLASSIC PLAYER STRAT (2) 1998-2005 *Custom Shop headstock logo, two-pivot vibrato, no string-guides, three Noiseless logo white pickups.*
- Fretted maple neck, or maple neck with rosewood fingerboard; 22 frets; truss-rod adjuster at headstock end; staggered height locking tuners.
- Body sunburst or colours.
- Three Noiseless logo white six-polepiece pickups (bridge pickup angled).
- Three controls (volume, two tone) and five-way selector, all on pickguard; jack socket in body face.
- Eight-screw white laminated plastic or anodised metal pickguard.
- Two-pivot bridge/vibrato unit.
Custom Shop production.

COLLECTORS EDITION STRATOCASTER (2) 1997 *Six-pivot vibrato, '1997' inlay at 12th fret position.*
- Maple neck with rosewood fingerboard; truss-rod adjuster at body end; one string-guide; oval-shape 1997 inlay at 12th fret.
- Body sunburst only.
- Three white six-polepiece pickups (bridge pickup angled).
- Three controls (volume, two tone) and five-way selector, all on pickguard; jack socket in body face.
- 11-screw tortoiseshell laminated plastic pickguard.
- Six-pivot bridge/vibrato unit.
- Gold-plated hardware.
Numbered factory production run of 1,997.

CONTEMPORARY STRAT (2) 1995-98 *Two-pivot vibrato, no string-guides, two single-coils and one humbucker, smaller body with slimmer horns.*
- Fretted maple neck, or maple neck with

rosewood fingerboard; 22 frets; truss-rod adjuster at headstock end; locking tuners; roller nut.
- Smaller body with slimmer horns; sunburst or colours.
- Two white six-polepiece pickups and one white coverless humbucker (at bridge).
- 11-screw white pearl laminated plastic pickguard.
- Two-pivot bridge/vibrato unit.
Also CONTEMPORARY STRAT FMT with figured-top body and two-pivot locking bridge/vibrato unit (1995-98). Custom Shop production.

CONTEMPORARY STRAT FMT *See previous listing.*

CUSTOM CLASSIC STRAT (2) 1999-current *22 frets, Custom Shop headstock logo, two-pivot vibrato, three white single-coils.*
Similar to AMERICAN STANDARD STRATOCASTER (see listing in earlier US Regular Stratocasters section), except:
- Custom Shop logo on headstock.
Custom Shop production.

DICK DALE STRATOCASTER (2) 1994-current *Signature on headstock.*
- Maple neck with rosewood fingerboard; truss-rod adjuster at body end; two string guides; Dick Dale signature on reverse headstock.
- Body gold only.
- Three white six-polepiece pickups (bridge pickup reverse-angled).
- One control (volume), three-way selector and two-way switch, all on pickguard; jack socket in body face.
- 11-screw white laminated plastic pickguard, metal covers over three 'spare' holes.
- Six-pivot bridge/vibrato unit.
Custom Shop production.

ELITE STRATOCASTER (2) 1983-84 *Single-pivot vibrato, three pushbutton switches.*
- Fretted maple neck, or maple neck with rosewood fingerboard; truss-rod adjuster at headstock end; two string-guides.
- Body sunburst or colours.
- Three white plain-top pickups (bridge pickup angled).
- Three controls (volume, two tone) and three pushbutton selectors, all on pickguard; side-mounted jack socket; active circuit.

- 11-screw white laminated plastic pickguard.
- Re-designed six-saddle bridge/tailpiece or single-pivot bridge/vibrato unit.

Also GOLD ELITE STRATOCASTER, with pearl tuner buttons and gold-plated hardware.
Also WALNUT ELITE STRATOCASTER, with walnut neck and ebony fingerboard, walnut body, pearl tuner buttons and gold-plated hardware.

ERIC CLAPTON STRATOCASTER first

version (2) 1988-2001 *Signature on headstock, three white plain-top pickups, active circuit.*

- Fretted maple neck; 22 frets; truss-rod adjuster at headstock end; one string-guide; Eric Clapton signature on headstock.
- Body various colours.
- Three white plain-top Lace Sensor pickups (bridge pickup angled).
- Three controls (volume, two tone) and five-way selector, all on pickguard; jack socket in body face; active circuit.
- Eight-screw white plastic pickguard.
- Six-pivot bridge/vibrato unit.

Earliest examples with 21 frets and/or mini-switch.

ERIC CLAPTON STRATOCASTER second

version (2) 2001-current *Signature on headstock, three Noiseless logo white pickups, active circuit.*
Similar to ERIC CLAPTON STRATOCASTER first version (see previous listing), except:
- Three Noiseless logo white six-polepiece pickups.

ERIC CLAPTON STRATOCASTER third

version (2) 2004-current *Signature on headstock rear, three Noiseless logo white pickups, Custom Shop headstock logo.*
Similar to ERIC CLAPTON STRATOCASTER first version (see earlier listing), except:
- Eric Clapton signature and Custom Shop logo on back of headstock.
- Three Noiseless logo white six-polepiece pickups.
- No active circuit.

Custom Shop production.

ERIC JOHNSON STRATOCASTER (2) 2005-

current *Engraved neckplate.*
- Fretted maple neck; truss-rod adjuster at body end; staggered height tuners; engraved neckplate.

- Body sunburst or colours.
- Three white six-polepiece pickups (bridge pickup angled).
- Three controls (volume, two tone) and five-way selector, all on pickguard; jack socket in body face.
- 8-screw white plastic pickguard.
- Six-pivot bridge/vibrato unit.

FLOYD ROSE CLASSIC STRAT HH (2)

1998-2002 *Two-pivot locking vibrato system, two humbuckers, three-screw fixing for each humbucker.*
Similar to FLOYD ROSE CLASSIC STRAT HSS (see later listing), except:
- Two white coverless humbuckers.

Known as STRAT SPECIAL WITH LOCKING TREMOLO HH (2002).

FLOYD ROSE CLASSIC STRAT HSS (2)

1998-2002 *Two-pivot locking vibrato system, two single-coils and one humbucker, three-screw fixing for humbucker.*
Similar to FLOYD ROSE CLASSIC STRATOCASTER (see later listing), except:
- Three-screw fixing for humbucker.
- No curved-ends humbucker cut-out in pickguard.

Known as STRAT SPECIAL WITH LOCKING TREMOLO HSS (2002).

FLOYD ROSE CLASSIC STRATOCASTER

(2) 1992-98 *Two-pivot locking vibrato system, two single-coils and one humbucker, curved-ends humbucker cut-out in pickguard.*
- Fretted maple neck, or maple neck with rosewood fingerboard; 22 frets; truss-rod adjuster at headstock end; single-bar string-guide; locking nut.
- Body sunburst or colours.
- Two white six-polepiece pickups and one white coverless humbucker (at bridge).
- Three controls (volume, two tone) and five-way selector, all on pickguard; jack socket in body face.
- 11-screw white laminated plastic pickguard.
- Two-pivot locking bridge/vibrato unit.

Replaced by FLOYD ROSE CLASSIC STRAT HSS (1998).

GOLD ELITE STRATOCASTER See earlier

ELITE STRATOCASTER listing.

GOLD/GOLD STRATOCASTER (2) 1981-83

Six-pivot vibrato, gold body and hardware.

Similar to STRAT (see later listing), except:
- Fretted maple neck only; 'Stratocaster' logo on headstock.
- Body gold only.
- Three controls (volume, two tone) and five-way selector.
- Normal-type six-pivot bridge/vibrato unit.
- Gold-plated hardware.

Some examples with pearl fingerboard position markers.

HENDRIX STRATOCASTER (2) 1980 *Six-*

pivot vibrato, large inverted headstock, normal logo.
- Fretted maple neck; truss-rod adjuster at body end; two string-guides; large reverse headstock; four-screw neckplate.
- Body with additional front contouring; white only.
- Three white six-polepiece pickups (bridge pickup angled).
- Three controls (volume, two tone) and five-way selector, all on pickguard; jack socket in body face.
- 11-screw white laminated plastic pickguard.
- Six-pivot bridge/vibrato unit.

Only 25 produced.

HIGHWAY ONE STRATOCASTER first

version (2) 2002-06 *Satin body finish, white pickguard, three white single-coils, small headstock.*
- Fretted maple neck, or maple neck with rosewood fingerboard; 22 frets; truss-rod adjuster at headstock end; two string-guides.
- Body various colours, satin finish.
- Three white six-polepiece pickups (bridge pickup angled).
- Three controls (volume, two tone) and five-way selector, all on pickguard; jack socket in body face.
- 11-screw white laminated plastic pickguard.
- Six-pivot bridge/vibrato unit.

HIGHWAY ONE STRATOCASTER second

version (2) 2006-current *Satin body finish, white pickguard, three white single-coils, large headstock.*
Similar to HIGHWAY ONE STRATOCASTER first version (see previous listing), except:
- Large headstock.

HIGHWAY ONE STRATOCASTER HSS

first version (2) 2003-06 *Satin body finish,*

large headstock, white pickguard, two white single-coils and one black humbucker.
Similar to HIGHWAY ONE STRATOCASTER first version (see earlier listing), except:
- Maple neck with rosewood fingerboard only; large headstock.
- Two white six-polepiece pickups and one black coverless humbucker (at bridge).

HIGHWAY ONE STRATOCASTER HSS

second version (2) 2006-current *Satin body finish, large headstock, white pickguard, two black single-coils and one black humbucker.*
Similar to HIGHWAY ONE STRATOCASTER HSS first version (see previous listing), except:
- Two black six-polepiece pickups and one black coverless humbucker (at bridge).
- Black plastic knobs.

HM STRAT first type (2) 1989-90 *Two-pivot locking vibrato system, two single-coils and one humbucker, black-face headstock.*
- Fretted maple neck, or maple neck with rosewood fingerboard; 25-inch scale, 24 frets; truss-rod adjuster at headstock end; locking nut; large flamboyant 'Strat' logo on black face headstock.
- Smaller body; various colours.
- Two black six-polepiece pickups and one black coverless humbucker (at bridge).
- Three controls (volume, two tone), five-way selector and coil-switch, all on body; side-mounted jack socket.
- No pickguard.
- Two-pivot locking bridge/vibrato unit.
- Black-plated hardware.

HM STRAT second type (2) 1989-90 *Two-pivot locking vibrato system, one angled Lace Sensor pickup and one humbucker.*
Similar to HM STRAT FIRST TYPE, except:
- One angled black plain-top Lace Sensor and one black coverless humbucker (at bridge).
- Two controls (volume, tone), three-way selector and coil-switch, all on body.
- Black laminated plastic pickguard.

HM STRAT third type (2) 1989-90 *Two-pivot locking vibrato system, two humbuckers.*
Similar to HM STRAT FIRST TYPE, except:
- Two black two coverless humbuckers.
- Two controls (volume, tone), three-way selector and coil-switch, all on body.

HM STRAT ULTRA (2) 1990-92 *Two-pivot locking vibrato system, four Lace Sensor pickups.*
Similar to HM STRAT FIRST TYPE, except:
- Ebony fingerboard with split-triangle markers.
- Four black plain-top Lace Sensor pickups (two at bridge).

INTERNATIONAL COLOUR
STRATOCASTER *See STRATOCASTER CBS SEVENTIES listing in earlier US Regular Stratocasters section.*

JEFF BECK STRATOCASTER first version
(2) 1991-2001 *Signature on headstock, four white plain-top pickups.*
- Maple neck with rosewood fingerboard; 22 frets; truss-rod adjuster at headstock end; locking tuners; roller nut; Jeff Beck signature on headstock.
- Body white, green or purple.
- Four white plain-top Lace Sensor pickups (two at bridge).
- Three controls (volume, two tone), five-way selector and pushbutton coil-switch, all on pickguard; jack socket in body face.
- 11-screw white laminated plastic pickguard.
- Two-pivot bridge/vibrato unit.

JEFF BECK STRATOCASTER second

version (2) 2001-current *Signature on headstock, three Noiseless logo white pickups.*
Similar to JEFF BECK STRATOCASTER first version (see previous listing), except:
- Body green or white.
- Three Noiseless logo white six-polepiece pickups (bridge pickup angled).
- Three controls (volume, two tone), five-way selector and push-switch, all on pickguard; jack socket in body face.

JEFF BECK SIGNATURE STRATOCASTER
(2) 2004-current *Signature on headstock rear, Custom Shop logo on headstock.*
Similar to JEFF BECK STRATOCASTER second version, except:
- Jeff Beck signature and Custom Shop logo on back of headstock.
Custom Shop production.

JIMI HENDRIX STRATOCASTER (2) 1997-
2000 *Mirror-image Fender Stratocaster logo on large inverted headstock.*

- Fretted maple neck; truss-rod adjuster at body end; one string-guide; mirror-image Fender Stratocaster logo on large reverse headstock.
- Left-handed body; white only.
- Three white six-polepiece pickups (bridge pickup reverse-angled).
- Three controls (volume, two tone) and five-way selector, all on pickguard; jack socket in body face.
- Left-handed 11-screw white laminated plastic pickguard.
- Left-handed six-pivot bridge/vibrato unit.

JOHN MAYER STRATOCASTER (2) 2005-
current *Signature on back of headstock.*
- Maple neck with rosewood fingerboard; truss-rod adjuster at body end; one string-guide (further up headstock); John Mayer signature on back of headstock.
- Body sunburst, gold with stripes, or white.
- Three white six-polepiece pickups (bridge pickup angled).
- Three controls (volume, two tone) and five-way selector, all on pickguard; jack socket in body face.
- 11-screw white or tortoiseshell laminated plastic pickguard.
- Six-pivot bridge/vibrato unit.

LONE STAR STRAT (2) 1996-2000 *Two-
pivot vibrato, two string-guides, two single-coils and one humbucker.*
Similar to AMERICAN STANDARD STRATOCASTER (see listing in earlier US Regular Stratocasters section), except:
- Two white six-polepiece pickups and one Seymour Duncan-logo white coverless humbucker (at bridge).
- 11-screw white pearl or tortoiseshell laminated plastic pickguard.

MARBLE STRATOCASTER (also unofficially
known as Bowling Ball Stratocaster) *See STRATOCASTER STANDARD SECOND VERSION listing in earlier US Regular Stratocasters section.*

MARK KNOPFLER STRATOCASTER (2)
2003-current *Signature on headstock.*
- Maple neck with rosewood fingerboard; truss-rod adjuster at body end; one string-guide; Mark Knopfler signature on headstock.
- Body red only.
- Three white six-polepiece pickups (bridge pickup angled).

- Three controls (volume, two tone) and five-way selector, all on pickguard; jack socket in body face.
- 11-screw white laminated plastic pickguard.
- Six-pivot bridge/vibrato unit.

MARY KAYE STRATOCASTER *See STRATOCASTER PRE-CBS listing in earlier US Regular Stratocasters section.*

RELIC FLOYD ROSE STRATOCASTER (2) 1998 *Two-pivot locking vibrato system, two white single-coils and one black humbucker, large headstock.*

- Fretted maple neck, or maple neck with rosewood fingerboard; truss-rod adjuster at body end; single-bar string-guide; locking nut; large headstock.
- Body black or white, distressed finish.
- Two white six-polepiece pickups and one black coverless humbucker (at bridge).
- Three controls (volume, two tone) and five-way selector, all on pickguard; jack socket in body face.
- 11-screw white laminated plastic pickguard.
- Two-pivot locking bridge/vibrato unit.
Custom Shop production.

RHINESTONE STRATOCASTER 1975 *Based on STRATOCASTER CBS SEVENTIES (see listing in earlier US Regular Stratocasters section) but with replacement bonded metal and fibreglass body from British sculptor Jon Douglas and specially ordered by Fender's UK agent in 1975. Front has heavy relief floral leaf scroll design, inset with rhinestones on some examples. Very small quantity produced. Unauthorised 1990s versions are identifiable by a plaque on back of body.*

RICHIE SAMBORA STRATOCASTER first version (2) 1993-99 *Signature on headstock.*

- Fretted maple neck, star position markers; 22 frets; truss-rod adjuster at headstock end; single-bar string-guide; locking nut; Richie Sambora signature on headstock.
- Body sunburst or white.
- Two white six-polepiece pickups and one white coverless humbucker (at bridge).
- Three controls (volume, two tone), five-way selector and push-switch, all on pickguard; jack socket in body face; active circuit.
- 11-screw white laminated plastic pickguard.

- Two-pivot locking bridge/vibrato unit.

RICHIE SAMBORA STRATOCASTER second version (2) 1999-2002 *Star position markers, three Noiseless logo white pickups.*

- Fretted maple neck, star position markers; 22 frets; truss-rod adjuster at headstock end.
- Body sunburst, red or white.
- Three Noiseless logo white six-polepiece pickups (bridge pickup angled).
- Three controls (volume, two tone), five-way selector and push-switch, all on pickguard; jack socket in body face; active circuit.
- 11-screw white laminated plastic pickguard.
- Six-pivot bridge/vibrato unit.

RITCHIE BLACKMORE STRATOCASTER (2) 1999-2005 *Signature on headstock, two white plain-top pickups.*

- Maple glued-in neck with rosewood fingerboard, with scalloping between frets; 22 frets; "bullet" truss-rod adjuster at headstock end; locking tuners; Ritchie Blackmore signature on large headstock.
- Body white only.
- Two white plain-top Lace Sensor pickups (bridge pickup angled).
- Three controls (volume, two tone) and five-way selector, all on pickguard; jack socket in body face.
- 11-screw white laminated plastic or anodised metal pickguard.
- Two-pivot bridge/vibrato unit.
Roland GK-2 synth pickup system option. Custom Shop production.

ROADHOUSE STRAT (2) 1997-2000 *Two-pivot vibrato, two string-guides, three single-coils, white pearl or tortoiseshell pickguard.* Similar to AMERICAN STANDARD STRATOCASTER (see listing in earlier US Regular Stratocasters section), except:

- Visually similar pickups but different specification.
- 11-screw white pearl or tortoiseshell laminated plastic pickguard.

ROBERT CRAY STRATOCASTER (2) 1992-current *Signature on headstock.*

- Maple neck with rosewood fingerboard; truss-rod adjuster at body end; one string-guide; Robert Cray signature on headstock.

- Body sunburst, silver or violet.
- Three white six-polepiece pickups (bridge pickup angled).
- Three controls (volume, two tone) and five-way selector, all on pickguard; jack socket in body face.
- 11-screw white laminated plastic pickguard.
- Six-saddle bridge with through-body stringing.
Also gold-plated hardware (1998-current). Custom Shop production.

ROBIN TROWER STRATOCASTER (2) 2005-current *Signature on back of large headstock.*

- Fretted maple neck only; "bullet" truss-rod adjuster at headstock end; one string-guide; Robin Trower signature on back of large headstock.
- Body various colours.
- Three white six-polepiece pickups (bridge pickup angled).
- Three controls (volume, two tone) and five-way selector, all on pickguard; jack socket in body face.
- 11-screw white laminated plastic pickguard.
- Six-pivot bridge/vibrato unit.
Custom Shop production.

RORY GALLAGHER STRATOCASTER (2) 2004-current *Ultra-distressed finished, one mismatching tuner.*

- Maple neck with rosewood fingerboard; truss-rod adjuster at body end; one mismatching tuner; two string-guides.
- Body sunburst, ultra-distressed finish.
- Three white six-polepiece pickups (bridge pickup angled).
- Three controls (volume, two tone) and five-way selector, all on pickguard; jack socket in body face.
- 11-screw white laminated plastic pickguard.
- Six-pivot bridge/vibrato unit.
Custom Shop production.

SET NECK STRATOCASTER first version (2) 1992-1995 *Two-pivot vibrato, no string-guides, four Lace Sensor pickups (two at bridge), glued-in neck.*

- Maple glued-in neck with ebony fingerboard; 22 frets; truss-rod adjuster at headstock end; locking tuners; roller nut.
- Body with figured top; sunburst or colours.
- Four white plain-top Lace Sensor pickups (two at bridge).

- Three controls (volume, two tone), five-way selector and coil-switch, all on pickguard; jack socket in body face.
- 11 screw white laminated plastic pickguard.
- Two-pivot bridge/vibrato unit.
Custom Shop production. Also Custom Shop limited edition.

SET NECK STRATOCASTER second version (2) 1995-98 1995 *Two-pivot vibrato, no string-guides, two single-coils and one humbucker, glued-in neck.*
Similar to SET NECK STRATOCASTER FIRST VERSION, except:
- Rosewood fingerboard.
- Sunburst or natural.
- Two white six-polepiece pickups and one white coverless humbucker (at bridge).
Custom Shop production.

SET NECK FLOYD ROSE STRATOCASTER (2) 1992-95 *Two-pivot locking vibrato system, two single-coils and one humbucker, reverse headstock, glued-in neck.*
- Maple glued-in neck with ebony fingerboard; 22 frets; truss-rod adjuster at headstock end; locking nut; black-face reverse headstock.
- Smaller body; sunburst or colours.
- Two black six-polepiece pickups and one black coverless humbucker (at bridge).
- Two controls (volume, tone) and five-way selector, all on body; side-mounted jack socket.
- No pickguard.
- Two-pivot locking bridge/vibrato unit.
- Black-plated or gold-plated hardware.
Custom Shop production.

SPECIAL EDITION 1993 STRATOCASTER (2) 1993 *Commemorative neckplate.*
Similar to AMERICAN STANDARD STRATOCASTER (see listing in earlier US Regular Stratocasters section), except:
- Commemorative neckplate.
- 11-screw white pearl laminated plastic pickguard.
- Gold-plated hardware.

SPECIAL EDITION 1994 STRATOCASTER (2) 1994 *Commemorative neckplate.*
Similar to AMERICAN STANDARD STRATOCASTER (see listing in earlier US Regular Stratocasters section), except:
- Commemorative neckplate.

- Body black or blond.
- 11-screw grey pearl or tortoiseshell laminated plastic pickguard.

STEVIE RAY VAUGHAN STRATOCASTER (2) 1992-current *Signature on headstock.*
- Maple neck with pao ferro fingerboard; truss-rod adjuster at body end; one string-guide; Stevie Ray Vaughan signature on headstock.
- Body sunburst only.
- Three white six-polepiece pickups (bridge pickup angled).
- Three controls (volume, two tone) and five-way selector, all on pickguard; jack socket in body face.
- Eight-screw black laminated plastic pickguard with 'SRV' engraving.
- Left-handed six-pivot bridge/vibrato unit.
- Gold-plated hardware.

STRAT (2) 1980-83 *Six-pivot vibrato, 'Strat' logo on headstock.*
- Fretted maple neck, or maple neck with rosewood fingerboard; truss-rod adjuster at body end; two string-guides; 'Strat' logo on re-styled headstock with face matching body colour.
- Body red, blue or white.
- Three white six-polepiece pickups (bridge pickup angled).
- Three controls (volume, tone, two-way rotary switch) and five-way selector, all on pickguard; jack socket in body face.
- 11-screw white laminated plastic pickguard.
- Re-designed six-pivot bridge/vibrato unit.
- Gold-plated brass hardware (early examples have chrome machine heads and polished brass hardware).
Also WALNUT STRAT, with fretted walnut neck (some with walnut neck and ebony fingerboard), walnut body, black laminated plastic pickguard, and gold-plated hardware (1981-83).

STRAT-O-SONIC DVI (2) 2003-04 *Model name on headstock, one large black six-polepiece pickup.*
- Maple neck with rosewood fingerboard; 22 frets; truss-rod adjuster at headstock end; staggered height locking tuners; black-face headstock.
- Semi-solid body; sunburst, blonde or red.
- One large black six-polepiece pickup (at bridge).
- Two controls (volume, tone) on body; side-mounted jack socket.

- Six-screw black laminated plastic pickguard.
- Six-saddle wrapover bridge/tailpiece.

STRAT-O-SONIC DVII (2) 2003-06 *Model name on headstock, two large black six-polepiece pickups.*
Similar to STRAT-O-SONIC DVI (see previous listing), except:
- Two large black six-polepiece pickups.
- Two controls (volume, tone) and three-way selector, all on body.

STRAT-O-SONIC HH (2) 2005-06 *Model name on headstock, two black humbuckers.*
Similar to STRAT-O-SONIC DVII (see previous listing), except:
- Two black coverless humbucker pickups.

STRAT PLUS (2) 1987-98 *Two-pivot vibrato, no string-guides, three same-type Lace Sensor pickups.*
- Fretted maple neck, or maple neck with rosewood fingerboard; 22 frets; truss-rod adjuster at headstock end; locking tuners; roller nut.
- Body sunburst or colours.
- Three same-type white plain-top Lace Sensor pickups (bridge pickup angled).
- Three controls (volume, two tone) and five-way selector, all on pickguard; jack socket in body face.
- 11-screw white or white pearl laminated plastic pickguard.
- Two-pivot bridge/vibrato unit.
Also with anodised aluminium hollow body option (1994-95).

STRAT PLUS DELUXE (2) 1989-98 *Two-pivot vibrato, no string-guides, three differing Lace Sensor pickups.*
Similar to STRAT PLUS, except:
- Three differing white plain-top Lace Sensor pickups (bridge pickup angled).
- 11-screw white, white pearl or tortoiseshell laminated plastic pickguard.
- Two-pivot bridge/vibrato unit.
Also with anodised aluminium hollow body option (1994-95).

STRAT PRO (2) 2006-current *Large headstock, roller nut, two-pivot vibrato.*
- Fretted maple neck, or maple neck with rosewood fingerboard; 22 frets (from 2007); truss-rod adjuster at body end; roller nut; large headstock.
- Body black or white, distressed finish.

- Three white six-polepiece pickups (bridge pickup angled).
- Three controls (volume, two tone) and five-way selector, all on pickguard; jack socket in body face.
- 11-screw white laminated plastic pickguard.
- Two-pivot bridge/vibrato unit.

Custom Shop production.

STRAT SPECIAL WITH LOCKING TREMOLO HH *See earlier FLOYD ROSE CLASSIC STRAT HH listing.*

STRAT SPECIAL WITH LOCKING TREMOLO HSS *See earlier FLOYD ROSE CLASSIC STRAT HSS listing.*

STRAT ULTRA (2) 1990-98 *Two-pivot vibrato, no string-guides, four Lace Sensor pickups (two at bridge), bolt-on neck.*
- Maple neck with ebony fingerboard; 22 frets; truss-rod adjuster at headstock end; locking tuners; roller nut.
- Body sunburst or colours.
- Four white plain-top Lace Sensor pickups (two at bridge).
- Three controls (volume, two tone), five-way selector and coil-switch, all on pickguard; jack socket in body face.
- 11-screw white or white pearl laminated plastic pickguard.
- Two-pivot bridge/vibrato unit.

Also with anodised aluminium hollow body option (1994-95).

SUB-SONIC STRATOCASTER HSS baritone first version (2) 2000-01 *'Sub-Sonic' on headstock, long-scale neck, white pearl pickguard, two Noiseless logo single-coils and one humbucker.*
- Fretted maple neck, or maple neck with rosewood fingerboard; 27-inch scale, 22 frets; truss-rod adjuster at body end; one string-guide; Sub-Sonic on headstock.
- Body sunburst or colours.
- Two Noiseless logo white six-polepiece pickups and one white coverless humbucker (at bridge).
- Three controls (volume, two tone) and five-way selector, all on pickguard; jack socket in body face.
- 11-screw white pearl laminated plastic pickguard.
- Six-saddle small bridge with through-body stringing.

Custom Shop production.

SUB-SONIC STRATOCASTER HSS baritone second version (2) 2001 *'Sub-Sonic' on headstock, long-scale neck, white pickguard, two single-coils and one humbucker.*
- Fretted maple neck, or maple neck with rosewood fingerboard; 27-inch scale, 22 frets; truss-rod adjuster at body end; one string-guide.
- Body sunburst or colours.
- Two white six-polepiece pickups and one white coverless humbucker (at bridge).
- Three controls (volume, two tone) and five-way selector, all on pickguard; jack socket in body face.
- 11-screw white laminated plastic pickguard.
- Six-saddle small bridge with through-body stringing.

SUB-SONIC STRATOCASTER HH baritone (2) 2000-01 *Sub-Sonic on headstock, long-scale neck, white pearl pickguard, two humbuckers.*
Similar to SUB-SONIC STRATOCASTER first version, except:
- Two white coverless humbuckers.

Custom Shop production.

US CONTEMPORARY STRATOCASTER (2) 1989-91 *Two-pivot locking vibrato system, two single-coils and one humbucker, straight-sided humbucker cut-out in pickguard.*
- Maple neck with rosewood fingerboard; 22 frets; truss-rod adjuster at headstock end; locking nut.
- Body sunburst or colours.
- Two white six-polepiece pickups and one white coverless humbucker (at bridge).
- Three controls (volume, two tone) and five-way selector, all on pickguard; jack socket in body face.
- 11-screw white laminated plastic pickguard.
- Two-pivot locking bridge/vibrato unit.

VINTAGE HOT ROD '57 STRAT (2) 2007-current *Two white six-polepiece pickups and one twin-blade pickup.*
- Fretted maple neck; truss-rod adjuster at body end; one string guide.
- Body sunburst, black or red.
- Two white six-polepiece pickups and one twin-blade pickup (angled at bridge).
- Three controls (volume, two tone) and five-way selector, all on pickguard; jack socket in body face.

- Eight-screw white plastic pickguard.
- Six-pivot bridge/vibrato unit.

VINTAGE HOT ROD '62 STRAT (2) 2007-current *Circuitry modifications.*
- Maple neck with rosewood fingerboard; truss-rod adjuster at body end; one string guide.
- Body sunburst, white or green.
- Three white six-polepiece pickups (bridge pickup angled).
- Three controls (volume, two tone) and five-way selector, all on pickguard; jack socket in body face.
- 11-screw white laminated plastic pickguard.
- Six-pivot bridge/vibrato unit.

Circuitry modifications as standard.

VOODOO STRATOCASTER (2) 1998-2000 *Large inverted headstock, reverse-angled bridge pickup, Jimi Hendrix image engraved neckplate.*
- Maple neck with maple or rosewood fingerboard; truss-rod adjuster at body end; one string-guide; Jimi Hendrix image engraved neckplate; large reverse headstock.
- Body sunburst, black or white.
- Three white six-polepiece pickups (bridge pickup reverse-angled).
- Three controls (volume, two tone) and five-way selector, all on pickguard; jack socket in body face.
- 11-screw white laminated plastic pickguard.
- Six-pivot bridge/vibrato unit.

WALNUT ELITE STRATOCASTER *See earlier ELITE STRATOCASTER listing.*

WALNUT STRAT *See earlier STRAT listing.*

YNGWIE MALMSTEEN STRATOCASTER first version (2) 1988-98 *Signature on small headstock, two-pivot vibrato.*
- Fretted maple neck, or maple neck with rosewood fingerboard, both with scalloping between frets; truss-rod adjuster at body end; one string-guide; brass nut; Yngwie Malmsteen signature on headstock.
- Body red, white or blue.
- Three white six-polepiece pickups (bridge pickup angled).
- Three controls (volume, two tone) and five-way selector, all on pickguard; jack

socket in body face.
- 11-screw white laminated plastic pickguard.
- ~~Two-pivot bridge/vibrato unit.~~

YNGWIE MALMSTEEN STRATOCASTER

second version (2) 1998-2006 *Signature on large headstock, six-pivot vibrato.*
Similar to YNGWIE MALMSTEEN STRATOCASTER first version (see previous listing), except:
- Yngwie Malmsteen signature on large headstock.
- Three controls (volume, two tone) and three-way selector, all on pickguard.
- Six-pivot bridge/vibrato unit.

YNGWIE MALMSTEEN STRATOCASTER

third version (2) 2007-current *Signature on large headstock, six-pivot vibrato, "bullet" truss-rod adjuster.*
Similar to YNGWIE MALMSTEEN STRATOCASTER second version (see previous listing), except:
- 'Bullet' truss-rod adjust at headstock end.

25th ANNIVERSARY STRATOCASTER (2)

1979-80 *'Anniversary' logo on body.*
Similar to STRATOCASTER CBS SEVENTIES (see listing in earlier US Regular Stratocasters section), except:
- Fretted maple neck only; truss-rod adjuster at body end; commemorative four-screw neckplate.
- Body silver (earliest examples white) with black 'Anniversary' logo.
- Six-pivot bridge/vibrato unit only.

'54 STRATOCASTER FMT (2) 1995-98

Replica of 1954-period original (see STRATOCASTER PRE-CBS listing in earlier US Regular Stratocasters section) but with figured body top. Gold-plated hardware option. Custom Shop production.

'60 STRATOCASTER FMT 1995-98 *Replica of 1960-period original (see STRATOCASTER PRE-CBS listing in earlier US Regular Stratocasters section) but with figured body top. Gold-plated hardware option. Custom Shop production.*

40th ANNIVERSARY 1954 STRATOCASTER 1994 *Replica of 1954-period original (see STRATOCASTER PRE-CBS listing in earlier US Regular Stratocasters section) but with commemorative*

neckplate. Numbered factory production run of 1,954.

50th ANNIVERSARY STRATOCASTER (2)

1996 *Commemorative neckplate.*
Similar to AMERICAN STANDARD STRATOCASTER (see listing in earlier US Regular Stratocasters section), except:
- Maple neck with rosewood fingerboard only; commemorative neckplate.
- Body sunburst only.
- Gold-plated hardware.
Numbered factory production run of 2,500. Also Custom Shop limited editions.

'68 REVERSE STRAT SPECIAL (2) 2002

Large inverted headstock, reverse-angled bridge pickup.
- Maple neck with maple fingerboard; truss-rod adjuster at body end; one string-guide; large reverse headstock.
- Body sunburst, black or white.
- Three white six-polepiece pickups (bridge pickup reverse-angled).
- Three controls (volume, two tone) and five-way selector, all on pickguard; jack socket in body face.
- 11-screw white laminated plastic pickguard.
- Six-pivot bridge/vibrato unit.

US-MADE TELECASTERS

US Telecasters are divided into three sections: US Regular; US Replica; and US Revised.

US REGULAR TELECASTERS

Listed here in chronological order are the models we regard as the standard versions of the Telecaster.

TELECASTER (1) 1951-83 *21 frets, slab single-cutaway body, two single-coils, three-saddle bridge.*
- Fretted maple neck (1951-59 and 1969-83), maple neck with rosewood fingerboard (1959-83), maple fingerboard official option (1967-69); truss-rod adjuster at body end; one string-guide (two from 1972).
- Slab single-cutaway body; originally blond only, later sunburst or colours.
- One plain metal-cover pickup (at neck) and one black six-polepiece pickup (angled in bridgeplate).
- Two controls (volume, tone; but originally volume, pickup blender) and three-way

selector, all on metal plate adjoining pickguard; side-mounted jack socket.
- Five-screw (eight-screw from 1959) black plastic pickguard (white plastic from 1954; white laminated plastic 1963-75 and 1981-83; black laminated plastic 1975-81).
- Three-saddle raised-sides bridge with through-body stringing (strings anchored at bridgeplate and not through body 1958-60).
Previously known as BROADCASTER (1950-51), but some transitional examples have no model name on the headstock and are unofficially known as NOCASTERS (see later listing in Other US-Made Models). Fender Bigsby bridge and vibrato tailpiece option (1967-74), no through-body string holes if unit factory-fitted. Also CUSTOM TELECASTER, with bound body (1959-72). Also PAISLEY RED TELECASTER, with red paisley-pattern body finish and clear plastic pickguard (1968-69). Also BLUE FLOWER TELECASTER, with blue floral-pattern body finish and clear plastic pickguard (1968-69). Also ROSEWOOD TELECASTER, with fretted rosewood neck, solid (later semi-solid) rosewood body and black laminated plastic pickguard (1969-72). Also ANTIGUA TELECASTER, with white/brown shaded body finish and matching-colour laminated plastic pickguard (1977-79). Also INTERNATIONAL COLOR TELECASTER, with special colour finishes, white laminated plastic pickguard and black-plated pickguard screws (1981).

TELECASTER STANDARD (1) 1983-84 *21 frets, slab single-cutaway body, two single-coils, six-saddle bridge/tailpiece.*
- Fretted maple neck; truss-rod adjuster at headstock end; two string-guides.
- Slab single-cutaway body; sunburst or colours.
- One plain metal-cover pickup at neck and one black six-polepiece pickup (angled in bridgeplate).
- Two controls (volume, tone) and three-way selector, all on metal plate adjoining pickguard; side-mounted jack socket.
- Five-screw (originally eight-screw) white plastic pickguard.
- Six-saddle flat bridge/tailpiece (no through-body stringing).
Also in red, yellow or blue streaked finish,

unofficially known as *Bowling Ball* or *Marble Telecaster (1984).*

AMERICAN STANDARD TELECASTER (1) 1988-2000 *22 frets, slab single-cutaway body, two single-coils, six-saddle bridge.*
- Fretted maple neck, or maple neck with rosewood fingerboard; 22 frets; truss-rod adjuster at headstock end; one string-guide.
- Slab single-cutaway body; sunburst or colours.
- One plain metal-cover pickup with visible height-adjustment screws (at neck) and one black six-polepiece pickup (angled in bridgeplate).
- Two controls (volume, tone) and three-way selector, all on metal plate adjoining pickguard; side-mounted jack socket.
- Eight-screw white laminated plastic pickguard.
- Six-saddle flat bridge with through-body stringing (earliest examples with raised-sides type).
Also with anodised aluminium hollow body option (1994-95).
Succeeded by AMERICAN TELECASTER (2000-current).

AMERICAN TELECASTER (1) 2000-current *Succeeded AMERICAN STANDARD TELECASTER (see previous listing).*

US REPLICA TELECASTERS
Listed here in alphabetical order are the models that replicate various standard-version US Regular Telecasters.

AMERICAN VINTAGE '52 TELECASTER 1998-current *Replica of 1952-period original (see TELECASTER listing in earlier US Regular Telecasters section).*

AMERICAN VINTAGE '52 TELE SPECIAL 1999-2001 *Replica of 1952-period original (see TELECASTER listing in earlier US Regular Telecasters section). Body sunburst only, gold-plated hardware.*

AMERICAN VINTAGE '62 CUSTOM TELECASTER 1999-current *Replica of 1962-period original with bound body (see TELECASTER listing in earlier US Regular Telecasters section).*

RELIC 50s NOCASTER 1996-98 *Distressed-finish replica of 1950s-period original with*

no model name on headstock (see *BROADCASTER listing in later Other US-made Models section). Custom Shop production.*

'51 NOCASTER 1999-current *Replica of 1951-period original with no model name on headstock (see TELECASTER listing in earlier US Regular Telecasters section). Offered with three finish distress degrees: N.O.S., Closet Classic and Relic. Custom Shop production.*

'52 TELECASTER 1983-84, 1986-98 *Replica of 1952-period original (see TELECASTER listing in earlier US Regular Telecasters section).*

50s TELECASTER 1996-98 *Replica of 1950s-period original (see TELECASTER listing in earlier US Regular Telecasters section). Gold-plated hardware option. Custom Shop production.*

'60 TELECASTER CUSTOM 2003-04 *Replica of 1960-period original with bound body (see TELECASTER listing in earlier US Regular Telecasters section). Offered with three finish distress degrees: N.O.S., Closet Classic and Relic. Custom Shop production.*

60s TELECASTER CUSTOM 1996-98 *Replica of 1960s-period original (see TELECASTER listing in earlier US Regular Telecasters section). Gold-plated hardware option. Custom Shop production.*

'63 TELECASTER 1999-current *Replica of 1963-period original (see TELECASTER listing in earlier US Regular Telecasters section). Offered with three finish distress degrees: N.O.S., Closet Classic and Relic. Custom Shop production.*

'67 TELECASTER 2005-current *Replica of 1967-period original (see TELECASTER listing in earlier US Regular Telecasters section). Offered with three finish distress degrees: N.O.S., Closet Classic and Relic. Custom Shop production.*

US REVISED TELECASTERS
Listed here in alphabetical order are the models we regard as revised and adapted versions of the standard-version US Regular Telecasters.

ALBERT COLLINS TELECASTER (1) 1990-current *Signature on headstock.*

- Maple neck with maple fingerboard; truss-rod adjuster at body end; one string-guide; Albert Collins signature on headstock.
- Slab single-cutaway bound body; natural only.
- One metal-cover six-polepiece humbucker (at neck) and one black six-polepiece pickup (angled in bridgeplate).
- Two controls (volume, tone) and three-way selector, all on metal plate adjoining pickguard; side-mounted jack socket.
- Eight-screw white laminated plastic pickguard.
- Six-saddle raised-sides bridge with through-body stringing.
Custom Shop production.

ALUMINUM-BODY TELECASTER (1) 1994-95 *Anodised aluminium hollow-body option on AMERICAN STANDARD TELECASTER (see listing in earlier US Regular Telecasters section).*

AMERICAN ASH TELECASTER (1) 2003-current *Five-screw pickguard, 22 frets.* Similar to AMERICAN TELECASTER (see listing in earlier US regular Telecasters section), except:
- Fretted maple neck only.
- Body sunburst or blonde.
- Five-screw white or black plastic pickguard.

AMERICAN CLASSIC TELECASTER first version (1) 1995-99 *Three single-coils (two white, one black), inverted control plate, five-way selector.*
Similar to AMERICAN STANDARD TELECASTER (see listing in earlier US Regular Telecasters section), except:
- Two white six-polepiece pickups and one black six-polepiece pickup (angled in bridgeplate).
- Two controls (volume, tone) and five-way selector, all on inverted control plate adjoining pickguard.
- Eight-screw white pearl or tortoiseshell laminated plastic pickguard.
Gold-plated hardware option.
Custom Shop production.

AMERICAN CLASSIC TELECASTER second version (1) 1999-2000 *Two single-coils, inverted control plate, three-way selector.*
Similar to AMERICAN CLASSIC TELECASTER first version (see earlier listing), except:

- One plain metal-cover pickup with visible height-adjustment screws (at neck) and one black six-polepiece pickup (angled in bridgeplate).
- Two controls (volume, tone) and three-way selector, all on inverted metal plate adjoining pickguard.
- Eight-screw white laminated plastic pickguard.

Custom Shop production.

AMERICAN DELUXE ASH TELECASTER

(1) 2004-current *Ash body, 22 frets, volume control with push-switch.*
Similar to AMERICAN DELUXE TELECASTER third version (see later listing), except:
- Fretted maple neck only.
- Unbound ash body; sunburst or blonde.
- Eight-screw black plastic pickguard.

AMERICAN DELUXE POWER TELE (1)

1999-2001 *Contoured bound body, two dual-concentric controls.*
Similar to AMERICAN DELUXE TELECASTER second version (see later listing), except:
- Two dual-concentric controls (volume, tone for magnetic and piezo pickups), three-way selector and mini-switch, all on metal plate adjoining pickguard.
- Fishman Power Bridge with six piezo-pickup saddles.

AMERICAN DELUXE TELECASTER first

version (1) 1998-99 *Contoured bound body, 22 frets, additional centre pickup.*
Similar to AMERICAN STANDARD TELECASTER (see listing in earlier US Regular Telecasters section), except:
- Contoured single-cutaway bound body.
- One plain metal-cover pickup with visible height-adjustment screws (at neck), one white six-polepiece pickup (in centre) and one black six-polepiece pickup (angled in bridgeplate).
- Two controls (volume, tone), five-way selector and mini-switch, all on metal plate adjoining pickguard.
- Eight-screw white or tortoiseshell laminated plastic pickguard.

AMERICAN DELUXE TELECASTER second

version (1) 1999-2003 *Contoured bound body, 22 frets, two single-coils.*
Similar to AMERICAN DELUXE TELECASTER first version (see previous

listing), except:
- One plain metal-cover pickup with visible height-adjustment screws (at neck) and one black six-polepiece pickup (angled in bridgeplate).
- Two controls (volume, tone) and three-way selector, all on metal plate adjoining pickguard.

AMERICAN DELUXE TELECASTER third

version (1) 2004-current *Contoured bound body, 22 frets, volume control with push-switch.*
Similar to AMERICAN DELUXE TELECASTER second version (see previous listing), except:
- One plain metal-cover pickup with visible height-adjustment screws (at neck) and one black six-polepiece pickup (angled in bridgeplate).
- Two controls (volume with push-switch, tone) and three-way selector, all on metal plate adjoining pickguard.
- Eight-screw white or tortoiseshell laminated plastic pickguard, or gold plastic pickguard.

AMERICAN DELUXE TELECASTER FMT

(1) 2004-06 *Figured top body, two humbuckers, no pickguard.*
- Maple neck with ebony fingerboard; 22 frets; truss-rod adjuster at headstock end; one string-guide.
- Single-cutaway body with figured top; sunburst or colours.
- Two black coverless humbuckers.
- Two controls (volume with push-switch, tone) and three-way selector, all on body; side-mounted jack socket.
- No pickguard.
- Six-saddle small bridge with through-body stringing.

Also AMERICAN DELUXE TELECASTER QMT, with quilted maple top (2004-06).

AMERICAN DELUXE TELECASTER QMT

See previous listing.

AMERICAN FAT TELE *See later U.S. FAT TELE listing.*

AMERICAN NASHVILLE B-BENDER TELE

See later Nashville B-Bender Tele listing.

AMERICAN STANDARD B-BENDER

TELECASTER (1) 1995-97 *Standard Tele pickup layout, 22 frets, B-Bender string-*

bending device installed.
Similar to AMERICAN STANDARD TELECASTER (see listing in earlier US Regular Telecasters section), except:
- Fretted maple neck only.
- Factory-fitted B-Bender built-in bending device for 2nd string.

AMERICAN TELECASTER HH first version

(1) 2003-04 *Two black coverless humbuckers, no pickguard.*
Similar to AMERICAN TELECASTER HS (see later listing), except:
- Two black coverless humbuckers.
- Six-saddle small bridge with through-body stringing.

AMERICAN TELECASTER HH second

version (1) 2004-06 *Two black coverless humbuckers, black pickguard.*
Similar to AMERICAN TELECASTER HS second version (see later listing), except:
- Two black coverless humbuckers.
- Six-saddle small bridge with through-body stringing.

AMERICAN TELECASTER HS first version

(1) 2003-04 *Coverless black humbucker at neck, no pickguard.*
- Fretted maple neck, or maple neck with rosewood fingerboard; 22 frets; truss-rod adjuster at headstock end; one string-guide.
- Slab single-cutaway body; various colours.
- One black coverless humbucker (at neck) and one black six-polepiece pickup (angled in bridgeplate).
- Two controls (volume, tone) and three-way selector, all on metal plate; side-mounted jack socket.
- No pickguard.
- Six-saddle flat bridge with through-body stringing.

AMERICAN TELECASTER HS second

version (1) 2004-06 *Coverless black humbucker at neck, black pickguard.*
Similar to AMERICAN TELECASTER HS first version (see previous listing), except:
- Two controls (volume with push-switch, tone) and three-way selector, all on metal plate.
- Eight-screw black plastic pickguard.

AMERICAN FAT TELE *See later U.S. FAT TELE listing.*

AMERICAN 60th ANNIVERSARY TELECASTER (1) 2006 *Commemorative neckplate, maple neck with rosewood fingerboard.*
Similar to AMERICAN TELECASTER (see listing in earlier US Regular Telecasters section), except:
- Maple neck with rosewood fingerboard only; commemorative headstock logo with jewel inlay; commemorative neckplate.

ANTIGUA TELECASTER *See TELECASTER listing in earlier US Regular Telecasters section.*

ANTIGUA TELECASTER CUSTOM *See later TELECASTER CUSTOM listing.*

ANTIGUA TELECASTER DELUXE *See later TELECASTER DELUXE listing.*

BAJO SEXTO TELECASTER baritone (1) 1992-98 *Model name on headstock, long-scale neck.*
- Fretted maple neck; 30.2-inch scale; 24 frets; truss-rod adjuster at body end; one string-guide; Bajo Sexto on headstock.
- Slab single-cutaway body; sunburst or blond.
- One plain metal-cover pickup (at neck) and one black six-polepiece pickup (angled in bridgeplate).
- Two controls (volume, tone) and three-way selector, all on metal plate adjoining pickguard; side-mounted jack socket.
- Five-screw black plastic pickguard.
- Three-saddle raised-sides bridge with through-body stringing.
Custom Shop production.

B-BENDER TELECASTER *See earlier AMERICAN STANDARD B-BENDER TELECASTER listing.*

BLACK & GOLD TELECASTER (1) 1981-83 *Normal Tele pickup layout, 21 frets, black body, gold hardware.*
Similar to 1981-period TELECASTER (see listing in earlier US Regular Telecasters section), except:
- Black-face headstock.
- Body black only.
- Black laminated plastic pickguard.
- Six-saddle heavy-duty small bridge with through-body stringing.
- Gold-plated brass hardware.

BLUE FLOWER TELECASTER *See TELECASTER listing in earlier US Regular Telecasters section.*

BOWLING BALL TELECASTER (also unofficially known as Marble Telecaster) *See TELECASTER STANDARD listing in earlier US Regular Telecasters section.*

BROADCASTER *See Other US-Made Models section.*

CALIFORNIA FAT TELE (1) 1997-98 *'California Series' on headstock, one humbucker and one single-coil.*
- Fretted maple neck; truss-rod adjuster at headstock end; one string-guide; 'California Series' on headstock.
- Slab single-cutaway body; sunburst or colours.
- One metal-cover six-polepiece humbucker (at neck) and one black six-polepiece pickup (angled in bridgeplate).
- Two controls (volume, tone) and three-way selector, all on metal plate adjoining pickguard; side-mounted jack socket.
- Eight-screw white laminated plastic pickguard.
- Six-saddle raised-sides bridge with through-body stringing.

CALIFORNIA TELE (1) 1997-current *'California Series' on headstock, two single-coils.*
Similar to CALIFORNIA FAT TELE (see previous listing), except:
- Fretted maple neck, or maple neck with rosewood fingerboard.
- One white six-polepiece pickup (at neck) and one black six-polepiece pickup (angled in bridgeplate).

CLARENCE WHITE TELECASTER (1) 1993-2001 *Signature on headstock.*
- Fretted maple neck; truss-rod adjuster at body end; Scruggs Peg banjo-style de-tuners for 1st and 6th strings; Clarence White signature on headstock.
- Slab single-cutaway body; sunburst only.
- One white six-polepiece pickup (at neck) and one black six-polepiece pickup (angled in bridgeplate).
- Two controls (volume, tone) and three-way selector, all on metal plate adjoining pickguard; side-mounted jack socket.
- Eight-screw tortoiseshell laminated plastic pickguard.

- Three-saddle raised-sides bridge with through-body stringing; factory-fitted B-Bender built-in bending device for 2nd string.
Custom Shop production.

CUSTOM CLASSIC TELECASTER (1) 2000-06 *Two single-coils, inverted control plate, four-way selector.*
Similar to AMERICAN CLASSIC TELECASTER second version (see earlier listing), except:
- Two controls (volume, tone) and four-way selector, all on inverted metal plate adjoining pickguard.
Custom Shop production.

CUSTOM ESQUIRE *See Other US-made Models.*

CUSTOM TELECASTER *See TELECASTER listing in earlier US Regular Telecasters section.*

DANNY GATTON TELECASTER (1) 1990-current *Signature on headstock.*
- Fretted maple neck; 22 frets; truss-rod adjuster at body end; one string-guide; Danny Gatton signature on headstock.
- Slab single-cutaway body; blond or gold.
- Two black twin-blade humbuckers (bridge pickup angled).
- Two controls (volume, tone) and three-way selector, all on metal plate adjoining pickguard; side-mounted jack socket.
- Five-screw cream plastic pickguard.
- Modified three-saddle raised-sides bridge with through-body stringing.
Custom Shop production.

DELUXE TELECASTER PLUS *See later TELECASTER PLUS listing.*

ELITE TELECASTER (1) 1983-84 *Two white plain-top humbuckers.*
- Fretted maple neck, or maple neck with rosewood fingerboard; truss-rod adjuster at headstock end; two string-guides.
- Slab single-cutaway bound body; sunburst or colours.
- Two white plain-top humbuckers.
- Four controls (two volume, two tone) and three-way selector, all on body; side-mounted jack socket; active circuit.
- White laminated plastic optional mini pickguard.
- Re-designed six-saddle bridge/tailpiece.

Also GOLD ELITE TELECASTER, with pearl tuner buttons and gold-plated hardware (1983-84). Also WALNUT ELITE TELECASTER, with walnut neck and ebony fingerboard, walnut body, pearl tuner buttons and gold-plated hardware (1983-84).

ESQUIRE *See Other US-made Models.*

FLAT HEAD TELECASTER (1) 2003-04
Name on headstock, 22 frets, one humbucker, single-cutaway body.
● Maple neck with ebony fingerboard; 22 frets; truss-rod adjuster at headstock end; staggered height locking tuners; no position markers except 'crossed pistons' inlay at 12th fret; Flat Head on headstock.
● Single-cutaway slab body; various colours.
● One black coverless humbucker.
● One control (volume) on body; side-mounted jack socket.
● No pickguard.
● Six-saddle small bridge with through-body stringing.
● Black-plated hardware
Custom Shop production.

FLAT HEAD TELECASTER HH (1) 2004-06
Name on headstock, 22 frets, two black plain-top humbuckers, single-cutaway body.
Similar to FLAT HEAD TELECASTER (see previous listing), except:
● Two black plain-top active humbuckers.
● One control (volume) and three-way selector, both on body.
Custom Shop production.

G.E. SMITH TELECASTER (1) 2007-current
Differing black position markers, cut down bridge, body-mounted bridge pickup.
● Fretted maple neck, differing pattern black position markers; truss-rod adjuster at body end; one string-guide.
● Slab single-cutaway body; red or blonde.
● One plain metal-cover pickup (at neck) and one black six-polepiece pickup (angled at bridge).
● Two controls (volume, tone) and three-way selector, all on metal plate adjoining pickguard; side-mounted jack socket.
● Five-screw white or black plastic pickguard.
● Three-saddle raised-sides cut-down bridge with through-body stringing.

GOLD ELITE TELECASTER *See previous listing.*

HIGHWAY ONE TELECASTER first version
(1) 2002-06 Satin finish, 22 frets, five-screw pickguard.
● Fretted maple neck, or maple neck with rosewood fingerboard; 22 frets; truss-rod adjuster at headstock end; one string-guide.
● Slab single-cutaway body; sunburst or colours, satin finish.
● One plain metal-cover pickup (at neck) and one black six-polepiece pickup (angled in bridgeplate).
● Two controls (volume, tone) and three-way selector, all on metal plate adjoining pickguard; side-mounted jack socket.
● Five-screw white plastic pickguard.
● Three-saddle raised-sides bridge with through-body stringing.

HIGHWAY ONE TELECASTER second version (1) 2006-current *Satin finish, 22 frets, eight-screw pickguard.*
Similar to HIGHWAY ONE TELECASTER first version (see previous listing), except:
● Eight-screw white laminate plastic pickguard.

HIGHWAY ONE TEXAS TELECASTER (1) 2003-current *Satin finish, 21 frets.*
Similar to HIGHWAY ONE TELECASTER (see earlier listing), except:
● Fretted maple neck only; 21 frets.
● Body sunburst or blonde, satin finish.

INTERNATIONAL COLOUR TELECASTER
See TELECASTER listing in earlier US Regular Telecasters section.

JAMES BURTON TELECASTER first version (1) 1990-2005 *Signature on headstock.*
● Fretted maple neck; truss-rod adjuster at body end; one string-guide; pearl tuner buttons; James Burton signature on headstock.
● Slab single-cutaway body; black with gold or red paisley-pattern, red or white.
● Three black plain-top Lace Sensor pickups (bridge pickup angled).
● Two controls (volume, tone) and five-way selector, all on metal plate; side-mounted jack socket.
● No pickguard.
● Six-saddle small bridge with through-body stringing.
● Black-plated or gold-plated hardware.

JAMES BURTON TELECASTER second version (1) 2006-current
Similar to JAMES BURTON TELECASTER first version (see previous listing), except:
● Body black with blue or red paisley flame pattern, white.
● Three black plain-top pickups.

JERRY DONAHUE TELECASTER (1) 1992-2001 *Signature on headstock.*
● Fretted maple neck; truss-rod adjuster at body end; one string-guide; Jerry Donahue signature on headstock.
● Slab single-cutaway body; sunburst, blue or red.
● Two black six-polepiece pickups (bridgeplate pickup angled).
● Two controls (volume, tone) and five-way selector, all on metal plate adjoining pickguard; side-mounted jack socket.
● Five-screw black laminated plastic pickguard.
● Three-saddle raised-sides bridge with through body stringing.
● Gold-plated hardware.
Custom Shop production.

JIMMY BRYANT TELECASTER (1) 2003-05
Decorative tooled leather pickguard overlay.
● Fretted maple neck; truss-rod adjuster at body end; one string-guide.
● Slab single-cutaway body; blonde only.
● One plain metal-cover pickup (at neck) and one black six-polepiece pickup (angled in bridgeplate).
● Two controls (volume, tone) and three-way selector, all on metal plate adjoining pickguard; side-mounted jack socket.
● Five-screw black plastic pickguard with decorative tooled leather overlay.
● Three-saddle raised sides bridge with through-body stringing.
Custom Shop production.

JOHN JORGENSON TELECASTER (1)
1998-2001 *Signature on headstock.*
● Maple neck with rosewood or ebony fingerboard; 22 frets; truss-rod adjuster at headstock end; no string-guide; locking tuners; John Jorgenson signature on headstock.
● Slab single-cutaway bound body; black or sparkle colours.
● Two plain metal-cover pickups (at neck)

and two black six-polepiece pickups (angled in bridgeplate).
- Two controls (volume, tone) and five-way selector, all on metal plate adjoining pickguard; side-mounted jack socket.
- Eight-screw clear plastic pickguard.
- Three-saddle raised-sides bridge with through-body stringing.
Custom Shop production.

J5:BIGSBY (1) 2003-current *Headstock with three tuners each side, Bigsby vibrato tailpiece.*
Similar to J5:HB TELECASTER (see following listing), except:
- One plain metal-cover pickup with visible height-adjustment screws (at neck) and one black six-polepiece pickup (angled in bridgeplate).
- Two controls (volume, tone) on metal plate adjoining pickguard.
- Six-saddle bridge, "F" logo Bigsby vibrato tailpiece.

J5:HB TELECASTER (1) 2003-current *Headstock with three tuners each side, humbucker at bridge.*
- Maple neck with rosewood fingerboard; 22 frets; truss-rod adjuster at headstock end; no string-guide; black-face three tuners-per-side headstock.
- Slab single-cutaway bound body; black only.
- One plain metal-cover pickup with visible height adjustment screws (at neck) and one black coverless humbucker (in bridgeplate).
- Two controls (both volume) on metal plate adjoining pickguard, three-way selector on body ; side-mounted jack socket.
- Eight-screw chromed pickguard.
- Six-saddle flat bridge with through-body stringing.
Custom Shop production.

MARBLE TELECASTER (also unofficially known as Bowling Ball Telecaster) *See* TELECASTER STANDARD *listing in earlier US Regular Telecasters section.*

MERLE HAGGARD TELE (1) 1997-current *Signature on headstock.*
- Fretted maple neck; 22 frets; truss-rod adjuster at body end; one string-guide; pearl tuner buttons; 'Tuff Dog Tele' inlay and Merle Haggard signature on headstock.

- Slab single-cutaway bound body; sunburst only.
- One plain metal-cover pickup (at neck) and one black six-polepiece pickup (angled in bridgeplate).
- Two controls (volume, tone) and four-way selector, all on metal plate adjoining pickguard; side-mounted jack socket.
- Seven-screw cream plastic re-styled pickguard.
- Six-saddle flat bridge with through-body stringing.
- Gold-plated hardware.
Custom Shop production.
Catalogue name varies: Merle Haggard Tribute Tuff Dog Tele (1997-2000); Merle Haggard Tribute Tele (2001-03); Merle Haggard Signature Telecaster (2004-current).

NASHVILLE B-BENDER TELE (1) 1998-current *Additional centre pickup, B-Bender string-bending device installed.*
Similar to AMERICAN STANDARD B-BENDER TELECASTER (see earlier listing), except:
- One plain metal-cover pickup with visible height-adjustment screws (at neck), one white six-polepiece pickup (in centre) and one black six-polepiece pickup (angled in bridgeplate).
- Two controls (volume, tone) and five-way selector, all on metal plate adjoining pickguard.
- Eight-screw white pearloid laminated plastic pickguard.
Known as American Nashville B-Bender Tele (2000-current).

NOCASTER *See* TELECASTER *listing in earlier US Regular Telecasters section.*

PAISLEY RED TELECASTER *See* TELECASTER *listing in earlier US Regular Telecasters section.*

ROSEWOOD TELECASTER *See* TELECASTER *listing in earlier US Regular Telecasters section.*

SET NECK TELECASTER (1) 1991-95 *Two coverless humbuckers, glued-in neck.*
- Mahogany glued-in neck with rosewood fingerboard (pao ferro from 1993); 22 frets; truss-rod adjuster at headstock end; two string-guides; neck and headstock face match body colour.
- Semi-solid slab single-cutaway bound

body; various colours.
- Two black coverless humbuckers.
- Two controls (volume, tone), three-way selector and coil-tap, all on body; side-mounted jack socket.
- No pickguard.
- Six-saddle small bridge with through-body stringing.
Custom Shop production.

SET NECK TELECASTER COUNTRY ARTIST (1) 1992-95 *One humbucker and one single-coil, glued-in neck.*
Similar to SET NECK TELECASTER, except:
- One black coverless humbucker (at neck) and one black six-polepiece pickup (angled in bridgeplate).
- Five-screw tortoiseshell laminated plastic small pickguard.
- Six-saddle flat bridge with through-body stringing.
- Gold-plated hardware.
Custom Shop production.

SET NECK TELECASTER FLOYD ROSE (1) 1991-92. *Two coverless humbuckers and one single-coil, glued-in neck, locking vibrato system.*
Similar to SET NECK TELECASTER, except:
- Ebony fingerboard; locking nut.
- Two black coverless humbuckers and one black six-polepiece pickup (in centre).
- Two controls (volume, tone), five-way selector and coil-tap, all on body; side-mounted jack socket.
- Two-pivot locking bridge/vibrato unit.
Custom Shop production.

SET NECK TELECASTER PLUS (1) 1991-92. *Two coverless humbuckers, glued-in neck, vibrato.*
Similar to SET NECK TELECASTER, except:
- Ebony fingerboard; locking tuners; roller nut.
- Two-pivot bridge/vibrato unit.
Custom Shop production.

SEYMOUR DUNCAN SIGNATURE ESQUIRE *See Other US-made Models.*

SPARKLE TELECASTER (1) 1992-95 *Coloured sparkle finish on body.*
- Fretted maple neck, or maple neck with rosewood fingerboard; truss-rod adjuster at body end; one string-guide.
- Slab single-cutaway body; sparkle colours.

- One plain metal-cover pickup (at neck) and one black six-polepiece pickup (angled in bridgeplate).
- Two controls (volume, tone) and three-way selector, all on metal plate adjoining pickguard; side-mounted jack socket.
- Eight-screw white laminated plastic pickguard.
- Three-saddle raised-sides bridge with through-body stringing.
Custom Shop production.

SPECIAL EDITION 1994 TELECASTER (1)
1994 *Commemorative neckplate.*
Similar to AMERICAN STANDARD TELECASTER (see listing in earlier US Regular Telecasters section), except:
- Body black or blond; commemorative neckplate.
- Eight-screw grey pearl or tortoiseshell laminated plastic pickguard.

SUB-SONIC TELE baritone (1) 2001-05
Sub-Sonic on headstock, long-scale neck.
- Fretted maple neck; 27-inch scale, 22 frets; truss-rod adjuster at body end; one string-guide; Sub-Sonic on headstock.
- Slab single-cutaway body; sunburst or colours.
- One plain metal cover pickup (at neck) and one black six-polepiece pickup (angled in bridgeplate).
- Two controls (volume, tone) and four-way selector, all on metal plate adjoining pickguard; side-mounted jack socket.
- Eight-screw white laminated plastic pickguard.
- Six-saddle bridge with through-body stringing.
Custom Shop production.

TELE JNR (1) 1995-2000 *Two large black rectangular pickups.*
- Mahogany glued-in neck with pao ferro fingerboard; 22 frets; truss-rod adjuster at headstock end; one string-guide; neck and headstock face match body colour.
- Semi-solid slab single-cutaway body; sunburst or colours.
- Two large black six-polepiece pickups.
- Two controls (volume, tone) and three-way selector, all on inverted metal plate adjoining pickguard; side-mounted jack socket.
- Small tortoiseshell plastic, or white pearl, tortoiseshell or black laminated plastic pickguard.

- Six-saddle small bridge with through-body stringing.
Custom Shop production.

TELE PLUS first version (1) 1990-95 *Three Lace Sensor pickups (two at bridge).*
- Fretted maple neck, or maple neck with rosewood fingerboard; 22 frets; truss-rod adjuster at headstock end; one string-guide.
- Slab single-cutaway body; sunburst or colours.
- Three black plain-top Lace Sensor pickups (two in single separate surround at bridge).
- Two controls (volume, tone), three-way selector and coil-switch, all on metal plate adjoining pickguard; side-mounted jack socket.
- Eight-screw white laminated plastic pickguard.
- Six-saddle small bridge with through-body stringing.

TELE PLUS second version (1) 1995-98 *Three Lace Sensor pickups (one angled in bridgeplate).*
- Fretted maple neck, or maple neck with rosewood fingerboard; 22 frets; truss-rod adjuster at headstock end; one string-guide.
- Slab single-cutaway bound body; sunburst or colours.
- Three plain-top Lace Sensor pickups (bridgeplate pickup angled).
- Two controls (volume, tone) and three-way selector, all on metal plate adjoining pickguard; side-mounted jack socket.
- Eight-screw white pearl or tortoiseshell laminated plastic pickguard.
- Six-saddle flat bridge with through-body stringing.

TELE PLUS DELUXE (1) 1991-92 *Three Lace Sensor pickups (two at bridge), vibrato.*
Similar to TELE PLUS FIRST VERSION, except:
- No string-guide; locking tuners; roller nut.
- Two-pivot bridge/vibrato unit.

TELE PRO (1) 2007-current *Five-screw pickguard, 22 frets, four-way selector.*
- Fretted maple neck, or maple neck with rosewood fingerboard; 22 frets; truss-rod adjuster at headstock end; one string-guide.
- Slab single-cutaway body; black or blonde.
- One plain metal-cover pickup (at neck)

and one black six-polepiece pickup (angled in bridgeplate).
- Two controls (volume, tone) and four-way selector, all on metal plate adjoining pickguard; side-mounted jack socket.
- Five-screw white plastic pickguard.
- Three-saddle raised-sides bridge with through-body stringing.

TELE-SONIC (1) 1998-2004 *Model name on headstock.*
- Maple neck with rosewood fingerboard; 24.75-inch scale, 22 frets; truss-rod adjuster at headstock end; one string-guide; black-face headstock.
- Semi-solid slab single-cutaway body; sunburst or red.
- Two black-top six-polepiece pickups.
- Four controls (two volume, two tone) and three-way selector, all on body; side-mounted jack socket.
- Six-screw black laminated plastic pickguard.
- Two-section wrapover bridge/tailpiece (six-saddle wrapover bridge/tailpiece from 2003).

TELE THINLINE (1) 2006-current *F-hole body, two single-coils, 12-screw white or black pickguard.*
- Fretted maple neck; truss-rod adjuster at body end; one string-guide.
- Semi-solid slab single-cutaway body with f-hole; black or blonde, offered with three finish distress degrees: N.O.S., Closet Classic and Relic.
- One plain metal-cover pickup (at neck) and one black six-polepiece pickup (angled in bridgeplate).
- Two controls (volume, tone) and three-way selector, all on pickguard; side-mounted jack socket.
- 12-screw white or black plastic pickguard.
- Three-saddle raised-sides bridge with through-body stringing.
Custom Shop production.

TELECASTER CUSTOM (1) 1972-81 *One humbucker and one single-coil, four controls.*
- Fretted maple neck, or maple neck with rosewood fingerboard; 'bullet' truss-rod adjuster at headstock end; two string-guides; three-screw neckplate.
- Slab single-cutaway body; sunburst or colours.

- One metal-cover split-polepiece humbucker (at neck) and one black six-polepiece pickup (angled in bridgeplate).
- Four controls (two volume, two tone) and three-way selector, all on pickguard; side-mounted jack socket.
- 16-screw black laminated plastic pickguard.
- Six-saddle raised-sides bridge with through-body stringing.

Earliest examples with 15-screw pickguard and/or three-saddle raised-sides bridge.

Also ANTIGUA TELECASTER CUSTOM, with white/brown shaded body finish and matching-colour laminated plastic pickguard (1977-79).

For Custom Telecaster (with bound body) see TELECASTER listing in earlier US Regular Telecasters section.

TELECASTER DELUXE (1) 1973-81 *Two covered humbuckers, normal Tele body.*
- Fretted maple neck; 'bullet' truss-rod adjuster at headstock end; two string-guides; large Stratocaster-style headstock; three-screw neckplate.
- Contoured single-cutaway body; sunburst or colours.
- Two metal-cover split-polepiece humbuckers.
- Four controls (two volume, two tone) and three-way selector, all on pickguard; side-mounted jack socket.
- 16-screw black laminated plastic pickguard.
- Six-saddle small bridge with through-body stringing.

Some examples with Stratocaster-type six-pivot bridge/vibrato unit.

Also ANTIGUA TELECASTER DELUXE, with white/brown shaded body finish and matching-colour laminated plastic pickguard (1977-79).

TELECASTER XII (1) 12-string 1995-98 *Model name on 12-string headstock.*
- Fretted maple neck, or maple neck with rosewood fingerboard; truss-rod adjuster at headstock end; one 'bracket' string-guide; six-tuners-per-side headstock.
- Slab single-cutaway body; sunburst or colours.
- One plain metal-cover pickup (at neck) and one black six-polepiece pickup (angled in bridgeplate).
- Two controls (volume, tone) and three-

way selector, all on metal plate adjoining pickguard; side-mounted jack socket.
- Five-screw black or white plastic, or white pearl laminated plastic pickguard.
- Twelve-saddle bridge with through-body stringing.

Custom Shop production.

THINLINE TELECASTER first version (1) 1968-71 *F-hole body, two single-coils, 12-screw white pearl pickguard.*
- Maple neck with maple fingerboard (fretted maple neck, or maple neck with rosewood fingerboard from 1969); truss-rod adjuster at body end; one string-guide.
- Semi-solid slab single-cutaway with f-hole; sunburst or colours.
- One plain metal-cover pickup with visible height-adjustment screws (at neck) and one black six-polepiece pickup (angled in bridgeplate).
- Two controls (volume, tone) and three-way selector, all on pickguard; side-mounted jack socket.
- 12-screw pearl laminated plastic pickguard.
- Three-saddle raised-sides bridge with through-body stringing.

THINLINE TELECASTER second version (1) 1971-79 *F-hole body, two humbuckers.* Similar to THINLINE TELECASTER FIRST VERSION, except:
- Fretted maple neck only; 'bullet' truss-rod adjuster at headstock; three-screw neckplate.
- Two metal-cover split-polepiece humbuckers.
- 12-screw black, white or white pearl laminated plastic re-styled pickguard.
- Six-saddle small bridge with through-body stringing.

U.S. FAT TELE (1) 1998-2000 *One humbucker and one single-coil, five-way selector.*
Similar to AMERICAN STANDARD TELECASTER (see listing in earlier US Regular Telecasters section), except:
- One metal-cover humbucker (at neck) and one black six-polepiece pickup (angled in bridgeplate).
- Two controls (volume, tone) and four-way selector, all on metal plate adjoining pickguard.

Known as AMERICAN FAT TELE (2001-03).

VINTAGE HOT ROD '52 TELE (1) 2007-current *Metal-cover small humbucker at neck.*
Similar to American Vintage '52 Telecaster (see listing in earlier US Replica Telecasters section), except:
- One plain metal-cover small humbucker (at neck) and one black six-polepiece pickup (angled in bridgeplate).

WALNUT ELITE TELECASTER *See earlier ELITE TELECASTER listing.*

WAYLON JENNINGS TRIBUTE TELECASTER (1) 1995-2003 *Signature on headstock.*
- Fretted maple neck; truss-rod adjuster at body end; one string-guide; pearl tuner buttons; Scruggs Peg banjo-style de-tuner for 6th string; 'W' inlay at 12th fret and Waylon Jennings signature on headstock.
- Slab single-cutaway bound body; black only with white leather inlay.
- One plain metal-cover pickup with visible height-adjustment screws (at neck) and one black six-polepiece pickup (angled in bridgeplate).
- Two controls (volume, tone) and three-way selector, all on metal plate adjoining pickguard; side-mounted jack socket.
- Eight-screw white laminated plastic pickguard.
- Six-saddle flat bridge with through-body stringing.

Custom Shop production.

WILL RAY TELECASTER (1) 1998-2001 *Signature on headstock, skull markers.*
- Maple neck with rosewood fingerboard, skull markers; 22 frets; truss-rod adjuster at headstock end; one string-guide; locking tuners; Will Ray signature on small Stratocaster-style headstock.
- Slab single-cutaway body; gold foil leaf on various colours.
- Two large rectangular white six-polepiece pickups (bridge pickup angled).
- Three controls (volume, two tone) and three-way selector, all on metal plate adjoining pickguard; side-mounted jack socket.
- Eight-screw white pearl laminated plastic re-styled pickguard.
- Modified three-saddle bridge with through-body stringing; optional Hipshot bending device on second string.

Custom Shop production.

50th ANNIVERSARY TELECASTER (1)
1996 *Commemorative neckplate.*
Similar to AMERICAN STANDARD TELECASTER (see listing in earlier US Regular Telecasters section), except:
- Fretted maple neck only; commemorative neckplate.
- Body sunburst only.
- Gold-plated hardware.
Numbered factory production run of 1,250.

'51 NOCASTER *See US Replica Telecasters.*

'59 ESQUIRE *See Other US-made Models.*

90s TELE THINLINE (1) 1997-2001 *F-hole body, 22 frets.*
- Fretted maple neck, or maple neck with rosewood fingerboard; 22 frets; truss-rod adjuster at headstock end; one string-guide.
- Semi-solid slab single-cutaway bound body; sunburst or colours.
- One plain metal-cover pickup with visible height-adjustment screws (at neck) and one black six-polepiece pickup (angled in bridgeplate)
- Two controls (volume, tone) and three-way selector, all on pickguard; side-mounted jack socket.
- 12-screw white pearl or tortoiseshell laminated plastic pickguard.
- Six-saddle flat bridge with through-body stringing.

1998 COLLECTORS EDITION TELECASTER (1) 1998 *Commemorative fingerboard inlay and neckplate.*
Similar to 50s TELECASTER (see listing in earlier US Replica Telecasters section), except:
- Fretted maple neck with commemorative inlay at 12th fret; commemorative neckplate.
- Body sunburst only.
- Five-screw white plastic pickguard.
- Gold-plated hardware.
Numbered factory production run of 1,998.

OTHER US-MADE MODELS
These are listed here in alphabetical order of model name.

AMERICAN VINTAGE '62 JAGUAR 1999-current *Replica of 1962-period original (see later JAGUAR listing).*

AMERICAN VINTAGE '62 JAZZMASTER
1999-current *Replica of 1962-period original (see later JAZZMASTER listing).*

ANTIGUA MUSTANG *See later MUSTANG listing.*

ARROW *See later SWINGER listing.*

BROADCASTER (1) 1950-51 *Forerunner of the TELECASTER (see listing in earlier US Regular Telecasters section) and very similar, but with Broadcaster model name on headstock, although some late examples have only the Fender logo, and these are unofficially known as NOCASTERS.*

BRONCO (5) 1967-80 *Model name on headstock, angled pickup at bridge.*
- Maple neck with rosewood fingerboard; 24-inch scale; truss-rod adjuster at body end; one string-guide; plastic tuner buttons (metal from 1975).
- Slab offset-waist body; red only (black or white from 1975).
- One black plain-top pickup (angled at bridge).
- Two controls (volume, tone) and jack socket, all on pickguard.
- 13-screw (15-screw from 1970) white laminated plastic pickguard (black laminated plastic from 1975).
- Six-saddle bridge/vibrato unit.

BULLET first version (12) 1981-83 *Model name on headstock, single-cutaway body, bridge on metal pickguard.*
- Fretted maple neck, or maple neck with rosewood fingerboard; truss-rod adjuster at body end; one string-guide; Telecaster-style headstock.
- Slab single-cutaway body; red or white.
- Two black or white plain-top pickups (neck pickup angled).
- Two controls (volume, tone), three-way selector and jack socket, all on pickguard.
- Six-screw (plus four at bridge) white- or black-painted metal pickguard.
- Six-saddle bridge, raised 'lip' of pickguard forms tailpiece.
Earliest examples use some Korean-made components.

BULLET DELUXE (12) 1981-83 *Model name on headstock, single-cutaway body, separate bridge.*

Similar to BULLET FIRST VERSION, except:
- Eight-screw white or black laminated plastic pickguard.
- Separate six-saddle bridge with through-body stringing.

BULLET second version (13) 1983 *Model name on headstock, offset-cutaway body, two single-coils, bridge on metal pickguard.*
- Fretted maple neck; truss-rod adjuster at body end; one string-guide; Telecaster-style headstock.
- Slab offset-cutaway body; red or white.
- Two white plain-top pickups (neck pickup angled).
- Two controls (volume, tone), three-way selector and jack socket, all on pickguard.
- Six-screw (plus four at bridge) white-painted metal pickguard.
- Six-saddle bridge, raised 'lip' of pickguard forms tailpiece.

BULLET H1 (13) 1983 *'Bullet' name on headstock, offset-cutaway body, one humbucker, bridge on metal pickguard.*
Similar to BULLET SECOND VERSION, except:
- One white plain-top humbucker (at bridge).
- Pushbutton coil-switch replaces three-way selector.

BULLET H2 (13) 1983 *'Bullet' name on headstock, offset-cutaway body, two humbuckers, separate bridge.*
Similar to BULLET SECOND VERSION, except:
- Sunburst or colours.
- Two white plain-top humbuckers.
- Three-way selector, plus two pushbutton coil-switches.
- Nine-screw white laminated plastic pickguard.
- Six-saddle separate bridge with through-body stringing.

BULLET S2 (13) 1983 *'Bullet' name on headstock, offset-cutaway body, two single-coils, separate bridge.*
Similar to BULLET SECOND VERSION, except:
- Sunburst or colours.
- Nine-screw white laminated plastic pickguard.
- Six-saddle separate bridge with through-body stringing.

BULLET S3 (13) 1983 *'Bullet' name on headstock, offset-cutaway body, three*

single-coils, separate bridge.
Similar to BULLET SECOND VERSION, except:
● Sunburst or colours.
● Three black or white plain-top pickups (bridge pickup angled).
● Five-way selector.
● Nine-screw white laminated plastic pickguard.
●   Six-saddle separate bridge with through-body stringing.

CLASSIC ROCKER (27) 2000-02 *Hollow single-cutaway body, two pickups, Bigsby vibrato tailpiece.*
● Maple glued-in neck with bound rosewood fingerboard, diamond markers; truss-rod adjuster at headstock end; three-tuners-per-side headstock.
● Hollow single-cutaway bound body with bound f-holes; black or red.
● Two white-top six-polepiece pickups.
● Four controls (three volume, one tone) and three-way selector, all on body; side-mounted jack socket.
● White plastic pickguard.
● Six-saddle metal-top bridge, Bigsby vibrato tailpiece.
Custom Shop production.

COMPETITION MUSTANG *See later* MUSTANG *listing.*

CORONADO I (6) 1966-69 *Model name on headstock, hollow twin-cutaway body, one pickup.*
● Maple neck with rosewood fingerboard; truss-rod adjuster at body end; plastic tuner buttons; single string-guide.
● Hollow twin-cutaway bound body with long f-holes; sunburst or colours.
● One metal-cover black-centre six-polepiece pickup (at neck).
● Two controls (volume, tone) on body; side-mounted jack socket.
● White or gold laminated plastic pickguard.
● Single-saddle wooden bridge, tailpiece; or six-saddle metal-top bridge, vibrato tailpiece.

CORONADO II (6) 1966-69 *Model name on headstock, hollow twin-cutaway body, two pickups.*
Similar to CORONADO I, except:
● Bound fingerboard, block markers.
● Bound long f-holes.
● Two pickups.

● Four controls (two volume, two tone) and three-way selector, all on body.
● Six-saddle metal-top bridge, tailpiece with F inlay; or six-saddle all-metal bridge, vibrato tailpiece.
Prototype examples with unbound dot-marker neck and three-tuners-per-side headstock; truss-rod adjuster at headstock end; unbound body; black laminated plastic pickguard; six-section tailpiece.

CORONADO II ANTIGUA (6) 1967-1971 *White/brown shaded hollow twin-cutaway body, two pickups.*
Similar to CORONADO II, except:
● Pearl tuner buttons.
● White/brown shaded finish.
● 'Antigua' on matching-colour laminated plastic pickguard.
● Six-saddle all-metal bridge, vibrato tailpiece only.

CORONADO II WILDWOOD (6) 1967-69 *Coloured wood hollow twin-cutaway body, two pickups.*
Similar to CORONADO II, except:
● Pearl tuner buttons.
● Six dye-injected colour combinations.
● 'Wildwood' on white laminated plastic pickguard.
● Six-saddle all-metal bridge, vibrato tailpiece only.

CORONADO XII 12-string (6) 1966-69 *Model name on 12-string headstock, hollow twin-cutaway body, two pickups.*
Similar to CORONADO II, except:
● One 'bracket' string-guide; six-tuners-per-side 'hockey stick' headstock.
● Six-saddle metal-top bridge, tailpiece with F inlay.

CORONADO XII ANTIGUA 12-string (6) 1967-71 *12-string headstock, white/brown shaded hollow twin-cutaway body, two pickups.*
Similar to CORONADO XII 12-string, except:
● Pearl tuner buttons.
● White/brown shaded finish.
● 'Antigua' on matching-colour laminated plastic pickguard.

CORONADO XII WILDWOOD 12-string (6) 1967-69 *12-string headstock, coloured wood hollow twin-cutaway body, two pickups.*
Similar to CORONADO XII 12-string, except:

● Pearl tuner buttons.
● Six dye-injected colour combinations.
● 'Wildwood' on white laminated plastic pickguard.

CUSTOM (8) 1969-70 *Model name on 'hockey stick' headstock.*
● Maple neck with bound rosewood fingerboard, block markers; truss-rod adjuster at body end; one 'bracket' string-guide; three-tuners-per-side 'hockey stick' headstock.
● Contoured offset-waist body with pointed base; sunburst only.
● Two black plain-top split pickups.
● Two controls (volume, tone) and jack socket, all on metal plate adjoining pickguard; four-way rotary selector on pickguard.
● 17-screw tortoiseshell laminated plastic pickguard.
● Six-saddle bridge with vibrato tailpiece.
Made using modified Electric XII parts, some with purpose-built necks. Some examples with MAVERICK *model name, not Custom, on headstock.*

CUSTOM ESQUIRE *See later* ESQUIRE *listing.*

CUSTOM TELECASTER *See* TELECASTER *listing in earlier US Regular Telecasters section.*

CUSTOM SHOP The Fender Custom Shop was established in 1987. It now produces general catalogue models, which are noted in the main US listing and indicated as 'Custom Shop production'. The Shop also makes limited-edition instruments, which over the years have variously been called Builder Select, Custom Team Built, Dealer Select, Limited Edition, Limited Release, Master Builder, Master Built, Master Design Limited Edition, Stock Team Built, Tribute Series, and probably more besides. These limited editions are clearly still big business, with the majority ordered by distributors or stores worldwide. Quantities of each item can range from tens to hundreds, and the number of models so far is considerable – making it impossible to identify and itemise all of them here, especially as Fender cannot supply complete records. Regardless of order size, all official Custom Shop instruments carry an identifying logo on the back of the headstock. Originally oval, the logo was later amended to the current 'V' shape.

D'AQUISTO DELUXE (16) 1995-2001
Hollow single-cutaway body, one pickup, wooden tailpiece.
- Maple glued-in neck with bound ebony fingerboard, block markers; 25.125-inch scale, 22 frets; truss-rod adjuster at headstock end; three-tuners-per-side headstock.
- Hollow archtop single-cutaway bound body with f-holes; sunburst, natural or red.
- One metal-cover six-polepiece humbucker (at neck).
- Two controls (volume, tone) on body; side-mounted jack socket.
- Bound wooden pickguard.
- Single-saddle wooden bridge, wooden tailpiece.
- Gold-plated hardware.
Custom Shop production

D'AQUISTO ELITE (16) 1994-95, 2000-01
Hollow single-cutaway body, one floating pickup, wooden tailpiece.
Similar to D'AQUISTO DELUXE, except:
- Split-block markers; ebony tuner buttons.
- Body sunburst or natural.
- Floating humbucker.
Custom Shop production

DUO-SONIC first version (3) 1956-64
Model name on headstock, neck pickup angled, bridge pickup straight.
- Fretted maple neck (maple neck with rosewood fingerboard from 1959); 22.5-inch scale, 21 frets; truss-rod adjuster at body end; plastic tuner buttons; one string-guide.
- Slab body; originally beige only, later sunburst or colours.
- Two plain-top pickups (neck pickup angled).
- Two controls (volume, tone), three-way selector and jack socket, all on pickguard.
- Eight-screw anodised metal pickguard (12-screw white or tortoiseshell laminated plastic from 1960).
- Three-saddle bridge/tailpiece.

DUO-SONIC second version (5) 1964-69
Model name on enlarged headstock, both pickups angled, two slide switches.
- Maple neck with rosewood fingerboard; 22.5-inch scale and 21 frets, or 24-inch

scale and 22 frets; enlarged headstock.
- Contoured offset-waist body; red, white, or blue.
- Two white or black plain top pickups (both angled).
- Two controls (volume, tone) and jack socket, all on metal plate adjoining pickguard; two selector slide-switches on pickguard.
- 12-screw white pearl or tortoiseshell laminated plastic re-styled pickguard.
- Enlarged three-saddle bridge/tailpiece.
Early examples with slab body. Version with 24-inch scale and 22 frets known as DUO-SONIC II (1964-69).

DUO-SONIC II See previous listing.

ELECTRIC XII 12-string (4) 1965-69 *Model name on 12-string 'hockey-stick' headstock.*
- Maple neck with rosewood fingerboard (bound from 1965), dot markers (blocks from 1966); truss-rod adjuster at body end; one 'bracket' string-guide; six-tuners-per-side 'hockey-stick' headstock.
- Contoured offset-waist body; sunburst or colours.
- Two black plain-top split pickups.
- Two controls (volume, tone) and jack socket, all on metal plate adjoining pickguard; four-way rotary selector on pickguard.
- 17-screw white pearl or tortoiseshell laminated plastic pickguard.
- 12-saddle bridge with through-body stringing.

ESQUIRE (1) 1950-69 *Model name on headstock, slab single-cutaway body, one pickup.*
- Fretted maple neck (1950-59 and 1969), maple neck with rosewood fingerboard (1959-69), maple fingerboard official option (1967-69); truss-rod adjuster at body end; one string-guide.
- Slab single-cutaway body; originally blond only, later sunburst or colours.
- One black six-polepiece pickup (angled in bridgeplate).
- Two controls (volume, tone) and three-way selector, all on metal plate adjoining pickguard; side-mounted jack socket.
- Five-screw (eight-screw from 1959) black plastic pickguard (white plastic from 1954; white laminated plastic from 1963).
- Three-saddle bridge with through-body stringing (strings anchored at bridgeplate

not through body 1958-60).
Very few earliest 'pre-production' examples without truss-rod, and some have second pickup at neck.
Also CUSTOM ESQUIRE, with bound body (1959-69).

FLAT HEAD SHOWMASTER (25) 2003-04
Name on headstock, 22 frets, one humbucker.
- Maple neck with ebony fingerboard; 22 frets; truss-rod adjuster at headstock end; staggered height locking tuners; no position markers except "crossed pistons" inlay at 12th fret; Flat Head on headstock.
- Body various colours.
- One black coverless humbucker.
- One control (volume) on body; side-mounted jack socket.
- No pickguard.
- Six-saddle small bridge with through-body stringing.
- Black-plated hardware.
Custom Shop production.

FLAT HEAD SHOWMASTER HH (25) 2004-06 *Name on headstock, 22 frets, two black plain-top humbuckers.*
Similar to FLAT HEAD SHOWMASTER (see previous listing), except:
- Two black plain top active humbuckers.
- One control (volume) and three-way selector, both on body.
Custom Shop production.

HIGHWAY ONE SHOWMASTER HH (25) 2003-04 *Name on headstock, 24 frets, two humbuckers.*
- Maple neck with rosewood fingerboard; 24 frets; truss-rod adjuster at headstock end; single-bar string-guide; locking nut.
- Body black, pewter or silver, satin finish.
- Two black coverless humbuckers.
- Two controls (volume, tone) and three-way selector, all on body; side-mounted jack socket.
- No pickguard.
- Two-pivot locking bridge/vibrato unit.

HIGHWAY ONE SHOWMASTER HSS (25) 2003-04 *Name on headstock, 24 frets, two single-coils and one humbucker.*
Similar to HIGHWAY ONE SHOWMASTER HH (see previous listing), except:
- Two black six-polepiece pickups and one black coverless humbucker.

Two controls (volume, tone) and five-way selector, all on body.

HIGHWAY ONE TORONADO (26) 2003-04 *Model name on headstock, two controls, two black coverless humbuckers.*
- Maple neck with rosewood fingerboard; 24.75-inch scale, 22 frets; truss-rod adjuster at headstock end; one string-guide.
- Contoured offset-waist body; black, pewter or silver, satin finish.
- Two black coverless humbuckers.
- Two controls (volume, tone) and three-way selector, all on body; side-mounted jack socket.
- Seven-screw black plastic pickguard.
- Six-saddle bridge, bar tailpiece.

JAGUAR (4) 1962-75 *Model name on headstock, three metal control plates.*
- Maple neck with rosewood fingerboard (bound from 1965), dot markers (blocks from 1966); 24-inch scale, 22 frets; truss-rod adjuster at body end; one string-guide.
- Contoured offset-waist body; sunburst or colours.
- Two rectangular white six-polepiece pickups, each with metal 'sawtooth' sides.
- Two controls (volume, tone) and jack socket, all on lower metal plate adjoining pickguard; slide-switch and two roller controls (volume, tone), all on upper metal plate adjoining pickguard; three slide-switches on metal plate inset into pickguard.
- Ten-screw white or tortoiseshell laminated plastic pickguard.
- Six-saddle bridge, spring-loaded string mute, vibrato tailpiece.
Some examples with gold-plated hardware.

JAZZMASTER (4) 1958-80 *Model name on headstock, two large rectangular pickups.*
- Maple neck with rosewood fingerboard (bound from 1965), dot markers (blocks from 1966); truss-rod adjuster at body end; one string-guide.
- Contoured offset-waist body; sunburst or colours.
- Two large rectangular white (black from 1977) six-polepiece pickups.
- Two controls (volume, tone), two rollers (volume, tone), three-way selector, slide-switch and jack socket, all on pickguard.

Nine-screw anodised metal pickguard (13-screw white or tortoiseshell laminated plastic from 1959; black laminated plastic from 1976).
- Six-saddle bridge, vibrato tailpiece.
Prototype examples with smaller headstock and/or fretted maple neck.
Some examples with gold-plated hardware.

LEAD I (11) 1979-82 *Model name on headstock, one humbucker pickup, two switches.*
- Fretted maple neck, or maple neck with rosewood fingerboard; truss-rod adjuster at body end; two string-guides.
- Body sunburst or colours.
- One black or white 12-polepiece humbucker (at bridge).
- Two controls (volume, tone), two two-way selectors and jack socket, all on pickguard.
- 11-screw black or white laminated plastic pickguard.
- Six-saddle bridge with through-body stringing.

LEAD II (11) 1979-82 *Model name on headstock, two single-coils, two switches.*
Similar to LEAD I, except:
- Two black or white six-polepiece pickups (both angled).
- One two-way selector, one three-way selector.

LEAD III (11) 1981-2 *Model name on headstock, two humbuckers, two switches.*
Similar to LEAD I, except:
- Two black or white 12-polepiece humbuckers.
- Two three-way selectors.

LTD (7) 1968-74 *Hollow single-cutaway body, metal tailpiece, one floating pickup.*
- Maple neck with bound ebony fingerboard, 'diamond-in-block' markers; 20 frets; truss-rod adjuster at body end; three-tuners-per-side headstock.
- Hollow single-cutaway bound body with carved top; sunburst or natural.
- One metal-cover six-polepiece humbucker (mounted on neck-end).
- Two controls (volume, tone) and jack socket, all on pickguard.
- Tortoiseshell laminated plastic pickguard.
- Single-saddle wooden bridge, tailpiece with F inlay.
- Gold-plated hardware.

MAVERICK *See earlier CUSTOM listing.*

MONTEGO I (7) 1968-74 *Hollow single-cutaway body, one pickup, metal tailpiece.*
- Maple neck with bound ebony fingerboard, 'diamond-in-block' markers; 20 frets; truss-rod adjuster at body end; three-tuners-per-side headstock.
- Hollow single-cutaway bound body with bound f-holes; sunburst or natural.
- One metal-cover six-polepiece humbucker (at neck).
- Two controls (volume, tone) on body; side-mounted jack socket.
- Black laminated plastic pickguard.
- Single-saddle wooden bridge, tailpiece with F inlay.

MONTEGO II (7) 1968-74 *Hollow single-cutaway body, two pickups, metal tailpiece.*
Similar to MONTEGO I, except:
- Two humbuckers.
- Four controls (two volume, two tone) and three-way selector, all on body.

MUSICLANDER *See later SWINGER listing.*

MUSICMASTER first version (3) 1956-64 *Model name on headstock, one angled pickup at neck.*
- Fretted maple neck (maple neck with rosewood fingerboard from 1959); 22.5-inch scale, 21 frets; truss-rod adjuster at body end; plastic tuner buttons; one string-guide.
- Slab body; originally beige only, later sunburst or colours.
- One plain-top pickup (angled at neck).
- Two controls (volume, tone) and jack socket, all on pickguard.
- Eight-screw anodised pickguard (12-screw white or tortoiseshell laminated plastic from 1960).
- Three-saddle bridge/tailpiece.

MUSICMASTER second version (5) 1964-75 *Model name on headstock, one angled pickup, controls on metal plate, enlarged headstock.*
- Maple neck with rosewood fingerboard (fretted maple neck option from 1970); 22.5-inch scale and 21 frets, or 24-inch scale and 22 frets (see note below); enlarged headstock.
- Contoured offset-waist body; red, white, or blue.
- One white or black plain-top pickup

(angled at neck).

- Two controls (volume, tone) and jack socket, all on metal plate adjoining pickguard.
- 12-screw white pearl or tortoiseshell laminated plastic re-styled pickguard.
- Enlarged three-saddle bridge/tailpiece.

Early examples with slab body. Version with 24-inch scale and 22 frets known as MUSICMASTER II *(1964-69), then just* MUSICMASTER *(1969-75).*

MUSICMASTER third version (5) 1975-80
Model name on headstock, one angled pickup at neck, controls on black pickguard.
Similar to MUSICMASTER SECOND VERSION, except:

- 24-inch scale, 22 frets only.
- Body black or white.
- One black plain-top pickup (angled at neck).
- Two controls (volume, tone) on pickguard.
- 15-screw black laminated plastic pickguard.

MUSICMASTER II *See earlier* MUSICMASTER SECOND VERSION *listing.*

MUSTANG (5) 1964-81 *Model name on headstock, two angled pickups, two slide switches, vibrato tailpiece.*

- Maple neck with rosewood fingerboard (fretted maple neck option from 1970); 22.5-inch scale and 21 frets (1964-69), or 24-inch scale and 22 frets; truss-rod adjuster at body end; plastic tuner buttons (metal from 1975); one string-guide (two from 1975).
- Contoured offset-waist body; sunburst or colours.
- Two white or black plain-top pickups (both angled).
- Two controls (volume, tone) and jack socket, all on metal plate adjoining pickguard; two selector slide-switches on pickguard.
- 12-screw white pearl or tortoiseshell laminated plastic pickguard (black laminated plastic from 1975).
- Six-saddle bridge with vibrato tailpiece.

Early examples with slab body.
Also ANTIGUA MUSTANG, *with white/brown shaded body finish and matching-colour laminated plastic pickguard (1977-79).*
Also COMPETITION MUSTANG, *with stripes on body (1968-73).*

NOCASTER *See earlier* BROADCASTER *listing.*

PRODIGY (15) 1991-93 *Prodigy on headstock, two single-coils and one humbucker, six-pivot bridge/vibrato unit.*

- Fretted maple neck, or maple neck with rosewood fingerboard; 22 frets; truss-rod adjuster at headstock end; one string-guide.
- Contoured offset-waist body; various colours.
- Two black six-polepiece pickups and one black coverless humbucker (at bridge).
- Two controls (volume, tone), five-way selector and jack socket, all on pickguard.
- Eight-screw black laminated plastic pickguard.
- Six-pivot bridge/vibrato unit.

PRODIGY II (15) 1991-92 *Prodigy on headstock, two single-coils and one humbucker, locking vibrato system.*
Similar to PRODIGY I, except:

- No string-guide; locking nut.
- Two-pivot locking bridge/vibrato unit.
- Chrome-plated or black-plated hardware.

ROBBEN FORD ELITE (18) 1994-2001
Signature on headstock, unbound fingerboard, twin-cutaway body.

- Mahogany glued-in neck with unbound ebony fingerboard (pao ferro from 1997); 24.625-inch scale, 22 frets; truss-rod adjuster at headstock end; three-tuners-per-side headstock.
- Twin-cutaway bound body; sunburst, black or red.
- Two metal-cover six-polepiece humbuckers.
- Four controls (two volume, two tone), three-way selector and coil-switch, all on body; side-mounted jack socket.
- Six-saddle bridge, fine-tuner tailpiece.

Custom Shop production.

ROBBEN FORD ULTRA FM (18) 1994-2001
Signature on headstock, bound fingerboard, twin-cutaway body.
Similar to ROBBEN FORD ELITE, except:

- Bound ebony fingerboard with split-block position markers.

Custom Shop production.

ROBBEN FORD ULTRA SP (18) 1994-2001
Signature on headstock, bound fingerboard, twin-cutaway body, gold-plated hardware.
Similar to ROBBEN FORD ELITE, except:

- Bound ebony fingerboard with split-block position markers; ebony tuner buttons.
- Semi-solid body.
- Gold-plated hardware.

Custom Shop production.

SEYMOUR DUNCAN SIGNATURE ESQUIRE (1) 2003-current *Signature on headstock.*

- Fretted maple neck; truss-rod adjuster at body end; one string-guide; Seymour Duncan signature on headstock.
- Slab single-cutaway body; sunburst only.
- One black six-polepiece pickup (angled in bridgeplate).
- Two controls (volume, tone) and three-way selector, all on metal plate adjoining pickguard; side-mounted jack socket.
- Five-screw white plastic pickguard.
- Three-saddle bridge with through-body stringing.

Custom Shop production.

SHOWMASTER ELITE (25) 2004-current
Model name on headstock, 22 frets, glued-in neck, two humbuckers, two-pivot vibrato.
Similar to SHOWMASTER FMT (see later listing), except:

- Mahogany glued-in neck with ebony fingerboard, ornate markers; pearl tuner buttons; black-face Telecaster-style headstock.
- Body brown or sunbursts.
- Two Seymour Duncan logo black coverless humbuckers.
- Two-pivot bridge/vibrato unit.

Body with figured carved top in various woods (FMT, LWT, QMT, SMT).
Custom Shop production.

SHOWMASTER ELITE HARD-TAIL (25) 2004-current *Model name on headstock, 22 frets, glued-in neck, two humbuckers, six-saddle wrapover bridge/tailpiece.*
Similar to SHOWMASTER ELITE (see previous listing), except:

- No roller nut.
- Six-saddle wrapover bridge/tailpiece.

Custom Shop production.

SHOWMASTER FMT (25) 1998-2005 *Model name on headstock, 22 frets, figured carved body top, two single-coils and one humbucker.*

- Fretted maple neck, or maple neck with rosewood fingerboard; 22 frets; truss-rod

adjuster at headstock end; staggered height locking tuners; roller nut.
- Body with figured carved top; sunburst or colours.
- Two black six-polepiece pickups and one black coverless humbucker (at bridge).
- Two controls (volume, tone) and five-way selector, all on body; side-mounted jack socket.
- No pickguard.
- Two-pivot bridge/vibrato unit (or two-pivot locking bridge/vibrato unit 1998-99).
Custom Shop production.

SHOWMASTER SET NECK FMT (25) 1999-2005 *Model name on headstock, 22 frets, glued-in neck, two single-soils and one humbucker.*
Similar to SHOWMASTER FMT (see previous listing), except:
- Maple glued-in neck with rosewood fingerboard only.
- Two-pivot locking bridge/vibrato unit only.
Custom Shop production.

SHOWMASTER SET NECK FMT HARD-TAIL (25) 1999-2005 *Model name on headstock, 22-frets, glued-in neck, two-section wrapover bridge/tailpiece.*
Similar to SHOWMASTER SET NECK FMT (see previous listing), except:
- No roller nut.
- Two-section wrapover bridge/tailpiece.
Custom Shop production.

SHOWMASTER STANDARD (25) 1999-2005 *Model name on headstock, 22 frets, carved body top.*
Similar to SHOWMASTER FMT (see earlier listing), except:
- Body with carved top; various colours.
- Two-pivot bridge/vibrato unit only.
Custom Shop production.

SHOWMASTER 7-STRING (25) 2000-01 *Model name on seven-string headstock.*
Similar to SHOWMASTER FMT (see earlier listing), except:
- Maple neck with rosewood fingerboard only; no roller nut; seven-string headstock.
- Body with carved top; various colours.
- Two-pivot bridge/vibrato unit only.

SHOWMASTER 7-STRING HARD-TAIL (25) 2000-01 *Model name on seven-string headstock, six-saddle bridge.*

Similar to SHOWMASTER 7-STRING (see previous listing), except:
- Two-section wrapover bridge/tailpiece.

STARCASTER (10) 1976-80 *Model name on 'hooked' headstock with black edging, semi-acoustic offset-waist body.*
- Fretted maple neck; 22 frets; 'bullet' truss-rod adjuster at headstock end; one 'bracket' string-guide; three-screw neckplate; black edging on headstock.
- Semi-acoustic offset-waist bound body with f-holes; sunburst or colours.
- Two metal-cover split-polepiece humbuckers.
- Five controls (two volume, two tone, master volume) and three-way selector, all on body; side-mounted jack socket.
- Black laminated plastic pickguard.
- Six-saddle bridge with through-body stringing.

STEEL GUITARS Fender's electric guitar lines also included at one time electric steel and pedal steel guitars. Non-pedal models included: Champ (1955-81); Champion (1949-52); Custom (1949-58); Deluxe (1946-49); Deluxe 6/Deluxe 8 (1950-81); Dual 6 Professional (1950-81); Dual 8 Professional (1946-57); Organ Button (1946-48); Princeton (1946-49); Stringmaster (1953-81); Student (1952-55); Studio Deluxe (1956-81). Pedal models included: Artist Dual 10/Single 10 (1976-81); Student Single 10 (1976-81); 400 (1958-76); 800 (1964-76); 1000 (1957-76); 2000 (1964-76).

STRAT-O-SONIC DVI *See US Revised Stratocasters.*

STRAT-O-SONIC DVII *See US Revised Stratocasters.*

STRAT-O-SONIC HH *See US Revised Stratocasters.*

SUB-SONIC *See US Revised Stratocasters and US Revised Telecasters.*

SWINGER (9) 1969 *Arrow-head-shape headstock, one angled pickup.*
- Maple neck with rosewood fingerboard; 22.5-inch scale, 21 frets; truss-rod adjuster at body end; one string-guide; 'arrow-head' shape headstock.
- Contoured offset-waist body with 'scoop' in base; various colours.

- One black plain-top pickup (angled at neck).
- Two controls (volume, tone) and jack socket, all on metal plate adjoining pickguard.
- 12-screw white pearl or tortoiseshell laminated plastic pickguard.
- Three-saddle bridge/tailpiece.
Made from modified Musicmaster and Mustang parts. Many examples have no Swinger logo on headstock. Also unofficially known as ARROW or MUSICLANDER.

TORONADO DVII (26) 2002-04 *Model name on black-face headstock, four controls, two black six-polepiece pickups.*
- Maple neck with rosewood fingerboard; 24-inch scale, 22 frets; truss-rod adjuster at headstock end; one string-guide; black-face headstock.
- Contoured offset-waist body; blonde or red.
- Two large black six-polepiece pickups.
- Four controls (two volume, two tone) and three-way selector, all on body; side-mounted jack socket.
- Seven-screw black laminated plastic pickguard.
- Six-saddle bridge, bar tailpiece.

TORONADO HH (26) 2002-04 *Model name on black-face headstock, four controls, two black coverless humbuckers.*
Similar to TORONADO DVII (see previous listing), except:
- Two black coverless humbuckers.

'59 ESQUIRE (1) 2003-06 *Replica of 1959-period original (see earlier ESQUIRE listing). No through-body stringing. Available with three finish distress degrees: N.O.S., Closet Classic and Relic. Custom Shop production.*

FENDER MEXICO

Each guitar has 'Made In Mexico' somewhere on the instrument.

MEXICO-MADE STRATOCASTERS

Mexican Stratocasters are divided into two sections: Mexico Replica; and Mexico Revised.

MEXICO REPLICA STRATOCASTERS

Listed here in alphabetical order are the Mexico-made models that replicate various standard-version US-made Stratocasters (see earlier US-made Regular Stratocasters section).

CLASSIC 50s STRATOCASTER 1999-current *Replica of 1950s-period original (see STRATOCASTER PRE-CBS listing in earlier US Regular Stratocasters section).*

CLASSIC 60s STRATOCASTER 1999-current *Replica of 1960s-period original (see STRATOCASTER PRE-CBS listing in earlier US Regular Stratocasters section).*

CLASSIC 70s STRATOCASTER 1999-current *Replica of 1970s-period original (see STRATOCASTER CBS listing in earlier US Regular Stratocasters section).*

MEXICO REVISED STRATOCASTERS

Listed here in alphabetical order are the models we regard as revised and adapted versions of the standard-version US-made Stratocasters (see earlier US-made Regular Stratocasters section).

BUDDY GUY POLKA DOT STRAT (2) 2002-current *Signature on headstock, black/white polka dot body finish.*
Similar to STANDARD STRATOCASTER (see later listing), except:
● Buddy Guy signature on headstock.
● Body black/white polka dot finish only.
● Three black six-polepiece pickups.
● Eight-screw black laminated plastic pickguard.

CHRIS REA CLASSIC STRATOCASTER (2) 1999 *Signature on headstock.*
Similar to CLASSIC 60s STRATOCASTER (see listing in earlier Mexico Replica Stratocasters section), except:
● Chris Rea signature on headstock.
● Body red only.

CLASSIC PLAYER 50s STRATOCASTER (2) 2006-current *Maple fingerboard, locking tuners, two-pivot vibrato.*
Similar to CLASSIC 50s STRATOCASTER (see listing in earlier Mexico Replica Stratocasters section), except:
● Locking tuners; neckplate with 'Custom Shop designed' logo.
● Body sunburst or gold.

● Two-pivot bridge/vibrato unit.

CLASSIC PLAYER 60s STRATOCASTER (2) 2006-current *Rosewood fingerboard, locking tuners, two-pivot vibrato.*
Similar to CLASSIC 60s STRATOCASTER (see listing in earlier Mexico Replica Stratocasters section), except:
● Locking tuners; neckplate with 'Custom Shop designed' logo.
● Body sunburst or blue.
● Two-pivot bridge/vibrato unit.

CONTEMPORARY STRATOCASTER *See later STRAT SPECIAL listing.*

DELUXE BIG BLOCK STRATOCASTER (2) 2005-06. *Block markers, black headstock face, chrome pickguard.*
● Maple neck with rosewood fingerboard, block markers; truss-rod adjuster at headstock end; one string-guide; black-face headstock.
● Body black only.
● Two black six-polepiece pickups and one black coverless humbucker (at bridge).
● Two controls (volume, tone) and five-way selector, all on pickguard; jack socket in body face.
● 11-screw chrome plastic pickguard.
● Six-pivot bridge/vibrato unit.

DELUXE DOUBLE FAT STRAT (2) 1999-2004 *Two-pivot vibrato, two black humbuckers, black pickguard, large headstock.*
Similar to DELUXE FAT STRAT (see later listing), except:
● Two black coverless humbuckers.
Known as DELUXE DOUBLE FAT STRAT HH (2002-03).
Known as DELUXE STRAT HH (2004).

DELUXE DOUBLE FAT STRAT FLOYD ROSE (2) 1998-2004 *Two-pivot locking vibrato system, two black humbuckers, black pickguard, large headstock.*
Similar to DELUXE FAT STRAT (see later listing), except:
● Single-bar string-guide; locking nut.
● Two black coverless humbuckers.
● Two-pivot locking bridge/vibrato unit.
Known as DELUXE DOUBLE FAT STRAT HH WITH LOCKING TREMOLO (2002-03).
Known as DELUXE STRAT HH WITH LOCKING TREMOLO (2004).

DELUXE DOUBLE FAT STRAT HH WITH LOCKING TREMOLO *See previous DELUXE DOUBLE FAT STRAT FLOYD ROSE listing.*

DELUXE FAT STRAT (2) 1999-2006 *Two-pivot vibrato, two black single-coils and one black humbucker, black pickguard, large headstock.*
● Maple neck with rosewood fingerboard; truss-rod adjuster at headstock end; one string-guide; large headstock.
● Body black or white.
● Two black six-polepiece pickups and one black coverless humbucker (at bridge).
● Three controls (volume, two tone) and five-way selector, all on pickguard; jack socket in body face.
● 11-screw black laminated plastic pickguard.
● Six-pivot bridge/vibrato unit.
Known as DELUXE FAT STRAT HSS (2002-03).
Known as DELUXE STRAT HSS (2004-06).

DELUXE FAT STRAT FLOYD ROSE (2) 1998-2005 *Two-pivot locking vibrato system, two black single-coils and one black humbucker, black pickguard, large headstock.*
Similar to DELUXE FAT STRAT (see previous listing), except:
● Single bar string-guide; locking nut.
● Two-pivot locking bridge/vibrato unit.
Known as DELUXE FAT STRAT HSS WITH LOCKING TREMOLO (2002-03).
Known as DELUXE STRAT HSS WITH LOCKING TREMOLO (2004-05).

DELUXE FAT STRAT HSS WITH LOCKING TREMOLO *See previous DELUXE FAT STRAT FLOYD ROSE listing.*

DELUXE PLAYER'S STRAT (2) 2004-current *Gold-plated hardware, push-switch, three Noiseless logo white pickups.*
Similar to STANDARD STRATOCASTER (see later listing), except:
● Three Noiseless logo white six-polepiece pickups.
● Three controls (volume, two tone), five-way switch and push-switch, all on pickguard.
● 11-screw tortoiseshell pickguard.
● Gold-plated hardware.

DELUXE POWER STRATOCASTER (2) 2006-current *Fishman Powerbridge vibrato, two volume controls, one tone control.*

Similar to STANDARD STRATOCASTER (see later listing), except:
- Two white six-polepiece pickups and one white coverless humbucker (at bridge).
- Three controls (volume, tone, piezo volume) and five-way switch, all on pickguard.
- 11-screw tortoiseshell pickguard.
- Six-pivot Fishman Powerbridge vibrato with six piezo pickup bridge saddles.

DELUXE POWERHOUSE STRAT (2) 1997-current *White pearl pickguard, active circuit.*
Similar to STANDARD STRATOCASTER (see later listing), except:
- Body various colours.
- Three controls (volume, tone, boost) and five-way selector, all on pickguard; active circuit.
- 11-screw white pearloid plastic pickguard.

DELUXE STRAT HH *See earlier DELUXE DOUBLE FAT STRAT listing.*

DELUXE STRAT HH WITH LOCKING TREMOLO *See earlier DELUXE DOUBLE FAT STRAT FLOYD ROSE listing.*

DELUXE STRAT HSS *See earlier DELUXE FAT STRAT listing.*

DELUXE STRAT HSS WITH LOCKING TREMOLO *See earlier DELUXE FAT STRAT FLOYD ROSE listing.*

DELUXE SUPER STRAT (2) 1997-2004 *Gold-plated hardware, push-switch.*
Similar to STANDARD STRATOCASTER (see earlier listing), except:
- Three controls (volume, two tone), five-way selector and push-switch, all on pickguard.
- 11-screw tortoiseshell laminated plastic pickguard.
- Gold-plated hardware.

FLOYD ROSE STANDARD STRATOCASTER (2) 1994-98 *Two-pivot locking vibrato system, two white single-coils and one white humbucker, white pickguard, small headstock, two controls.*
Similar to STANDARD STRATOCASTER (see later listing), except:
- Single-bar string-guide; locking nut.
- Body black or white.
- Two white six-polepiece pickups and one white coverless humbucker (at bridge).
- Two controls (volume, tone) and five-way selector, all on pickguard.
- Two-pivot locking bridge/vibrato unit.
Also known as SQUIER SERIES FLOYD ROSE STANDARD STRATOCASTER, with small Squier Series logo on headstock (1994-96).

GOLD SISTER STRATOCASTER (2) 2007
Gold body and headstock face
Similar to STANDARD STRATOCASTER HSS (see later listing) except:
- Fretted maple neck only; gold-faced headstock.
- Body gold only.
- Two black six-polepiece pickups and one black coverless humbucker (at bridge).
- Two controls (volume, tone) and five-way selector, all on pickguard.
- Chromed pickguard.

HANK MARVIN CLASSIC STRATOCASTER (2) 2000 *Signature on headstock.*
Similar to CLASSIC 50s STRATOCASTER (see listing in earlier Mexico Replica Stratocasters section), except:
- Hank Marvin signature on headstock.
- Body red only.
- Six-pivot bridge/vibrato unit with special design vibrato arm.
Limited edition of 250.

HANK MARVIN STRATOCASTER (2) 1997 *Signature on body.*
Similar to TRADITIONAL STRATOCASTER (see later listing), except:
- Fretted maple neck only; Hank Marvin signature on body.
- Body red only.
Limited edition of 300.

JIMMIE VAUGHAN TEX-MEX STRATOCASTER (2) 1997-current *Signature on back of headstock.*
Similar to STANDARD STRATOCASTER (see later listing), except:
- Fretted maple neck only; Jimmie Vaughan signature on back of headstock.
- 11-screw white plastic pickguard.
- Modified control operation.

RICHIE SAMBORA STANDARD STRATOCASTER (2) 1994-2002 *Signature on headstock.*
Similar to STANDARD STRATOCASTER (see later listing), except:
- Maple neck with rosewood fingerboard only; single-bar string-guide; locking nut; Richie Sambora signature on headstock.
- Body various colours.
- Two white six-polepiece pickups and one white coverless humbucker (at bridge).
- Two-pivot locking bridge/vibrato unit.

ROBERT CRAY STRATOCASTER (2) 2003-current *Signature on headstock.*
Similar to CLASSIC 60s STRATOCASTER (see listing in earlier Mexico Replica Stratocasters section), except:
- Robert Cray signature on headstock.
- Body sunburst, silver or violet.
- Six-saddle bridge with through-body stringing.

SILVER SISTER STRATOCASTER (2) 2007
Silver body and headstock face
Similar to STANDARD STRATOCASTER HSS (see later listing) except:
- Maple neck with rosewood fingerboard only; silver-faced headstock.
- Body silver only.
- Gold anodised metal pickguard.

SPECIAL STRATOCASTER *See later STANDARD STRATOCASTER listing.*

SPLATTER STRATOCASTER (2) 2003
Coloured splatter finish on body and pickguard.
Similar to STANDARD STRATOCASTER (see later listing), except:
- Body various colours, splatter finish.
- 11-screw plastic pickguard in splatter finish matching body colour.

SQUIER SERIES FLOYD ROSE STANDARD STRATOCASTER *See earlier FLOYD ROSE STANDARD STRATOCASTER listing.*

SQUIER SERIES STANDARD STRATOCASTER *See later TRADITIONAL STRATOCASTER listing.*

STANDARD FAT STRAT (2) 1999-current *Modern-style 'thick' Fender headstock logo in silver, two single-coils and one humbucker, six-pivot vibrato.*
Similar to STANDARD STRATOCASTER (see later listing), except:
- Two white six-polepiece pickups and one white coverless humbucker (at bridge).
Known as STANDARD STRATOCASTER HSS (2004-current).

STANDARD FAT STRAT FLOYD ROSE (2)
1999-current *Two-pivot locking vibrato system, two white single-coils and one white humbucker, white pickguard, small headstock, three controls.*
Similar to STANDARD STRATOCASTER (see later listing), except:
- Maple neck with rosewood fingerboard only; single-bar string-guide; locking nut.
- Two white six-polepiece pickups and one white coverless humbucker (at bridge).
- Two-pivot locking bridge/vibrato unit.
Known as STANDARD FAT STRAT WITH LOCKING TREMOLO (2002-03).
Known as STANDARD STRATOCASTER HSS WITH LOCKING TREMOLO (2004-current).

STANDARD FAT STRAT WITH LOCKING TREMOLO *See previous STANDARD FAT STRAT FLOYD ROSE listing.*

STANDARD ROLAND READY STRAT (2)
1998-current *Six-pivot vibrato, one string-guide, extra slim white pickup at bridge.*
Similar to STANDARD STRATOCASTER (see later listing), except:
- Maple neck with rosewood fingerboard only.
- Additional slim white plain-top Roland synthesiser pickup (at bridge).
- Three controls (volume, tone, synth volume), five-way selector, two push-buttons and mini-switch, all on pickguard; jack socket in body face; side-mounted multi-pin synth output.

STANDARD SATIN STRATOCASTER (2)
2003-06 *Satin body finish, small headstock, white black pickguard, three black single-coils.*
Similar to STANDARD STRATOCASTER (see later listing), except:
- Body various colours, satin finish.
- Three black six-polepiece pickups.
- 11-screw black laminated plastic pickguard.

STANDARD STRATOCASTER (2) 1991-current *Modern-style 'thick' Fender headstock logo in silver, three single-coils, six-pivot vibrato.*
- Fretted maple neck, or maple neck with rosewood fingerboard; truss-rod adjuster at headstock end; one string-guide.
- Body sunburst or colours.
- Three white six-polepiece pickups (bridge pickup angled).

- Three controls (volume, two tone) and five-way selector, all on pickguard; jack-socket in body face.
- 11-screw white laminated plastic pickguard.
- Six-pivot bridge/vibrato unit.
Originally known as SPECIAL STRATOCASTER in UK.

STANDARD STRATOCASTER FMT (2)
2005-06 *Figured-top body, no pickguard, three black six-polepiece pickups.*
- Maple neck with rosewood fingerboard; truss-rod adjuster at headstock end; one string guide.
- Body with figured top; cherry sunburst or tobacco sunburst.
- Three black six-polepiece pickups (bridge pickup angled).
- Two controls (volume, tone) and five-way selector, all on body; side-mounted jack socket.
- No pickguard.
- Six-pivot bridge/vibrato unit.

STANDARD STRATOCASTER HH (2) 2004-06 *Two-pivot vibrato, two black humbuckers, black pickguard, small headstock.*
Similar to STANDARD STRATOCASTER (see earlier listing), except:
- Maple neck with rosewood fingerboard only.
- Two black coverless humbuckers.
- 11-screw black laminated plastic pickguard.

STANDARD STRATOCASTER HSS *See earlier STANDARD FAT STRAT listing.*

STANDARD STRATOCASTER HSS WITH LOCKING TREMOLO *See earlier STANDARD FAT STRAT FLOYD ROSE listing.*

STANDARD 60th ANNIVERSARY STRATOCASTER (2) 2006 *Commemorative neckplate, fretted maple neck.*
Similar to STANDARD STRATOCASTER (see earlier listing), except:
- Fretted maple neck only; commemorative neckplate.
- Body silver grey only.

STRAT SPECIAL (2) 1994-96 *Black pickups and pickguard.*
Similar to STANDARD STRATOCASTER (see previous listing), except:

- Two black six-polepiece pickups and one black coverless humbucker (at bridge).
- Two controls (volume, tone), five-way selector and coil-switch, all on pickguard.
- 11-screw black laminated plastic pickguard.
- Black-plated hardware
Known as CONTEMPORARY STRATOCASTER in UK.

TEX-MEX STRAT (2) 1996-97 *Vintage-style 'thin' Fender headstock logo in gold, three single-coils.*
Similar to STANDARD STRATOCASTER (see earlier listing), except:
- Headstock with vintage-style Fender headstock logo in gold.
Fitted with different specification, visually similar pickups.

TEX-MEX STRAT SPECIAL (2) 1997
Vintage-style 'thin' Fender headstock logo in gold, two single-coils and one humbucker.
Similar to STANDARD STRATOCASTER (see earlier listing), except:
- Two white six-polepiece pickups and one white coverless humbucker (at bridge).

TOM DELONGE STRATOCASTER (2) 2001-03 *One humbucker, one control.*
- Maple neck with rosewood fingerboard; truss-rod adjuster at headstock end; one string-guide; large headstock; Tom Delonge engraved neckplate.
- Body various colours.
- One white coverless humbucker (at bridge).
- One control (volume) on pickguard; jack socket in body face.
- 11-screw white or white pearl laminated plastic pickguard.
- Six-saddle small bridge with through-body stringing.

TRADITIONAL STRATOCASTER (2) 1996-98 *Modern-style 'thick' Fender headstock logo in black, three single-coils.*
- Fretted maple neck, or maple neck with rosewood fingerboard; truss-rod adjuster at headstock end; one string-guide.
- Body black, red, or white.
- Three white six-polepiece pickups (bridge pickup angled).
- Three controls (volume, two tone) and five-way selector, all on pickguard; jack-socket in body face.
- 11-screw white laminated plastic pickguard.

● Six-pivot bridge/vibrato unit.
Previously known as SQUIER SERIES STANDARD STRATOCASTER, with small Squier Series logo on headstock (1994-96).

TRADITIONAL FAT STRAT (2) 1996-98
Modern-style 'thick' Fender headstock logo in black, two single-coils and one humbucker.
Similar to TRADITIONAL STRATOCASTER (see previous listing), except:
● Two white six-polepiece pickups and one white coverless humbucker (at bridge).

50th ANNIVERSARY GOLDEN STRATOCASTER (2) 2004 *Gold-finish body.*
Similar to CLASSIC 50s STRATOCASTER (see listing in earlier Mexico Replica Stratocasters section), except:
● Body gold only.

MEXICO-MADE TELECASTERS
Mexican Telecasters are divided into two sections: Mexico Replica; and Mexico Revised.

MEXICO REPLICA TELECASTERS
Listed here in alphabetical order are the Mexico-made models that replicate various standard-version US-made Telecasters (see earlier US-made Regular Telecasters section).

CLASSIC 50s TELECASTER 1999-2006
Replica of 1950s-period original (see TELECASTER listing in earlier US Regular Telecasters section).

CLASSIC 60s TELECASTER 2001-current
Replica of 1960s-period original (see TELECASTER listing in earlier US Regular Telecasters section).

CLASSIC '69 TELECASTER THINLINE
1998-current *Replica of 1969-period original (see listing in earlier US Revised Telecasters section).*

CLASSIC '72 TELECASTER CUSTOM
1999-current *Replica of 1972-period original (see listing in earlier US Revised Telecasters section).*

CLASSIC '72 TELECASTER DELUXE 2004-current *Replica of 1972-period original (see listing in earlier US Revised Telecasters section).*

CLASSIC '72 TELECASTER THINLINE
1999-current *Replica of 1972-period original (see listing in earlier US Revised Telecasters section).*

MEXICO REVISED TELECASTERS
Listed here in alphabetical order are the Mexico-made models that we regard as revised and adapted versions of standard-version US-made Telecasters (see earlier US-made Regular Telecasters section).

CLASSIC PLAYER BAJA TELECASTER (1) 2006-current
Similar to CLASSIC 50s TELECASTER (see listing in earlier Mexico Replica Telecasters section), except:
● Neckplate with 'Custom Shop designed' logo.
● Body blonde or sand.
● Two controls (volume with push-switch, tone) and four-way selector, all on metal plate adjoining pickguard.

CLASSIC 50s ESQUIRE *See Other Mexico-made Models.*

CONTEMPORARY TELECASTER *See later TELE SPECIAL listing.*

DELUXE BIG BLOCK TELECASTER (1) 2005-06 *Block markers, black headstock face, chrome pickguard.*
● Maple neck with rosewood fingerboard, block markers; truss-rod adjuster at headstock end; one string-guide; black-face headstock.
● Body black only.
● Two plain metal-cover pickups with visible height adjustment screws (at neck and in centre) and one black six-polepiece pickup (angled in bridgeplate).
● Two controls (volume, tone) and five-way selector, all on metal plate adjoining pickguard; side-mounted jack socket.
● Eight-screw chrome plastic pickguard.
● Six-saddle flat bridge with through-body stringing.

DELUXE NASHVILLE TELE (1) 1997-current *White six-polepiece pickup in centre position.*
Similar to STANDARD TELECASTER (see later listing), except:
● Fretted maple neck, or maple neck with rosewood fingerboard.
● Body sunburst or colours.
● One plain metal-cover pickup with visible

height-adjustment screws (at neck), one white six-polepiece pickup (in centre) and one black six-polepiece pickup (angled in bridgeplate).
● White six-polepiece pickup (in centre).
● Two controls (volume, tone) and five-way selector.
● Eight-screw tortoiseshell laminated plastic pickguard.
● Six-saddle raised-sides bridge with through-body stringing.

DELUXE NASHVILLE POWER TELE (1) 1999-current *White six-polepiece pickup in centre position, one dual-concentric control.*
Similar to DELUXE NASHVILLE TELE (see earlier listing), except:
● One dual-concentric control (volume, tone for magnetic pickups), one control (volume for piezo pickups) and five-way selector.
● Fishman Power Bridge with six piezo-pickup saddles.

JAMES BURTON STANDARD TELECASTER (1) 1995-current *Signature on headstock.*
Similar to STANDARD TELECASTER (see later listing), except:
● James Burton signature on headstock.
● Eight-screw white plastic pickguard.
● Six-saddle raised-sides bridge with through-body stringing.

JOHN 5 TELECASTER (1) 2004-current
Headstock with three tuners each side, humbucker at bridge.
● Maple neck with rosewood fingerboard; 22 frets; truss-rod adjuster at headstock end; no string-guide; black-face, three-tuners-per-side headstock.
● Slab single-cutaway bound body; black only.
● One plain metal-cover pickup with visible height adjustment screws (at neck) and one black coverless humbucker (in bridgeplate).
● Two controls (volume, tone) on metal plate adjoining pickguard; three-way selector on body; side-mounted jack socket.
● Eight-screw chrome plastic pickguard.
● Six-saddle flat bridge with through-body stringing.

J5 TRIPLE TELE DELUXE (1) 2007-current
Three split-polepiece humbuckers.
● Maple neck with rosewood fingerboard;

22 frets; truss-rod adjuster at headstock end; no string-guide; black-face large Stratocaster-style headstock.
- Contoured single-cutaway bound body; black only.
- Three metal-cover split-polepiece humbuckers.
- Two controls (volume, tone) and three-way selector, all on pickguard; side-mounted jack socket.
- 13-screw chromed pickguard.
- Six-pivot bridge/vibrato unit.

MUDDY WATERS TELECASTER (1) 2001-current *Custom Telecaster on headstock, amplifier-type black plastic control knobs.*
Similar to CLASSIC 60s TELECASTER (see listing in earlier Mexico Replica Telecasters section), except:
- Custom Telecaster on headstock.
- Body red only.
- Nine-screw white plastic pickguard.
- Amplifier-type black plastic control knobs.

SPECIAL TELECASTER *See later STANDARD TELECASTER listing.*

SQUIER SERIES STANDARD TELECASTER
See later TRADITIONAL TELECASTER listing.

STANDARD TELECASTER (1) 1991-current *Modern-style 'thick' Fender headstock logo in silver, two single-coils.*
- Fretted maple neck; truss-rod adjuster at headstock end; one string-guide.
- Slab single-cutaway body; sunburst or colours.
- One plain metal-cover pickup with visible height-adjustment screws (at neck) and one black six-polepiece pickup (angled in bridgeplate).
- Two controls (volume, tone) and three-way selector, all on metal plate adjoining pickguard; side-mounted jack socket.
- Eight-screw white laminated plastic pickguard.
- Six-saddle flat bridge/tailpiece (no through-body stringing).
Originally known as SPECIAL TELECASTER in UK.

TELE SPECIAL (1) 1994-96 *Humbucker at neck, black pickguard.*
Similar to STANDARD TELECASTER (see previous listing), except:
- One metal-cover six-polepiece humbucker (at neck) and one black six-polepiece pickup (angled in bridgeplate).

- Two controls (volume, tone) and five-way selector.
- Eight-screw black laminated plastic pickguard.
- Six-saddle raised-sides bridge with through-body stringing.
Known as CONTEMPORARY TELECASTER in UK.

TEX-MEX TELE SPECIAL (1) 1997
Humbucker at neck, white pickguard.
Similar to STANDARD TELECASTER (see earlier listing), except:
- One metal-cover six-polepiece humbucker (at neck) and one black six-polepiece pickup (angled in bridgeplate).
- Two controls (volume, tone) and five-way selector.
- Six-saddle raised-sides bridge with through-body stringing.

TRADITIONAL TELECASTER (1) 1996-98
Modern-style 'thick' Fender headstock logo in black, two single-coils.
Similar to vintage-style Telecaster, except:
- Fretted maple neck; truss-rod adjuster at headstock end; one string-guide.
- Slab single-cutaway body; black, red or white.
- One plain metal-cover pickup with visible height-adjustment screws (at neck) and one black six-polepiece pickup (angled in bridgeplate).
- Two controls (volume, tone) and three-way selector, all on metal plate adjoining pickguard; side-mounted jack socket.
- Eight-screw white laminated plastic pickguard.
- Six-saddle flat bridge/tailpiece (no through-body stringing).
Previously known as SQUIER SERIES STANDARD TELECASTER, with small Squier Series logo on headstock (1994-96).

OTHER MEXICO-MADE MODELS
These are listed here in alphabetical order of the model name.

CLASSIC 50s ESQUIRE 2005-current *Replica of 1950s-period original (see ESQUIRE listing in earlier Other US made Models section).*

CYCLONE (5) 1998-2006 *Name on headstock, one angled single-coil and one humbucker.*
- Maple neck with rosewood fingerboard;

24.75-inch scale, 22 frets; truss-rod adjuster at headstock end; one string-guide.
- Contoured offset-waist body, sunburst or colours.
- One white six-polepiece pickup (angled at neck) and one white/black coverless humbucker (at bridge).
- Two controls (volume, tone) and jack socket, all on metal plate adjoining pickguard; three-way selector on pickguard.
- Nine-screw white pearl laminated plastic pickguard.
- Six-pivot bridge/vibrato unit.

CYCLONE HH (5) 2003-05 *Name on headstock, two humbuckers.*
Similar to CYCLONE (see previous listing), except:
- Two black coverless humbuckers.
- Nine-screw white pearl or black laminated plastic pickguard.

CYCLONE II (5) 2002-2006 *Name on headstock, three angled single-coils.*
Similar to CYCLONE (see earlier listing), except:
- Body blue or red, with stripes.
- Three rectangular white six-polepiece pickups, each with metal 'sawtooth' sides, all angled.
- Two controls (volume, tone) and jack socket, all on metal plate adjoining pickguard; three slide-switches on metal plate inset into pickguard.

DUO-SONIC (3) 1993-97 *Model name on headstock, 20-fret neck, two angled pickups.*
- Fretted maple neck; 22.7-inch scale, 20 frets; truss-rod adjuster at body end; one string-guide.
- Slab offset-cutaway body; black, red or white.
- Two white six-polepiece pickups (both angled).
- Two controls (volume, tone), three-way selector and jack socket, all on pickguard.
- 12-screw white plastic pickguard.
- Three-saddle bridge/tailpiece.
Based on US original (see DUO-SONIC FIRST VERSION listing in earlier Other US-made Models section).

TORONADO (26) 1998-2004 *Model name on headstock, four controls, two metal-cover humbuckers.*

- Maple neck with rosewood fingerboard; 24.75-inch scale, 22 frets; truss-rod adjuster at headstock end; one string-guide.
- Contoured offset-waist body; sunburst or colours.
- Two metal-cover humbuckers.
- Four controls (two volume, two tone) on body; three-way selector on pickguard; side-mounted jack socket.
- Ten-screw tortoiseshell or white pearl laminated plastic pickguard.
- Six-saddle bridge with through-body stringing.

TORONADO HH (26) 2005-06 *Model name on headstock, four controls, two black coverless humbuckers.*
Similar to TORONADO (see previous listing), except:
- Body various colours.
- Two black coverless humbuckers.
- Four controls (two volume, two tone) and three-way selector, all on body.
- Seven-screw black laminated plastic pickguard.
- Six-saddle bridge, bar tailpiece.

FENDER JAPAN

This section lists only the models marketed outside of Japan, all of which have 'Made In Japan' or 'Crafted in Japan' somewhere on the instrument. It does not cover the guitars produced solely for the Japanese market, which include numerous interpretations of Fender's established designs and many combinations of construction, components, and cosmetics. The periods of availability for models sold in Japan often differ greatly to those of the same models officially sold in export markets. These export models, listed here, often appear to come and go, usually because demand from a particular distributor fluctuates. For that reason, certain Japanese models are irregularly removed from and then replaced in Fender's catalogues in the USA and Europe – while manufacture of the model in Japan might well remain continuous. This interrupted availability is confusing from a Western point of view and makes it difficult to accurately pin down the true periods of production. We have reflected this in the listing by simply showing a start date followed by 'onwards'.

JAPAN-MADE STRATOCASTERS
Japanese Stratocasters are divided into two sections: Japan Replica; and Japan Revised.

JAPAN REPLICA STRATOCASTERS
Listed here in alphabetical order are the Japan-made models for sale outside Japan that replicate various standard-version US-made Stratocasters (see earlier US-made Regular Stratocasters section).

ANTIGUA STRATOCASTER 2004 *Replica of 1977-period US original with white/brown shaded body finish and matching pickguard (see STRATOCASTER CBS SEVENTIES listing in earlier US Regular Stratocasters section).*

STRATOCASTER '68 1988-onwards *Replica of 1968-period US original (see STRATOCASTER CBS SIXTIES listing in earlier US-made Regular Stratocasters section).*

STRATOCASTER '72 1985-onwards *Replica of 1972-period US original (see STRATOCASTER CBS SEVENTIES listing in earlier US-made Regular Stratocasters section).*

50s STRATOCASTER 1985-onwards *Replica of 1957-period US original (see STRATOCASTER PRE-CBS listing in earlier US-made Regular Stratocasters section). Also version with six-saddle bridge and through-body stringing. Previously known in UK as SQUIER SERIES '57 STRATOCASTER, with small Squier Series logo on headstock (1982-83). Sold under the actual Squier brandname (1983-85) and new Fender version introduced in 1985, although Japanese market manufacture continuous since 1982. Foto Flame fake figured wood finish option (1992-94).*

60s STRATOCASTER 1985-onwards *Replica of 1962-period US original (see STRATOCASTER PRE-CBS listing in earlier US-made Regular Stratocasters section). Previously known in UK as SQUIER SERIES '62 STRATOCASTER, with small Squier Series logo on headstock (1982-83). Sold under the actual Squier brandname (1983-85) and*

new Fender version introduced in 1985, although Japanese market manufacture continuous since 1982. Foto Flame fake figured wood finish option (1992-94).

JAPAN REVISED STRATOCASTERS
Listed here in alphabetical order are the Japan-made models for sale outside Japan that we regard as revised and adapted versions of the standard-version US-made Stratocasters (see earlier US-made Regular Stratocasters section).

AERODYNE CLASSIC STRATOCASTER (2) 2006-current *Aerodyne Series on headstock, figured carved body top.*
Similar to AERODYNE STRATOCASTER first version (see next listing), except:
- Aerodyne Series on matching colour headstock face.
- Bound body with figured carved top; various colours.
- Three white six-polepiece pickups (bridge pickup angled).
- 11-screw white laminated plastic pickguard.

AERODYNE STRATOCASTER first version (2) 2004 *Aerodyne Series on headstock, three pickups, black pickguard.*
- Maple neck with rosewood fingerboard; 22 frets; truss-rod adjuster at headstock end; one string-guide; Aerodyne Series on black-face headstock.
- Bound body with carved top; black only.
- Three black six-polepiece pickups (bridge pickup angled).
- Three controls (volume, two tone) and five-way selector, all on pickguard; jack socket in body face.
- 11-screw black laminated plastic pickguard.
- Six-pivot bridge/vibrato unit.

AERODYNE STRATOCASTER second version (2) 2005-06 *Aerodyne Series on headstock, three pickups, no pickguard.*
Similar to AERODYNE STRATOCASTER first version (see previous listing), except:
- Three controls (volume, two tone) and five-way selector, all on body; side-mounted jack socket.
- No pickguard.

BLUE FLOWER STRATOCASTER first version (2) 1988-93 *Blue floral-pattern body finish, large headstock.*

Similar to STRATOCASTER '72 (see listing in earlier Japan Replica Stratocasters section), except:

- Fretted maple neck only.
- Body blue floral-pattern only.
- Eleven-screw blue floral-pattern pickguard.

BLUE FLOWER STRATOCASTER second version (2) 2003 *Blue floral-pattern body finish, small headstock.*
Similar to BLUE FLOWER STRATOCASTER first version, except:

- Small headstock; truss-rod adjuster at body end,

CONTEMPORARY STRATOCASTER first type (2) 1985-87 *One humbucker, normal logo, black neck.*

- Maple neck with rosewood fingerboard; 22 frets; truss-rod adjuster at headstock end; string-clamp; black neck.
- Body various colours.
- One black coverless humbucker (at bridge).
- One control (volume) on body; side-mounted jack socket.
- No pickguard.
- Two -pivot bridge/vibrato unit.
- Black-plated hardware.

CONTEMPORARY STRATOCASTER second type (2) 1985-87 *Two humbuckers, black neck.*
Similar to CONTEMPORARY STRATOCASTER FIRST VERSION, except:

- Two black coverless humbuckers.
- Two controls (volume, tone) and three-way selector, all on pickguard.
- 11-screw black plastic pickguard.

CONTEMPORARY STRATOCASTER third type (2) 1985-87 *Two single-coils and one humbucker, black neck,*
Similar to CONTEMPORARY STRATOCASTER FIRST VERSION, except:

- Two black six-polepiece pickups and one black coverless humbucker (at bridge).
- Two controls (volume, tone), five-way selector and coil-switch, all on pickguard.
- 11-screw black plastic pickguard.

CONTEMPORARY STRATOCASTER fourth type (2) 1985-87 *Lever-type locking nut, two single-coils and one black coverless humbucker.*
Similar to CONTEMPORARY STRATOCASTER FIRST VERSION, except:

- Two string-guides; lever-type locking nut; black-face headstock.
- Two black six-polepiece pickups and one black coverless humbucker (at bridge).
- Two controls (volume, tone), five-way selector and coil-switch, all on pickguard.
- 11-screw black plastic pickguard.
- Chrome-plated hardware.

CONTEMPORARY STRATOCASTER DELUXE first type (2) 1985-87 *Two humbuckers, normal colour neck.*
Similar to CONTEMPORARY STRATOCASTER FIRST VERSION, except:

- Two string-guides; lever-type locking nut; black-face headstock.
- Two black cover humbuckers.
- Two controls (volume, tone), three-way selector and coil-switch, all on pickguard.
- 11-screw black plastic pickguard.
- Chrome-plated hardware.

CONTEMPORARY STRATOCASTER DELUXE second type (2) 1985-87 *Two single-coils and one covered humbucker.*
Similar to CONTEMPORARY STRATOCASTER FIRST VERSION, except:

- Two string-guides; lever-type locking nut; black-face headstock.
- Two black six-polepiece pickups and one black cover humbucker (at bridge).
- Two controls (volume, tone), five-way selector and coil-switch, all on pickguard.
- 11-screw black plastic pickguard.
- Chrome-plated hardware.

FIXED-BRIDGE STRATOCASTER *See later STANDARD STRATOCASTER SECOND VERSION listing, and 50S STRATOCASTER listing in earlier Replica Stratocasters section.*

FLOYD ROSE HRR STRATOCASTER *See later HRR STRATOCASTER listing.*

FLOYD ROSE STANDARD STRATOCASTER (2) 1994-96 *Two single-coils and one coverless humbucker, normal colour neck, locking vibrato system.*

- Maple neck with rosewood fingerboard; truss-rod adjuster at headstock end; single-bar string-guide; locking nut.
- Body with Foto Flame fake figured wood finish; sunburst, blue or red.
- Two white six-polepiece pickups and one white coverless humbucker (at bridge).
- Two controls (volume, tone) and five-way

selector, all on pickguard; jack socket in body face.

- 11-screw white laminated plastic pickguard.
- Two-pivot locking bridge/vibrato unit.

Also known as SQUIER SERIES FLOYD ROSE STANDARD STRATOCASTER, with small Squier Series logo on headstock (1992-96).

FOTO FLAME STRATOCASTER (2) 1995-96 *Three single-coils, 21 frets, fake figured wood finish.*
Similar to 60S STRATOCASTER (see listing in earlier Japan Replica Stratocasters section), except:

- Foto Flame fake figured wood finish neck.
- Foto Flame fake figured wood finish body; sunbursts and natural.
- 11-screw white or white pearl laminated plastic pickguard.

HANK MARVIN STRATOCASTER (2) 1996-97 *Signature on headstock.*
Similar to 50S STRATOCASTER (see listing in earlier Japan Replica Stratocasters section), except:

- Hank Marvin signature on headstock.
- Body red only.

HM POWER STRAT first type (2) 1988-89 *One humbucker, black-face headstock with large flamboyant 'Strat' logo.*

- Fretted maple neck, or maple neck with rosewood fingerboard; 25-inch scale, 24 frets; truss-rod adjuster at headstock end; locking nut; flamboyant 'Strat' logo on black face headstock.
- Smaller body; various colours.
- One black coverless humbucker (at bridge).
- Two controls (volume, tone) and coil-switch, all on body; side-mounted jack socket.
- No pickguard.
- Two -pivot locking bridge/vibrato unit.
- Black-plated hardware.

Some examples with International Series logo on headstock.

HM POWER STRAT second type (2) 1988-89 *Two single-coils and one humbucker, black-face headstock with large flamboyant 'Strat' logo.*
Similar to HM POWER STRAT FIRST VERSION, except:

- Two black six-polepiece pickups and one

black coverless humbucker (at bridge).
- Three controls (volume, two tone), five-way selector and coil-switch, all on body.

HM STRAT first type (2) 1991-92 *Black-face headstock with 'stencil'-style 'Strat' logo.*
- Fretted maple neck, or maple neck with rosewood fingerboard; 25.1-inch scale, 24 frets; truss-rod adjuster at headstock end; single-bar string-guide; locking nut; 'stencil'-style Strat logo on black-face headstock.
- Smaller body; various colours.
- Two black six-polepiece pickups and one black coverless humbucker (at bridge).
- Two controls (volume, tone) and five-way selector, all on body; side-mounted jack socket.
- No pickguard.
- Two -pivot locking bridge/vibrato unit.
- Black-plated hardware.

HM STRAT second type (2) 1991-92 *Drooped black-face headstock with long 'streamlined' Fender logo.*
- Fretted maple neck, or maple neck with rosewood fingerboard; 25.1-inch scale, 22 frets; truss-rod adjuster at headstock end; single-bar string-guide; locking nut; long 'streamlined' Fender logo on drooped black-face headstock.
- Smaller body; various colours.
- Two black coverless humbuckers and one black six-polepiece pickup (in centre).
- Two controls (volume, tone) and five-way selector, all on pickguard; side-mounted jack socket
- Eight-screw black laminated plastic pickguard.
- Two -pivot locking bridge/vibrato unit.
- Black-plated hardware.

HRR STRATOCASTER (2) 1990-94 *22 frets, three controls on pickguard with rectangular hole for humbucker, locking bridge/vibrato system.*
- Fretted maple neck, or maple neck with rosewood fingerboard; 22 frets; truss-rod adjuster at headstock end; single-bar string-guide; locking nut.
- Body sunburst or colours.
- Two white six-polepiece pickups and one coverless humbucker (at bridge).
- Three controls (volume, two tone) and five-way selector, all on pickguard; jack socket in body face.
- 11-screw white plastic or laminated

plastic pickguard.
- Two -pivot locking bridge/vibrato unit.
Also known as FLOYD ROSE HRR STRATOCASTER (1992-94). Foto Flame fake figured wood finish option (1992-94).

IRON MAIDEN SIGNATURE STRATOCASTER (2) 2001-02 *Iron Maiden on headstock.*
- Fretted maple neck only; 22 frets; truss-rod adjuster at headstock end; single-bar string-guide; locking nut; Iron Maiden on headstock.
- Body black only.
- Two black twin-blade humbuckers and one small black 12-polepiece humbucker (angled at bridge).
- Three controls (volume, two tone) and five-way selector, all on pickguard; jack socket in body face.
- 11-screw mirror plastic pickguard.
- Two-pivot locking bridge/vibrato unit.

JERRY DONAHUE HELLECASTERS STRATOCASTER (2) 1997-98 *Signature on headstock, 'Hellecasters' inlay at 12th fret.*
- Fretted maple neck; truss-rod adjuster at headstock end; one string-guide; roller nut; 'Hellecasters' inlay at 12th fret; Jerry Donahue signature on headstock.
- Body blue only.
- Three white six-polepiece pickups (bridge pickup angled).
- Three controls (volume, tone, two-way rotary switch) and five-way selector, all on pickguard; jack socket in body face.
- 11-screw blue sparkle laminated plastic pickguard.
- Six-pivot bridge/vibrato unit.

JOHN JORGENSON HELLECASTER (2) 1997-98 *Signature and model name on headstock, three split pickups.*
- Maple neck with rosewood fingerboard, gold sparkle dot markers; 22 frets; truss-rod adjuster at headstock end; locking tuners; 'Hellecasters' inlay at 12th fret; John Jorgenson signature on large Stratocaster reverse headstock.
- Body black sparkle only.
- Three black plain-top split pickups (bridge pickup angled).
- Three controls (volume, two tone) and five-way selector, all on pickguard; jack socket in body face.
- 11-screw gold sparkle laminated plastic pickguard.

- Two -pivot bridge/vibrato unit.
- Gold-plated hardware.

MATTHIAS JABS STRATOCASTER (2) 1998 *Ringed planet position markers.*
- Maple neck with rosewood fingerboard, ringed planet position markers; 22 frets; truss-rod adjuster at headstock end; locking tuners; scroll inlay at 12th fret.
- Body red only.
- Two white six-polepiece pickups and one white coverless humbucker (at bridge).
- Three controls (two volume, tone) and five-way selector, all on pickguard; jack socket in body face.
- 11-screw white plastic pickguard.
- Six-pivot bridge/vibrato unit.

PAISLEY STRATOCASTER (2) 1988-onwards *Pink paisley-pattern body finish.* Similar to STRATOCASTER'72 (see listing in earlier Japan Replica Stratocasters section), except:
- Fretted maple neck only.
- Body pink paisley-pattern only.
- Eleven-screw pink paisley-pattern pickguard.

RICHIE SAMBORA PAISLEY STRATOCASTER (2) 1996 *Signature on headstock, black paisley-pattern body finish.*
- Fretted maple neck, star markers; 22 frets; truss-rod adjuster at headstock end; pearl tuner buttons; single-bar string-guide; locking nut; Richie Sambora signature on headstock.
- Body black paisley-pattern only.
- Two black six-polepiece pickups and one black coverless humbucker (at bridge).
- Three controls (volume, two tone) and five-way selector, all on pickguard; jack socket in body face.
- 11-screw black paisley laminated plastic pickguard.
- Two-pivot locking bridge/vibrato unit.

RITCHIE BLACKMORE STRATOCASTER (2) 1997-98 *Signature on headstock, centre pickup missing, only cover installed.*
- Maple neck with scalloped rosewood fingerboard; 'bullet' truss-rod adjuster at headstock end; two string-guides; Ritchie Blackmore signature on large headstock.
- Body white only.
- Two black six-polepiece pickups (bridge

pickup angled); centre pickup missing, cover only installed.
- Three controls (volume, two tone) and three-way selector, all on pickguard, jack socket in body face.
- 11-screw white laminated plastic pickguard.
- Six-pivot bridge/vibrato unit.

SHORT-SCALE STRATOCASTER (2) 1989-95 *Two controls, 22 frets.*
- Fretted maple neck, or maple neck with rosewood fingerboard; 24-inch scale, 22 frets; truss-rod adjuster at headstock end; one string-guide.
- Body sunburst or colours.
- Three white six-polepiece pickups (bridge pickup angled).
- Two controls (volume, tone) and five-way selector, all on pickguard; jack socket in body face.
- Eight-screw white laminated plastic pickguard.
- Two-pivot bridge/vibrato unit.

SPECIAL STRATOCASTER *UK designation for STANDARD STRATOCASTER SECOND VERSION (see later listing).*

SQUIER SERIES FLOYD ROSE STANDARD STRATOCASTER 1992-96 *See earlier FLOYD ROSE STANDARD STRATOCASTER listing.*

SQUIER SERIES '57 STRATOCASTER *See 50S STRATOCASTER listing in earlier Japan Replica Stratocasters section.*

SQUIER SERIES '62 STRATOCASTER *See 60S STRATOCASTER listing in earlier Japan Replica Stratocasters section.*

STANDARD STRATOCASTER first version (2) 1985-89 *22 frets, two-pivot bridge/vibrato unit.*
- Fretted maple neck, or maple neck with rosewood fingerboard; 22 frets; truss-rod adjuster at headstock end; string clamp (locking nut from 1988).
- Body sunburst or colours.
- Three white six-polepiece pickups (bridge pickup angled).
- Three controls (volume, two tone) and five-way selector, all on pickguard; jack socket in body face.
- 11-screw white laminated plastic pickguard.
- Two-pivot bridge/vibrato unit (locking type from 1988).

STANDARD STRATOCASTER second version (2) 1988-91 *21 frets, two string-guides.*
Similar to 50s STRATOCASTER and 60S STRATOCASTER (see listings in earlier Japan Replica Stratocasters section), except:
- Two string-guides.
Also version with six-saddle bridge and through-body stringing.
Previously sold under Squier brandname (1986-88). Production moved to Mexico from 1991 (see STANDARD STRATOCASTER listing in earlier Mexico-made Stratocasters section). Known as SPECIAL STRATOCASTER in UK.

STRAT XII 12-string (2) 1988-onwards *12-string headstock, offset-cutaway body.*
- Maple neck with rosewood fingerboard; 24.75-inch scale, 22 frets; truss-rod adjuster at body end; one 'bracket' string-guide; six-tuners-per-side headstock.
- Body sunburst or colours.
- Three white six-polepiece pickups (bridge pickup angled).
- Three controls (volume, two tone) and five-way selector, all on pickguard; jack socket in body face.
- 11-screw white laminated plastic pickguard.
- 12-saddle bridge with through-body stringing.

THE VENTURES STRATOCASTER (2) 1996 *The Ventures logo on headstock, three Lace Sensor pickups.*
- Maple neck with bound rosewood fingerboard, block markers; 22 frets; truss-rod adjuster at body end; one string-guide; The Ventures logo on black-face headstock.
- Body black only.
- Three white plain-top Lace Sensor pickups (pickup at bridge is angled).
- Three controls (volume, tone, boost) and five-way selector, all on pickguard; jack socket in body face; active circuit.
- 11-screw white pearl laminated plastic pickguard.
- Six-pivot bridge/vibrato unit.
- Gold-plated hardware.
Optional Ventures logo for body.

YNGWIE MALMSTEEN STANDARD STRATOCASTER (2) 1991-94 *Signature on headstock.*

- Scalloped fretted maple neck; 'bullet' truss-rod adjuster at headstock end; two string-guides; three-screw neckplate.
- Body black, blue, or white.
- Three black six-polepiece pickups (pickup at bridge is angled).
- Three controls (volume, two tones) and five-way selector, all on pickguard; jack socket in body face.
- 11-screw white laminated plastic pickguard.
- Six-pivot bridge/vibrato unit.

JAPAN-MADE TELECASTERS
Japanese Telecasters are divided into two sections: Japan Replica and Japan Revised.

JAPAN REPLICA TELECASTERS
Listed here in alphabetical order are the Japan-made models for sale outside Japan that replicate various standard-version US-made Telecasters (see earlier US-made Regular Telecasters and US-made Revised Telecasters sections).

ANTIGUA TELECASTER 2004 *Replica of 1977-period US original with white/brown shaded body finish and matching pickguard (see TELECASTER listing in earlier US Regular Telecasters section).*

BLUE FLOWER TELECASTER 1986-onwards *Replica of 1969-period US original with blue floral pattern-finish body (see TELECASTER listing in earlier US-made Regular Telecasters section).*

CUSTOM TELECASTER '62 1985-onwards *Replica of 1962-period US original with bound-body (see TELECASTER listing in earlier US-made Regular Telecasters section). Foto Flame fake figured wood finish option (1994-96).*

PAISLEY TELECASTER 1986-onwards *Replica of 1969-period US original with paisley-pattern body finish (see TELECASTER listing in earlier US-made Regular Telecasters section).*

ROSEWOOD TELECASTER 1986-onwards *Replica of 1969-period US original with rosewood neck and body (see TELECASTER listing in earlier US-made Regular Telecasters section).*

TELECASTER CUSTOM '72 1986-onwards *Replica of 1972-period US original with humbucker and single-coil (see TELECASTER CUSTOM listing in earlier US-made Revised Telecasters section).*

THINLINE TELECASTER '69 1986-onwards *Replica of 1969-period US original with two single-coils (see THINLINE TELECASTER FIRST VERSION listing in earlier US-made Revised Telecasters section).*

THINLINE TELECASTER '72 1986-onwards *Replica of 1972-period US original with two humbuckers (see THINLINE TELECASTER SECOND VERSION listing in earlier US-made Revised Telecasters section).*

50s TELECASTER 1990-onwards *Replica of 1952-period US original (see TELECASTER listing in earlier US-made Regular Telecasters section). Previously known in UK as SQUIER SERIES '52 TELECASTER, with small Squier Series logo on headstock (1982-83). Sold under the actual Squier brandname (1983-85) and new Fender version introduced in 1990, although Japanese market manufacture continuous since 1982. Foto Flame fake figured wood finish option (1994).*

JAPAN REVISED TELECASTERS

Listed here in alphabetical order are the Japan-made models for sale outside Japan that we regard as revised and adapted versions of the standard-version US-made Telecasters (see earlier US-made Regular Telecasters).

AERODYNE TELE (1) 2004-06 *Aerodyne Series on headstock, two pickups.*
- Maple neck with rosewood fingerboard; 22 frets; truss-rod adjuster at headstock end; one string guide; Aerodyne Series on black-face headstock.
- Single-cutaway bound body with carved top; black only.
- One large black rectangular six-polepiece pickup (at neck) and one black six-polepiece pickup (angled in bridgeplate).
- Two controls (volume, tone) and three-way selector, all on body; side-mounted jack socket.
- No pickguard.
- Six-saddle flat bridge with through-body stringing.

BUCK OWENS TELECASTER (1) 1998 *Signature on headstock, red, silver and blue sparkle striped body front.*
- Maple neck with rosewood fingerboard; truss-rod adjuster at body end; one string- guide; red, silver and blue sparkle striped headstock face; Buck Owens signature on headstock.
- Slab single-cutaway bound body; red, silver and blue sparkle striped front.
- One plain metal-cover pickup (at neck) and one black six-polepiece pickup (angled in bridgeplate).
- Two controls (volume, tone) and three-way selector, all on metal plate adjoining pickguard; side-mounted jack socket.
- Eight-screw gold pickguard.
- Three-saddle raised-sides bridge with through-body stringing.
- Gold-plated hardware.

CONTEMPORARY TELECASTER first type (1) 1985-87 *Black neck, two humbuckers.*
- Maple neck with rosewood fingerboard; 22 frets; truss-rod adjuster at headstock end; string clamp; black neck.
- Slab single-cutaway body; various colours.
- Two black coverless humbuckers.
- Two controls (volume, tone), three-way selector and coil-switch, all on body; side-mounted jack socket.
- No pickguard.
- Two -pivot bridge/vibrato unit.
- Black-plated hardware.

CONTEMPORARY TELECASTER second type (1) 1985-87 *Black neck, two single-coils and one humbucker.*
Similar to CONTEMPORARY TELECASTER FIRST VERSION, except:
- Two black six-polepiece pickups and one black coverless humbucker (at bridge).
- Two controls (volume, tone) and three mini-switches, all on body.

CUSTOM ESQUIRE *See Other Japan-made Models,*

ESQUIRE *See Other Japan-made Models.*

FOTO FLAME TELECASTER (1) 1995-96 *Fake figured wood finish on neck and body; two single-coils.*
Similar to 60s TELECASTER (see later listing), except:
- Foto Flame fake figured wood finish

body; sunbursts or natural.

FRANCIS ROSSI SIGNATURE TELECASTER (1) 2003-04 *Signature on headstock.*
- Fretted maple neck; truss-rod adjuster at body end; one string-guide; Francis Rossi signature on headstock.
- Slab single-cutaway body with circular hole; black with green front only, satin finish.
- Three white plain-top pickups (bridge pickup angled in cut-down bridgeplate).
- Two controls (volume, tone) and five-way selector, all on metal plate adjoining pickguard; side-mounted jack socket.
- Eight-screw white laminated plastic pickguard.
- Six-saddle small bridge with through-body stringing.

HMT ACOUSTIC-ELECTRIC first version (1) 1991-94 *Stratocaster-style headstock, wooden-base bridge.*
- Maple neck with rosewood fingerboard; 25.1-inch scale, 22 frets; truss-rod adjuster at headstock end; one string-guide; large Stratocaster-style headstock with black-face.
- Enlarged semi-solid slab single-cutaway bound body with f-hole; sunburst or colours.
- One black plain-top Lace Sensor (angled at neck) and piezo pickup (in bridge).
- Three controls (volume, tone, pan,) all on body; side-mounted jack socket; active circuit.
- No pickguard.
- Single-saddle wooden-base bridge.

HMT ACOUSTIC-ELECTRIC second version (1) 1995-97 *Telecaster headstock, wooden-base bridge.*
Similar to HMT ACOUSTIC-ELECTRIC FIRST VERSION (see previous entry), except:
- Telecaster headstock.
- Body sunburst or black.
- One black plain-top pickup (angled at neck) and piezo pickup (in bridge).

HMT TELECASTER first version (1) 1991-92 *Stratocaster-style headstock, F-hole body, two humbuckers.*
- Maple neck with rosewood fingerboard; 25.1-inch scale, 22 frets; truss-rod adjuster at headstock end; Stratocaster-style black-face headstock.
- Larger semi-solid slab single-cutaway

bound body with f-hole; sunburst or colours.
- Two black coverless humbuckers.
- Two controls (volume, tone), three-way selector and coil-switch, all on body; side-mounted jack socket.
- No pickguard.
- Six-saddle small bridge with through-body stringing.

HMT TELECASTER second version (1) 1991-92 *Drooped headstock with long 'streamlined' Fender logo, f-hole body, angled Lace Sensor and humbucker.*
Similar to HMT TELECASTER FIRST VERSION, except:
- Split-triangle markers; locking nut; long 'streamlined' Fender logo on drooped black-face headstock.
- One black plain-top Lace Sensor pickup (angled at neck) and one black coverless humbucker (at bridge).
- Two-pivot locking bridge/vibrato unit.

JD TELECASTER (1) 1992-99 *'JD' on headstock, black six-polepiece pickup at neck.*
- Fretted maple neck; truss-rod adjuster at body end; one string-guide; Jerry Donahue initials on headstock.
- Slab single-cutaway bound body; sunburst or colours.
- Two black six-polepiece pickups (bridgeplate pickup angled).
- Two controls (volume, tone) and five-way selector, all on metal plate adjoining pickguard; side-mounted jack socket.
- Eight-screw black laminated plastic pickguard.
- Three-saddle raised-sides bridge with through-body stringing.
Based on signature model of US Custom Shop.

NOKIE EDWARDS TELECASTER (1) 1996 *Signature on headstock, two twin-blade humbuckers.*
- Maple neck with ebony fingerboard; 22 frets; truss-rod adjuster at body end; brass nut; optional Scruggs Peg banjo-style de-tuner for 6th string; Nokie Edwards signature on headstock.
- Single-cutaway body with figured front; natural only.
- Two black twin-blade humbucker pickups.
- Two controls (volume, tone) and three-way selector, all on body, side-mounted jack socket.

- No pickguard.
- Six-saddle small bridge with through-body stringing.
- Gold-plated hardware.
Optional Nokie Edwards logo for body.

RICHIE KOTZEN SIGNATURE TELECASTER (1) 2005-06 *Signature on headstock.*
- Fretted maple neck; truss-rod adjuster at headstock end; one string-guide; Richie Kotzen signature on headstock.
- Contoured single-cutaway bound body; sunburst or green.
- One plain metal-cover pickup with visible height-adjustment screws (at neck) and one black twin-blade humbucker (angled in bridgeplate).
- One control (volume), pickup mode rotary switch and three-way selector, all on metal plate adjoining pickguard; side-mounted jack socket.
- Eight-screw white plastic or white pearl laminated plastic pickguard.
- Six-saddle flat bridge with through-body stringing.
- Gold-plated hardware

RICK PARFITT SIGNATURE TELECASTER (1) 2003-04 *Signature on headstock.*
- Maple neck with rosewood fingerboard; truss-rod adjuster at body end; one string-guide; Rick Parfitt signature on headstock.
- Slab single-cutaway body; white only, satin finish.
- One plain metal-cover pickup (at neck) and one black six-polepiece pickup (angled in cut down bridgeplate).
- Two controls (volume, tone) and three-way selector, all on metal plate adjoining pickguard; side-mounted jack socket.
- Eight-screw black plastic pickguard.
- Four-saddle wrapover bridge/tailpiece with through-body stringing.
- Some hardware gold-plated.

SPECIAL TELECASTER *UK designation for* STANDARD TELECASTER *(see later listing).*

SQUIER SERIES '52 TELECASTER *See 50s* TELECASTER *listing in earlier Japan Replica Telecasters section.*
STANDARD TELECASTER (1) 1988-91 *Two string-guides, five-screw pickguard, six-saddle bridge/tailpiece with no through-body stringing.*

- Fretted maple neck; truss-rod adjuster at body end; two string-guides.
- Slab single-cutaway body; black or blond.
- One plain metal cover pickup (at neck) and one black six-polepiece pickup (angled in bridgeplate).
- Two controls (volume, tone) and three-way selector, all on metal plate adjoining pickguard; side-mounted jack socket.
- Five-screw white plastic pickguard.
- Six-saddle flat bridge/tailpiece with no through-body stringing.
Previously marketed under the Squier brandname (1985-88). Production moved to Mexico from 1991 (see STANDARD STRATOCASTER *listing in earlier Mexico-made Stratocasters section). Known as* SPECIAL TELECASTER *in UK.*

WILL RAY JAZZ-A-CASTER (1) 1997-98 *Signature and model name on headstock, two large white pickups.*
- Maple neck with rosewood fingerboard, triangle markers; 22 frets; truss-rod adjuster at headstock end; one string guide; locking tuners; 'Hellecasters' inlay at 12th fret; Will Ray signature on small Stratocaster-style headstock.
- Slab single-cutaway body; gold foil leaf only.
- Two large white rectangular six-polepiece pickups (bridge pickup angled).
- Two controls (volume, tone) and four-way selector, all on metal plate adjoining pickguard; side-mounted jack socket.
- Eight-screw white pearl laminated plastic pickguard.
- Modified six-saddle bridge with through-body stringing; Hipshot bending device on 2nd string.

50s TELECASTER WITH BIGSBY (1) 2005-06 *Fretted maple neck, 'F' logo Bigsby vibrato tailpiece.*
Similar to 50s TELECASTER (see listing in earlier Japan Replica Telecasters section), except:
- Body natural or blonde.
- Six-saddle bridge, 'F' logo Bigsby vibrato tailpiece.

60s TELECASTER (1) 1994 *Fake figured wood finish on neck and body; two single-coils.*
- Foto flame fake figured wood finish neck with rosewood fingerboard; truss-rod adjuster at body end; one string-guide.
- Slab single-cutaway, Foto Flame fake

figured wood finish body; natural only.
- One plain metal-cover pickup (at neck) and one black six-polepiece pickup (angled in bridgeplate).
- Two controls (volume, tone) and three-way selector, all on metal plate adjoining pickguard; side-mounted jack socket.
- Eight-screw white or white pearl laminated plastic pickguard.
- Three-saddle raised-sides bridge with through-body stringing.

Known as FOTO FLAME TELECASTER (1995-96); see earlier listing.

60s TELECASTER WITH BIGSBY (1) 2005-current *Bound body, rosewood fingerboard, 'F' logo Bigsby vibrato tailpiece.*
Similar to 60s TELECASTER (see earlier listing), except:
- Bound body; sunburst or red.?
- Six-saddle bridge, 'F' logo Bigsby vibrato tailpiece.

90s TELECASTER CUSTOM (1) 1995-98 *Black or white bound body with matching headstock face, pearl pickguard, gold-plated hardware.*
- Maple neck with rosewood fingerboard; truss-rod adjuster at body end; one string-guide; black- or white-face headstock.
- Slab single-cutaway bound body; black or white.
- One plain metal cover pickup (at neck) and one black six-polepiece pickup (angled in bridgeplate).
- Two controls (volume, tone) and three-way selector, all on metal plate adjoining pickguard; side-mounted jack socket.
- Eight-screw grey or white pearl laminated plastic pickguard.
- Six-saddle flat bridge with through-body stringing.
- Gold-plated hardware.

90s TELECASTER DELUXE (1) 1995-98 *Contoured body, three six-polepiece pickups, reversed control plate.*
- Maple neck with rosewood fingerboard; truss-rod adjuster at body end; one string-guide.
- Single-cutaway body; sunburst or colours.
- Two white six-polepiece pickups (neck and centre) and one black six-polepiece pickup (angled in bridgeplate).
- Two controls (volume, tone) and five-way

selector, all on reversed metal plate adjoining pickguard; side-mounted jack socket.
- Eight-screw white pearl laminated plastic pickguard.
- Six-saddle flat bridge with through-body stringing.

Foto Flame fake figured wood finish option (1995-96).

OTHER JAPAN-MADE MODELS

Listed here in alphabetical order are the other Japan-made models for sale outside Japan.

ANTIGUA JAGUAR *See later JAGUAR listing.*

COMPETITION MUSTANG *See later MUSTANG listing.*

CUSTOM ESQUIRE 1986-onwards *Replica of 1962-period US original with bound body (see ESQUIRE listing in earlier Other US-made Models section).*

D'AQUISTO ELITE (16) 1984, 1989-94 *Hollow single-cutaway body, one pickup, wooden tailpiece.*
Similar to D'AQUISTO STANDARD (next listing), except:
- Bound ebony fingerboard, block markers; ebony tuner buttons.
- One black 12-polepiece humbucker pickup (one metal-cover six-polepiece humbucker 1989-94).
- Two controls (volume, tone) on body.
- Gold-plated hardware.

D'AQUISTO STANDARD (16) 1984 *Hollow single-cutaway body, two pickups, wooden tailpiece.*
- Maple glued-in neck with bound rosewood fingerboard; 24.75-inch scale, 20 frets; truss-rod adjuster at headstock end; pearl tuner buttons; three-tuners-per-side headstock.
- Hollow archtop single-cutaway bound body with f-holes; sunburst, natural or black.
- Two black 12-polepiece humbuckers.
- Four controls (two volume, two tone) and three-way selector, all on body; side-mounted jack socket.
- Bound floating wooden pickguard.

- Single-saddle wooden bridge, wooden tailpiece.

ELAN I (21) 1993 *Three-tuners-per-side headstock, EL on truss-rod cover, offset-cutaway body, two humbuckers.*
- Mahogany glued-in neck with bound ebony fingerboard; 25.1-inch scale, 22 frets; truss-rod adjuster at headstock end; pearl tuner buttons; three-tuners-per-side headstock; neck matches body colour; EL on truss-rod cover.
- Offset-cutaway carved-top bound body; sunburst or colours.
- Two black coverless humbuckers.
- Two controls (volume, tone) and five-way selector, all on body; side-mounted jack socket.
- Six-saddle bridge with through-body stringing.

Previously with 'Heartfield' or 'Heartfield by Fender' on headstock as part of Elan series.

ESPRIT STANDARD (18) 1984 *Three-tuners-per-side headstock, twin-cutaway body, two humbuckers.*
- Maple glued-in neck with bound rosewood fingerboard; 24.75-inch scale, 22 frets; truss-rod adjuster at headstock end; three-tuners-per-side headstock; neck matches body colour.
- Semi-solid twin-cutaway bound body; sunburst or black.
- Two black 12-polepiece humbucker pickups.
- Two controls (volume, tone) and three-way selector, all on body; side-mounted jack socket.
- Six-saddle bridge, tailpiece.

ESPRIT ELITE (18) 1984 *Three-tuners-per-side headstock, Elite on truss-rod cover, twin-cutaway body, two humbuckers.*
Similar to ESPRIT STANDARD, except:
- Snowflake position markers; pearl tuner buttons; Elite on truss-rod cover.
- Sunburst or colours.
- Four controls (two volume, two tone), three-way selector and coil-switch, all on body.
- Fine-tuner tailpiece.

ESPRIT ULTRA (18) 1984 *Three-tuners-per-side headstock, Ultra on truss-rod cover, twin-cutaway body, two humbuckers.*
Similar to ESPRIT STANDARD, except:
- Bound ebony fingerboard, split-block

position markers; ebony tuner buttons; Ultra on truss-rod cover.
- Sunburst or colours.
- Four controls (two volume, two tone), three-way selector and coil-switch, all on body.
- Fine-tuner tailpiece.
- Gold-plated hardware.

ESQUIRE 1986-onwards *Replica of 1954-period US original (see ESQUIRE listing in earlier Other US-made Models section).*

FLAME STANDARD (17) 1984 *Three-tuners-per-side headstock, offset-cutaway body, two humbuckers.*
Similar to ESPRIT STANDARD (see earlier listing), except:
- Semi-solid offset-cutaway smaller body.

FLAME ELITE (17) 1984 *Three-tuners-per-side headstock, Elite on truss-rod cover, offset-cutaway body, two humbuckers.*
Similar to ESPRIT ELITE (see earlier listing), except:
- Semi-solid offset-cutaway smaller body.

FLAME ULTRA (17) 1984 *Three-tuners-per-side headstock, Ultra on truss-rod cover, offset-cutaway body, two humbuckers.*
Similar to ESPRIT ULTRA (see earlier listing), except:
- Semi-solid offset-cutaway smaller body.

JAG-STANG (24) 1996-onwards *Model name on headstock, angled single-coil and humbucker.*
- Maple neck with rosewood fingerboard; 24-inch scale, 22 frets; truss-rod adjuster at body end; one string-guide.
- Contoured offset-waist body; blue or red.
- One white six-polepiece pickup (at neck) and one white coverless humbucker (at bridge), both angled.
- Two controls (volume, tone) and jack socket, all on metal plate adjoining pickguard; two selector slide-switches on pickguard.
- 10-screw white pearl laminated plastic pickguard.
- Six-saddle bridge with vibrato unit.

JAGUAR 1986-onwards *Replica of early 1960s-period US original (see JAGUAR listing in earlier Other US-made Models section). Gold-plated hardware option (1994). Foto*

Flame fake figured wood finish option (1994-96). Also ANTIGUA JAGUAR, with white/brown shaded body finish and matching pickguard (2004).

JAGUAR BARITONE CUSTOM (4) 2004-06 *Model name on headstock, long-scale neck.*
Similar to Jaguar (see previous listing), except:
- 21 frets, 28.5-inch scale; truss-rod adjuster at headstock end.
- Body sunburst only.
- Nine-screw tortoiseshell laminated plastic pickguard.
- Six-saddle bridge, bar tailpiece.
Known as JAGUAR BASS VI CUSTOM (2006).

JAGUAR BARITONE HH (4) 2005-current *Black-face headstock, long-scale neck, two metal-cover humbuckers, one metal control plate.*
Similar to JAGUAR BARITONE CUSTOM (see previous listing), except:
- Black-face headstock.
- Body black only.
- Two metal cover humbuckers.
- Two controls (volume, tone) and jack socket, all on metal plate adjoining pickguard: three-way selector on pickguard.
- 11-screw black laminated plastic pickguard.

JAGUAR HH (4) 2005-current *Special on black-face headstock, two metal-cover humbuckers, three metal control plates.*
Similar to JAGUAR (see earlier listing), except:
- Truss-rod adjuster at headstock end; black-face headstock.
- Body black only.
- Two metal-cover humbuckers.
- Nine-screw black plastic pickguard.

JAZZMASTER 1986-onwards *Replica of early 1960s-period US original (see JAZZMASTER listing in earlier Other US-made Models section). Gold-plated hardware option (1994). Foto Flame fake figured wood finish option (1994-96).*

KATANA (19) 1985-86 *Model name on headstock, wedge-shape body.*
- Maple glued-in neck with bound rosewood fingerboard, offset triangle markers; 24.75-inch scale, 22 frets; truss-rod adjuster at headstock end; string

clamp; arrow-head-shape headstock; neck matches body colour.
- Bevelled-edge wedge-shape body; various colours.
- Two black coverless humbuckers.
- Two controls (volume, tone) and three-way selector, all on body; side-mounted jack socket.
- Two -pivot bridge/vibrato unit.

MASTER SERIES *See earlier listings for D'AQUISTO, ESPRIT and FLAME models.*

MUSTANG 1986-onwards *Replica of 1969-period US original with 24-inch scale (see MUSTANG listing in earlier Other US-made Models section). Also COMPETITION MUSTANG, with stripes on body (2002-03)*

PERFORMER (20) 1985-86 *Model name on headstock, two angled white plain-top pickups.*
- Maple neck with rosewood fingerboard; 24 frets; truss-rod adjuster at headstock end; string clamp; 'arrow-head' shape headstock.
- Contoured offset waist body with 'hooked' horns; sunburst or colours.
- Two white plain-top humbuckers (both angled).
- Two controls (volume, tone), three-way selector and coil-switch, all on pickguard; side-mounted jack socket.
- 10-screw white laminated plastic pickguard.
- Two -pivot bridge/vibrato unit.

ROBBEN FORD (18) 1989-94 *Name on truss-rod cover.*
Similar to ESPRIT ULTRA (see earlier listing), except:
- Robben Ford on truss-rod cover.
- Body sunburst, natural or black.
- Two black coverless humbucker pickups.

RR-58 (22) 1993 *RR on truss-rod cover, two humbuckers, fixed bridge.*
- Mahogany glued-in neck with rosewood fingerboard; 24.75-inch scale, 22 frets; truss-rod adjuster at headstock end; neck matches body colour; RR on truss-rod cover.
- Body blond, green, or red.
- Two black plain-top humbuckers.
- Two controls (volume, tone) and five-way selector, all on body; side-mounted jack socket.

- Four-screw black laminated plastic pickguard.
- Six-saddle bridge with through-body stringing.

Previously with 'Heartfield' or 'Heartfield by Fender' on headstock as part of RR series.

TALON (23) 1993 *Model name on reverse headstock.*
- Maple neck with rosewood fingerboard, triangle markers; 25.1-inch scale, 24 frets; truss-rod adjuster at headstock end; single-bar string-guide; locking nut; reverse pointed black-face headstock.
- Body various colours.
- Two black coverless humbuckers and one black six-polepiece pickup (in centre).
- Two controls (volume, tone) and five-way selector, all on body; side-mounted jack socket.
- Nine-screw black laminated plastic pickguard.
- Two -pivot locking bridge/vibrato unit.
- Black-plated hardware.

Previously with 'Heartfield' or 'Heartfield by Fender' on headstock as part of Talon series (Talon V).

THE VENTURES JAZZMASTER (4) 1996 *The Ventures logo on headstock, two large white pickups.*
- Maple neck with bound rosewood fingerboard, block markers; 22 frets; truss-rod adjuster at body end; two string guides; The Ventures logo on black-face headstock.
- Contoured offset-waist body; black only.
- Two large white rectangular six-polepiece pickups.
- Two controls (volume, tone), three-way selector and jack socket, all on pickguard.
- 11-screw white pearl laminated plastic pickguard.
- Six-saddle bridge, vibrato tailpiece.
- Gold-plated hardware.

Optional Ventures logo for body.

'65 MUSTANG REISSUE 2006-current *Replica of 1965-period original with 24-inch scale (see MUSTANG listing in earlier Other US-made Models section).*

FENDER KOREA

Many models made in Korea for Fender bear the Squier brandname and so are outside the scope of this reference section. However, some have prominently featured the Fender logo, and these are listed here. All have 'Made in Korea' somewhere on the instrument.

KOREA-MADE STRATOCASTERS

KOA STRATOCASTER (2) 2006-current *Rosewood fingerboard, white pearl pickguard.*
- Maple neck with rosewood fingerboard; 22 frets; truss-rod adjuster at headstock end; two string-guides.
- Body with Koa veneer top; sunburst only.
- Three white six polepiece pickups (bridge pickup angled).
- Three controls (volume, two tone) and five-way selector, all on pickguard; jack socket in body face.
- 11-screw white pearl laminated plastic pickguard.
- Two-pivot bridge/vibrato unit.

LITE ASH STRATOCASTER (2) 2004-current *Maple neck with maple fingerboard, three Seymour Duncan logo black single-coils, black pickguard.*
- Maple neck with maple fingerboard; 22 frets; truss-rod adjuster at headstock end; two string-guides.
- Body natural, black or white.
- Three Seymour Duncan logo black six-polepiece pickups (bridge pickup angled).
- Three controls (volume, two tone) and five-way selector, all on pickguard; jack socket in body face.
- 11-screw black plastic pickguard.
- Two-pivot bridge/vibrato unit.

SQUIER SERIES STANDARD STRATOCASTER (2) 1992-94 *Small Squier Series logo on headstock.*
- Fretted maple neck, or maple neck with rosewood fingerboard; 21 frets; truss-rod adjuster at headstock end; two string-guides; small Squier Series logo on headstock.
- Body various colours.
- Three white six-polepiece pickups (bridge pickup angled).
- Three controls (volume, two tone) and

five-way selector, all on pickguard; jack socket in body face.
- 11-screw white plastic pickguard.
- Six-pivot bridge/vibrato unit.

Replaced by Mexican-made version in 1994 (see TRADITIONAL STRATOCASTER in earlier Mexico-made Stratocasters section).

TIE-DYE STRAT HS (2) 2005 *Multi-coloured body front, matching headstock face.*
- Maple neck with rosewood fingerboard, no front markers; 22 frets; truss-rod adjuster at headstock end; two string-guides; multi-colour headstock face.
- Body black, multi-colour front, two colour combinations only.
- One black six-polepiece pickup (at neck) and one black coverless humbucker (at bridge).
- Two controls (volume, tone) and three-way selector, all on body; side-mounted jack socket.
- No pickguard.
- Two-pivot bridge/vibrato unit.
- Black-plated hardware.

KOREA-MADE TELECASTERS

BLACKOUT TELECASTER HH (1) 2004 *Glued-in neck, no front markers, two Seymour Duncan humbuckers.*
- Maple glued-in neck with rosewood fingerboard, no front markers; 22 frets; truss-rod adjuster at headstock end; two string-guides.
- Single-cutaway body; black or blue.
- Two Seymour Duncan logo black coverless humbuckers.
- Two controls (volume, tone) and three-way selector, all on body; side-mounted jack socket.
- No pickguard.
- Six-saddle small bridge with through-body stringing.
- Black-plated hardware.

CUSTOM TELECASTER FMT HH (1) 2003-04 *Glued-in neck, bound body with figured top.*
- Maple glued-in neck with bound rosewood fingerboard; 22 frets; truss-rod adjuster at headstock end; two string-guides.
- Single-cutaway bound body with figured top; various colours.
- Two black coverless humbuckers.
- Two controls (volume, tone with pull

switch) and three-way selector, all on body; side-mounted jack socket.
- No pickguard.
- Six-saddle small bridge with through-body stringing.
- Smoked chrome-plated hardware.

ESQUIRE CUSTOM CELTIC *See Other Korea-made Models.*

ESQUIRE CUSTOM GT *See Other Korea-made Models.*

ESQUIRE CUSTOM SCORPION *See Other Korea-made Models.*

KOA TELECASTER (1) 2006-current
Rosewood fingerboard, white pearl pickguard.
- Maple neck with rosewood fingerboard; 22 frets; truss-rod adjuster at headstock end; two string-guides.
- Body with Koa veneer top; sunburst only.
- One plain metal-cover pickup (at neck) and one Seymour Duncan logo black six-polepiece pickup (angled in bridgeplate).
- Two controls (volume, tone) and three-way selector, all on metal plate adjoining pickguard; side-mounted jack socket.
- Eight-screw white pearl laminated plastic pickguard.
- Three-saddle raised-sides bridge/tailpiece with through-body stringing.

LITE ASH TELECASTER (1) 2004-current
Maple neck with maple fingerboard, black pickguard.
- Maple neck with maple fingerboard; 22 frets; truss-rod adjuster at headstock end; two string-guides.
- Slab single-cutaway body; natural, black or white.
- One plain metal-cover pickup (at neck) and one Seymour Duncan logo black six-polepiece pickup (angled in bridgeplate).
- Two controls (volume, tone) and three-way selector, all on metal plate adjoining pickguard; side-mounted jack socket.
- Eight-screw black plastic pickguard.
- Three-saddle raised-sides bridge/tailpiece with no through-body stringing.

SQUIER SERIES STANDARD TELECASTER
(1) 1992-94 *Small Squier Series logo on headstock.*
- Fretted maple neck; 21 frets; truss-rod

adjuster at headstock end; one string-guide; small Squier Series logo on headstock.
- Slab single-cutaway body; black, blue, red or white.
- One plain metal cover pickup with visible height-adjustment screws (at neck) and one black six-polepiece pickup (angled in bridgeplate).
- Two controls (volume, tone) and three-way selector, all on metal plate adjoining pickguard; side-mounted jack socket.
- Eight-screw white plastic pickguard.
- Six-saddle flat bridge/tailpiece with no through-body stringing.
Replaced by Mexican-made version in 1994 (see TRADITIONAL TELECASTER in earlier Mexico-made Telecasters section).

OTHER KOREA-MADE MODELS

ESQUIRE CUSTOM CELTIC (1) 2003 *Celtic design inlay at 12th fret, single-cutaway body.*
- Mahogany glued-in neck with rosewood fingerboard; 22 frets, truss-rod adjuster at headstock end; two string-guides; no front markers except Celtic design inlay at 12th fret.
- Single-cutaway contoured body; silver only, satin finish.
- One black coverless humbucker (at bridge).
- One control (volume) on body; side-mounted jack socket.
- No pickguard.
- Six-saddle small bridge with through-body stringing.
- Black-plated hardware.

ESQUIRE CUSTOM GT (1) 2003 *Centre striped single cutaway body.*
- Mahogany glued-in neck with bound rosewood fingerboard; 22 frets; truss-rod adjuster at headstock end; two string-guides.
- Single-cutaway contoured bound body; blue, red or silver, with centre stripes.
- One black coverless humbucker (at bridge).
- One control (volume) on body; side-mounted jack socket.
- No pickguard.
- Six-saddle small bridge with through-body stringing.
- Black-plated hardware.

ESQUIRE CUSTOM SCORPION (1) 2003
Scorpion inlay at 12th fret, single-cutaway body.
- Mahogany glued-in neck with bound rosewood fingerboard; 22 frets; truss-rod adjuster at headstock end; two string-guides; no front markers except Scorpion inlay at 12th fret.
- Single-cutaway contoured bound body; black only.
- One black coverless humbucker (at bridge).
- One control (volume) on body; side-mounted jack socket.
- No pickguard.
- Six-saddle small bridge with through-body stringing.
- Black-plated hardware.

SHOWMASTER BLACKOUT (25) 2004-05
Glued-in neck, no front markers, two Seymour Duncan humbuckers.
Similar to SHOWMASTER H (see later listing), except:
- Body black or blue.
- Two Seymour Duncan logo black coverless humbuckers.
- Two controls (volume, tone) and five-way selector, all on body.

SHOWMASTER CELTIC H (25) 2003 *Celtic design inlay at 12th fret, offset cutaway body.*
- Maple glued-in neck with rosewood fingerboard; 24 frets; truss-rod adjuster at headstock end; two string-guides; locking tuners; no front markers except Celtic design inlay at 12th fret.
- Body silver only, satin finish.
- One black coverless humbucker (at bridge).
- One control (volume) on body; side-mounted jack socket.
- No pickguard.
- Six-saddle small bridge with through-body stringing.
- Black-plated hardware.

SHOWMASTER DELUXE HH WITH TREMOLO (25) 2003 *Glued-in neck, no front markers, bound gold body.*
Similar to SHOWMASTER HH WITH TREMOLO (see later listing), except:
- Bound body; gold only.
- Two white coverless humbuckers.
- Chrome-plated hardware.

SHOWMASTER FAT-HH (25) 2004-05
Glued-in neck, front markers, figured ash-top body, two Seymour Duncan logo humbuckers.
Similar to SHOWMASTER H (see later listing), except:
- Front markers.
- Body with figured ash top; sunburst only.
- Two Seymour Duncan logo black coverless humbuckers.
- Two controls (volume, tone) and five-way selector, all on body.
- Chrome-plated hardware.

SHOWMASTER FAT-SSS (25) 2004-05
Glued-in neck, fingerboard front markers, figured ash-top body, three Seymour Duncan logo single-coils.
Similar to SHOWMASTER FAT-HH (see previous listing), except:
- Three Seymour Duncan logo black six-polepiece pickups (bridge pickup angled).

SHOWMASTER FMT-HH (25) 2005-current
Glued-in neck, fingerboard front markers, figured maple-top body, two Seymour Duncan humbuckers.
Similar to SHOWMASTER H (see later listing), except:
- Dot front markers.
- Body with figured maple top; sunburst or natural.
- Two Seymour Duncan logo black coverless humbuckers.
- Two controls (volume, tone) and five-way selector, all on body.
- Chrome-plated hardware.

SHOWMASTER H WITH TREMOLO (25)
2003 *Glued-in neck, no fingerboard front markers, one black humbucker.*
- Maple glued-in neck with rosewood fingerboard, no front markers; 24 frets; truss-rod adjuster at headstock end; two string-guides; locking tuners.
- Body silver only, satin finish.
- One black coverless humbucker (at bridge).
- One control (volume) on body; side-mounted jack socket.
- No pickguard.
- Two-pivot bridge/vibrato unit.
- Black-plated hardware.

SHOWMASTER HH WITH TREMOLO (25)
2003 *Glued-in neck, no fingerboard front markers, two black humbuckers.*

Similar to SHOWMASTER H (see previous listing), except:
- Maple glued-in neck with bound rosewood fingerboard.
- Bound body; black only.
- Two black coverless humbuckers.
- Two controls (volume, tone) and five-way selector, all on body.

SHOWMASTER QBT-HH (25) 2004-current
Glued-in neck, fingerboard front markers, figured bubinga-top body, two Seymour Duncan logo humbuckers.
Similar to SHOWMASTER H (see earlier listing), except:
- Front markers.
- Body with figured bubinga top; brown only.
- Two Seymour Duncan logo black coverless humbuckers.
- Two controls (volume, tone) and five-way selector, all on body.
- Chrome-plated hardware.

SHOWMASTER QBT-SSS (25) 2004-05
Glued-in neck, fingerboard front markers, figured bubinga-yop body, three Seymour Duncan logo single-coils.
Similar to SHOWMASTER QBT-HH (see previous listing), except:
- Three Seymour Duncan logo single-coils.

SHOWMASTER QMT-HH (25) 2005-current
Glued-in neck, fingerboard front markers, figured maple-top body, two Seymour Duncan logo humbuckers.
Similar to SHOWMASTER QBT-HH (see earlier listing), except:
- Body with figured maple top; sunbursts only.

SHOWMASTER SCORPION HH (25) 2003
Scorpion inlay at 12th fret, offset cutaway body.
- Maple glued-in neck with bound rosewood fingerboard; 24 frets; truss-rod adjuster at headstock end; two string-guides; locking tuners; no fingerboard front markers except Scorpion inlay at 12th fret.
- Bound body; black only.
- Two black coverless humbuckers.
- Two controls (volume, tone) and five-way selector, all on body; side-mounted jack socket.
- No pickguard.
- Six-saddle small bridge with through-

body stringing.
- Black-plated hardware.

SO-CAL SPEED SHOP (25) 2005 *So-Cal logo on body, red/white graphic finish.*
- Maple neck with rosewood fingerboard; 22 frets; truss-rod adjuster at headstock end; two string-guides; matching colour headstock, neck and fingerboard.
- Body red/white graphic finish only.
- One black coverless humbucker (at bridge).
- One control (volume) on body; side-mounted jack socket.
- No pickguard.
- Six-saddle small bridge with through-body stringing.

TC-90 THINLINE (28) 2004-current *Twin-cutaway body with f-hole.*
- Maple glued-in neck with rosewood fingerboard; 22 frets; truss-rod adjuster at headstock end; two string-guides; Telecaster style headstock with matching colour face.
- Semi-solid slab twin-cutaway body with f-hole; redburst or white.
- Two large black six-polepiece pickups.
- Two controls (volume, tone) and three-way selector, all on body; side-mounted jack socket.
- Six-screw black laminated plastic pickguard.
- Six-saddle bridge, bar tailpiece.

TORONADO GT HH (26) 2005-06 *Striped body, four controls, two Seymour Duncan black humbuckers.*
- Maple neck with rosewood fingerboard; 24.75-inch scale, 22 frets; truss-rod adjuster at headstock end; two string-guides; matching colour headstock face.
- Contoured offset-waist body; various colours, with stripes.
- Two Seymour Duncan logo black coverless humbuckers.
- Four controls (two volume, two tone) and three-way selector, all on body.
- No pickguard.
- Six-saddle bridge, bar tailpiece.

FENDER-RELATED BRANDS

HEARTFIELD

This brandname appeared on a series of instruments started in 1989 and built by Fujigen, the factory responsible then for much of Fender Japan's production. As part of a reciprocal arrangement, Heartfield was distributed through Fender Musical Instruments US. The line, designed by both Fender US and Fender Japan, featured models considered too radical to bear the Fender brand, although some did have 'Heartfield by Fender' on the headstock. The guitars were phased out in 1993, and in this final year selected examples did appear with a Fender brand only; these have been included here in the Fender Japan section.

REGAL

From the late 1950s into the early 1960s the Harmony company of Chicago supplied instruments and amplification for exclusive distribution by Fender. Bearing the Regal brandname, this line included electric guitars. Some examples also carried the Fender logo on the truss-rod cover, occasionally accompanied by an 'F' symbol on the pickguard.

SQUIER

The first instruments with this brandname appeared in the early 1980s and were Japanese-made Fenders exported into Europe, but soon they were sold elsewhere and later made elsewhere.

The brandname was borrowed from the US Fender-owned V.C. Squier string company. Fender's policy is that the Squier catalogue caters for lower pricepoints, maintaining the company's ever-expanding market coverage – but not by cheapening the Fender name itself.

The Squier logo, supported by a small but important 'by Fender' line, appeared on an increasing number of models during the its first decade. At first these originated in Japan, but escalating production costs meant a move to cheaper manufacturing sources. Korea came on line in 1985, and India made a brief appearance in the late 1980s on early Squier II models (or their

Sunn equivalents – another borrowed brandname) before returning to the roster in 2007.

Fender's facility in Mexico helped out too in the early 1990s, and more recently China, Indonesia, and India have entered the picture, providing entry-level electrics with the kudos of a Fender connection. Periodic returns to Japanese production have yielded impressive results, such as the Silver and Vista series, while the Pro Tone line and more recent efforts offer evidence of improving Korean quality.

The continuing success story of Squier makes this a very important support brand for Fender, exhibiting a level of design and build quality that regularly exceeds its apparent status as a second-string line.

CHRONOLOGY 1950-2007

This listing is designed to show in chronological order the production-model electric guitars that have "Fender" as their main logo/brandname, and that have been manufactured in the US, Japan, Korea, and Mexico between 1950 and early 2007.

The start date shown is the year that production commenced for each model in the country of manufacture, regardless of different start dates elsewhere. The finish date is the final year that each model was available in the US and/or Europe.

KEY

aka means also known as
-current indicates a model still in production at the time of writing
-onwards indicates a Japanese-made model with fluctuating availability outside Japan
US manufacture unless noted:
(J) indicates Japanese manufacture
(K) indicates Korean manufacture
(M) indicates Mexican manufacture

Broadcaster	1950-51
Esquire	1950-69
Nocaster	1951
Telecaster	1951-83
Stratocaster (pre-CBS)	1954-65

Duo-Sonic (1st version)	1956-64
Musicmaster (1st version)	1956-64
Jazzmaster	1958-80
Custom Esquire	1959-69
Custom Telecaster	1959-72
Jaguar	1962-75
Duo-Sonic (2nd version)	1964-69
Duo-Sonic II	1964-69
Musicmaster (2nd version)	1964-75
Musicmaster II	1964-69
Mustang (regular scale)	1964-81
Mustang (short scale)	1964-69
Electric XII	1965-69
Stratocaster (CBS Sixties)	1965-71
Coronado I	1966-69
Coronado II	1966-69
Coronado XII	1966-69
Bronco	1967-80
Coronado II Antigua	1967-71
Coronado II Wildwood	1967-69
Coronado XII Antigua	1967-71
Coronado XII Wildwood	1967-69
Blue Flower Telecaster	1968-69
Competition Mustang	1968-73
LTD	1968-74
Montego I	1968-74
Montego II	1968-74
Paisley Red Telecaster	1968-69
Thinline Telecaster (1st version)	1968-71
Custom (aka Maverick)	1969-70
Musicmaster (2nd version)	1969-75
Rosewood Telecaster	1969-72
Swinger (aka Arrow or Musiclander)	1969
Stratocaster (CBS Seventies)	1971-81
Thinline Telecaster (2nd version)	1971-79
Telecaster Custom	1972-81
Telecaster Deluxe	1973-81
Musicmaster (3rd version)	1975-80
Rhinestone Stratocaster	1975
Starcaster	1976-80
Antigua Mustang	1977-79
Antigua Stratocaster	1977-79

Antigua Telecaster	1977-79
Antigua Telecaster Custom	1977-79
Antigua Telecaster Deluxe	1977-79
Lead I	1979-82
Lead II	1979-82
25th Anniversary Stratocaster	1979-80
Hendrix Stratocaster	1980
Strat	1980-83
Black & Gold Telecaster	1981-83
Bullet (1st version)	1981-83
Bullet Deluxe	1981-83
Gold/Gold Stratocaster	1981-83
International Color Stratocaster	1981
International Color Telecaster	1981
Lead III	1981-82
Stratocaster Standard (1st version)	1981-83
Walnut Strat	1981-83
Squier Series '57 Stratocaster (J)	1982-83
Squier Series '62 Stratocaster (J)	1982-83
Squier Series '52 Telecaster (J)	1982-83
Bullet (2nd version)	1983
Bullet H1	1983
Bullet H2	1983
Bullet S2	1983
Bullet S3	1983
Elite Stratocaster	1983-84
Elite Telecaster	1983-84
Gold Elite Stratocaster	1983-84
Gold Elite Telecaster	1983-84
Stratocaster Standard (2nd version)	1983-84
Telecaster Standard	1983-84
Walnut Elite Stratocaster	1983-84
Walnut Elite Telecaster	1983-84
'52 Telecaster	1983-84, 86-98
'57 Stratocaster	1983-85, 86-98
'62 Stratocaster	1983-85, 86-98
Bowling Ball Stratocaster (aka Marble Stratocaster)	1984
Bowling Ball Telecaster (aka Marble Telecaster)	1984
D'Aquisto Elite (J)	1984, 1989-94
D'Aquisto Standard (J)	1984
Esprit (Standard, Elite, Ultra) (J)	1984
Flame (Standard, Elite, Ultra) (J)	1984
Contemporary Stratocaster (4 variations) (J)	1985-87
Contemporary Stratocaster Deluxe (2 variations) (J) 1985-87	
Contemporary Telecaster (2 variations) (J)	1985-87
Custom Telecaster '62 (J)	1985-onwards
Katana (J)	1985-86
Performer (J)	1985-86

Standard Stratocaster (1st version) (J)	1985-89
Stratocaster '72 (J)	1985-onwards
50s Stratocaster (J)	1985-onwards
60s Stratocaster (J)	1985-onwards
American Standard Stratocaster	1986-2000
Blue Flower Telecaster (J)	1986-onwards
Custom Esquire (J)	1986-onwards
Esquire (J)	1986-onwards
Jaguar (J)	1986-onwards
Jazzmaster (J)	1986-onwards
Mustang (J)	1986-onwards
Paisley Telecaster (J)	1986-onwards
Rosewood Telecaster (J)	1986-onwards
Telecaster Custom '72 (J)	1986-onwards
Thinline Telecaster '69 (J)	1986-onwards
Thinline Telecaster '72 (J)	1986-onwards
Strat Plus	1987-98
American Standard Telecaster	1988-2000
Blue Flower Stratocaster (1st version) (J)	1988-93
Eric Clapton Stratocaster (1st version)	1988-2001
HM Power Strat (2 variations) (J)	1988-89
Paisley Stratocaster (J)	1988-onwards
Standard Stratocaster (2nd version) (J)	1988-91
Standard Telecaster (J)	1988-91
Strat XII (J)	1988-onwards
Yngwie Malmsteen Stratocaster (1st version)	1988-98
Stratocaster '68 (J)	1988-onwards
American Standard Deluxe Stratocaster	1989-90
HM Strat (3 variations)	1989-90
Robben Ford (J)	1989-94
Short-Scale Stratocaster (J)	1989-95
Strat Plus Deluxe	1989-98
US Contemporary Stratocaster	1989-91
Albert Collins Telecaster	1990-current
Danny Gatton Telecaster	1990-current
HM Strat Ultra	1990-92
HRR Stratocaster (J)	1990-94
James Burton Telecaster (1st version)	1990-2005
Strat Ultra	1990-98
Tele Plus (1st version)	1990-95
50s Telecaster (J)	1990-onwards
HM Strat (2 variations) (J)	1991-92
HMT Acoustic-Electric (1st version) (J)	1991-94
HMT Telecaster (2 variations) (J)	1991-92
Jeff Beck Stratocaster (1st version)	1991-2001
Prodigy	1991-93
Prodigy II	1991-92
Set Neck Telecaster	1991-95
Set Neck Telecaster Floyd Rose	1991-92
Set Neck Telecaster Plus	1991-92

Standard Stratocaster (M)	1991-current
Standard Telecaster (M)	1991-current
Tele Plus Deluxe	1991-92
Yngwie Malmsteen Standard Stratocaster (J)	1991-94
American Classic Stratocaster	1992-99
Bajo Sexto Telecaster baritone	1992-98
Floyd Rose Classic Stratocaster	1992-98
Floyd Rose HRR Stratocaster (J)	1992-94
JD Telecaster (J)	1992-99
Jerry Donahue Telecaster	1992-2001
Robert Cray Stratocaster	1992-current
Set Neck Stratocaster (1st version)	1992-95
Set Neck Floyd Rose Stratocaster	1992-95
Set Neck Telecaster Country Artist	1992-95
Sparkle Telecaster	1992-95
Squier Series Floyd Rose Standard Stratocaster (J)	1992-96
Squier Series Standard Stratocaster (K)	1992-94
Squier Series Standard Telecaster (K)	1992-94
Stevie Ray Vaughan Stratocaster	1992-current
50s Stratocaster Foto Flame (J)	1992-94
60s Stratocaster Foto Flame (J)	1992-94
'54 Stratocaster	1992-98
'60 Stratocaster (1st version)	1992-98
Clarence White Telecaster	1993-2001
Duo-Sonic (M)	1993-97
Elan 1 (J)	1993
Richie Sambora Stratocaster (1st version)	1993-99
RR-58 (J)	1993
Special Edition 1993 Stratocaster	1993
Talon (J)	1993
Aluminum-Body Stratocaster (various models)	1994-95
Aluminum-Body Telecaster	1994-95
D'Aquisto Elite	1994-95, 2000-01
Dick Dale Stratocaster	1994-current
Floyd Rose Standard Stratocaster (M)	1994-98
Floyd Rose Standard Stratocaster (J)	1994-96
Jaguar Foto Flame (J)	1994-96
Jazzmaster Foto Flame (J)	1994-96
Richie Sambora Standard Stratocaster (M)	1994-2002
Robben Ford Elite	1994-2001
Robben Ford Ultra FM	1994-2001
Robben Ford Ultra SP	1994-2001
Special Edition 1994 Stratocaster	1994
Special Edition 1994 Telecaster	1994
Squier Series Floyd Rose Standard Stratocaster (M)	1994-96
Squier Series Standard Stratocaster (M)	1994-96
Squier Series Standard Telecaster (M)	1994-96
Strat Special (M)	1994-96
Tele Special (M)	1994-96
40th Anniversary 1954 Stratocaster	1994
50s Telecaster Foto Flame	1994
60s Telecaster Foto Flame (J)	1994

American Classic Telecaster (1st version)	1995-99
American Standard B-Bender Telecaster	1995-97
American Standard Roland GR-Ready Stratocaster	1995-98
Bonnie Raitt Stratocaster	1995-2001
Buddy Guy Stratocaster	1995-current
Carved Top Strat	1995-98
Contemporary Strat	1995-98
Contemporary Strat FMT	1995-98
D'Aquisto Deluxe	1995-2001
Foto Flame Stratocaster (J)	1995-96
Foto Flame Telecaster (J)	1995-96
90s Telecaster Deluxe Foto Flame (J)	1995-96
HMT Acoustic-Electric (2nd version) (J)	1995-97
James Burton Standard Telecaster (M)	1995-current
Set Neck Stratocaster (2nd version)	1995-98
Tele Jnr	1995-2000
Tele Plus (2nd version)	1995-98
Telecaster XII	1995-98
Waylon Jennings Tribute Telecaster	1995-2003
'54 Stratocaster FMT	1995-98
'60 Stratocaster FMT	1995-98
90s Telecaster Custom (J)	1995-98
90s Telecaster Deluxe (J)	1995-98

Hank Marvin Stratocaster (J)	1996-97
Jag-Stang (J)	1996-onwards
Lone Star Strat	1996-2000
Nokie Edwards Telecaster (J)	1996
Relic 50s Nocaster	1996-98
Relic 50s Stratocaster	1996-98
Relic 60s Stratocaster	1996-98
Richie Sambora Paisley Stratocaster (J)	1996
Tex-Mex Strat (M)	1996-97
The Ventures Jazzmaster (J)	1996
The Ventures Stratocaster (J)	1996
Traditional Fat Strat (M)	1996-98
Traditional Stratocaster (M)	1996-98
Traditional Telecaster (M)	1996-98
'58 Stratocaster	1996-98
'69 Stratocaster (1st version)	1996-98
50s Telecaster	1996-98
60s Telecaster Custom	1996-98
50th Anniversary Stratocaster	1996
50th Anniversary Telecaster	1996

Big Apple Strat	1997-2000
California Fat Strat	1997-98
California Fat Tele	1997-98
California Strat	1997-98
California Tele	1997-98
Collectors Edition Stratocaster	1997
Deluxe Nashville Tele (M)	1997-current
Deluxe Powerhouse Strat (M)	1997-current
Deluxe Super Strat (M)	1997-2004
Hank Marvin Stratocaster (M)	1997
Jerry Donahue Hellecasters Stratocaster (J)	1997-98

Jimi Hendrix Stratocaster	1997-2000
Jimmie Vaughan Tex-Mex Stratocaster (M)	1997-current
John Jorgenson Hellecaster (J)	1997-98
Merle Haggard Tele	1997-current
Ritchie Blackmore Stratocaster (J)	1997-98
Roadhouse Strat	1997-2000
Tex-Mex Strat Special (M)	1997
Tex-Mex Tele Special (M)	1997
Will Ray Jazz-A-Caster (J)	1997-98
90s Tele Thinline	1997-2001

American Deluxe Fat Strat	1998-2003
American Deluxe Fat Strat/Locking Trem	1998-2003
American Deluxe Stratocaster (1st version)	1998-2003
American Deluxe Telecaster (1st version)	1998-99
American Standard Stratocaster Hard-Tail	1998-2000
American Vintage '52 Telecaster	1998-current
American Vintage '57 Stratocaster	1998-current
American Vintage '62 Stratocaster	1998-current
Big Apple Strat Hard-Tail	1998-2000
Buck Owens Telecaster (J)	1998
Carved Top Strat HH	1998
Carved Top Strat HSS	1998
Classic Player Strat	1998-2005
Classic '69 Telecaster Thinline (M)	1998-current
Cyclone (M)	1998-2006
Deluxe Double Fat Strat Floyd Rose (M)	1998-2004
Deluxe Fat Strat Floyd Rose (M)	1998-2005
Floyd Rose Classic Strat HH	1998-2002
Floyd Rose Classic Strat HSS	1998-2002
John Jorgenson Telecaster	1998-2001
Matthias Jabs Stratocaster (J)	1998
Nashville B-Bender Tele	1998-current
N.O.S. ('65) Strat	1998
Relic Floyd Rose Stratocaster	1998
Showmaster FMT	1998-2005
Standard Roland Ready Strat (M)	1998-current
Tele-Sonic	1998-2004
Toronado (M)	1998-2004
U.S. Fat Tele / American Fat Tele	1998-2000, 01-03
Voodoo Stratocaster	1998-2000
Will Ray Telecaster	1998-2001
Yngwie Malmsteen Stratocaster (2nd version)	1998-2006
1998 Collectors Edition Telecaster	1998

American Classic Telecaster (2nd version)	1999-2000
American Deluxe Telecaster (2nd version)	1999-2003
American Deluxe Power Tele	1999-2001
American Vintage '52 Tele Special	1999-2001
American Vintage '62 Custom Telecaster	1999-current
American Vintage '62 Jaguar	1999-current
American Vintage '62 Jazzmaster	1999-current
Chris Rea Classic Stratocaster (M)	1999
Classic 50s Stratocaster (M)	1999-current

Classic 50s Telecaster (M)	1999-2006
Classic 60s Stratocaster (M)	1999-current
Classic 70s Stratocaster (M)	1999-current
Classic '72 Telecaster Custom (M)	1999-current
Classic '72 Telecaster Thinline (M)	1999-current
Custom Classic Strat	1999-current
Deluxe Double Fat Strat (M)	1999-2004
Deluxe Fat Strat (M)	1999-2006
Deluxe Nashville Power Tele (M)	1999-current
Richie Sambora Stratocaster (2nd version)	1999-2002
Ritchie Blackmore Stratocaster	1999-2005
Showmaster Set Neck FMT	1999-2005
Showmaster Set Neck FMT Hard-Tail	1999-2005
Showmaster Standard	1999-2005
Standard Fat Strat (M)	1999-current
Standard Fat Strat Floyd Rose (M)	1999-current
'51 Nocaster (Closet Classic/N.O.S./Relic)	1999-current
'56 Stratocaster (Closet Classic/N.O.S./Relic)	1999-current
'60 Stratocaster (2nd version) (Closet Classic/N.O.S./Relic)	1999-current
'63 Telecaster (Closet Classic/N.O.S./Relic)	1999-current
'69 Stratocaster (2nd version) (Closet Classic/N.O.S./Relic)	1999-current

American Stratocaster	2000-current
American Stratocaster Hard-Tail	2000-06
American Double Fat Strat	2000-03
American Double Fat Strat Hard-Tail	2000-03
American Fat Strat Texas Special	2000-03
American Strat Texas Special	2000-03
American Telecaster	2000-current
Classic Rocker	2000-02
Custom Classic Telecaster	2000-06
Hank Marvin Classic Stratocaster (M)	2000
Showmaster 7-string	2000-01
Showmaster 7-string Hard-Tail	2000-01
Sub-Sonic Stratocaster HH baritone	2000-01
Sub-Sonic Stratocaster HSS baritone (1st version)	2000-01

American Fat Tele	2001-03
Classic 60s Telecaster (M)	2001-current
Eric Clapton Stratocaster (2nd version)	2001-current
Iron Maiden Signature Stratocaster (J)	2001-02
Jeff Beck Stratocaster (2nd version)	2001-current
Muddy Waters Telecaster (M)	2001-current
Sub-Sonic Stratocaster HSS baritone (2nd version)	2001
Sub-Sonic Tele baritone	2001-05
Tom Delonge Stratocaster (M)	2001-03

Buddy Guy Polka Dot Strat (M)	2002-current
Competition Mustang (J)	2002-03
Cyclone II (M)	2002-06
Deluxe Double Fat Strat HH (M)	2002-03

Deluxe Double Fat Strat HH With Locking Tremolo (M)	2002-03
Deluxe Fat Strat HSS (M)	2002-03
Deluxe Fat Strat HSS With Locking Tremolo (M)	2002-03
Highway One Stratocaster (1st version)	2002-06
Highway One Telecaster (1st version)	2002-06
Standard Fat Strat With Locking Tremolo (M)	2002-03
Strat Special With Locking Tremolo HH	2002
Strat Special With Locking Tremolo HSS	2002
Toronado DVII	2002-04
Toronado HH	2002-04
'68 Reverse Strat Special	2002

American Ash Telecaster	2003-current
American Stratocaster HH	2003-06
American Stratocaster HH Hard-Tail	2003-05
American Stratocaster HSS	2003-current
American Telecaster HH (1st version)	2003-04
American Telecaster HS (1st version)	2003-04
Blue Flower Stratocaster (2nd version) (J)	2003
Custom Telecaster FMT HH (K)	2003-04
Cyclone HH (M)	2003-05
Esquire Custom Celtic (K)	2003
Esquire Custom GT (K)	2003
Esquire Custom Scorpion (K)	2003
Flat Head Showmaster	2003-04
Flat Head Telecaster	2003-04
Francis Rossi Signature Telecaster (J)	2003-04
Highway One Showmaster HH	2003-04
Highway One Showmaster HSS	2003-04
Highway One Stratocaster HSS (1st version)	2003-06
Highway One Texas Telecaster	2003-current
Highway One Toronado	2003-04
J5:Bigsby	2003-current
J5:HB Telecaster	2003-current
Jimmy Bryant Telecaster	2003-05
Mark Knopfler Stratocaster	2003-current
Rick Parfitt Signature Telecaster (J)	2003-04
Robert Cray Stratocaster (M)	2003-current
Showmaster Celtic H (K)	2003
Showmaster Deluxe HH With Tremolo (K)	2003
Showmaster H With Tremolo (K)	2003
Showmaster HH With Tremolo (K)	2003
Showmaster Scorpion HH (K)	2003
Seymour Duncan Signature Esquire	2003-current
Splatter Stratocaster (M)	2003
Standard Satin Stratocaster (M)	2003-06
Strat-O-Sonic DVI	2003-04
Strat-O-Sonic DVII	2003-06
'59 Esquire	2003-06
'60 Telecaster Custom (Closet Classic/N.O.S./Relic)	2003-04
'65 Stratocaster (Closet Classic/N.O.S./Relic)	2003-06

Aerodyne Stratocaster (1st version) (J)	2004
Aerodyne Tele (J)	2004-06

American Deluxe Ash Stratocaster	2004-current
American Deluxe Ash Telecaster	2004-current
American Deluxe Stratocaster (2nd version)	2004-current
American Deluxe Stratocaster FMT HSS	2004-current
American Deluxe Stratocaster HSS	2004-current
American Deluxe Stratocaster HSS LT	2004-06
American Deluxe Stratocaster QMT HSS	2004-current
American Deluxe Stratocaster V Neck	2004-current
American Deluxe Telecaster (3rd version)	2004-current
American Deluxe Telecaster FMT	2004-06
American Deluxe Telecaster QMT	2004-06
American Deluxe 50th Anniversary Stratocaster	2004
American Telecaster HH (2nd version)	2004-06
American Telecaster HS (2nd version)	2004-06
American 50th Anniversary Stratocaster	2004
Antigua Jaguar (J)	2004
Antigua Stratocaster (J)	2004
Antigua Telecaster (J)	2004
Blackout Telecaster HH (K)	2004
Classic '72 Telecaster Deluxe (M)	2004-current
Deluxe Player's Strat (M)	2004-current
Deluxe Strat HH (M)	2004
Deluxe Strat HH With Locking Tremolo (M)	2004
Deluxe Strat HSS (M)	2004-06
Deluxe Strat HSS With Locking Tremolo (M)	2004-05
Eric Clapton Stratocaster (3rd version)	2004-current
Flat Head Showmaster HH	2004-06
Flat Head Telecaster HH	2004-06
Jaguar Baritone Custom (J)	2004-06
Jeff Beck Signature Stratocaster	2004-current
John 5 Telecaster (M)	2004-current
Lite Ash Stratocaster (K)	2004-current
Lite Ash Telecaster (K)	2004-current
Rory Gallagher Stratocaster	2004-current
Showmaster Blackout (K)	2004-05
Showmaster Elite FMT/LWT/QMT/SMT	2004-current
Showmaster Elite Hard-Tail	2004-current
Showmaster Fat-HH (K)	2004-05
Showmaster Fat-SSS (K)	2004-05
Showmaster QBT-HH (K)	2004-current
Showmaster QBT-SSS (K)	2004-05
Standard Stratocaster HH (M)	2004-06
Standard Stratocaster HSS (M)	2004-current
Standard Stratocaster HSS With Locking Tremolo (M)	2004-current
TC-90 Thinline (K)	2004-current
50th Anniversary Golden Stratocaster (M)	2004
'66 Stratocaster (Closet Classic/N.O.S./Relic)	2004-current

Aerodyne Stratocaster (2nd version) (J)	2005-06
Classic 50s Esquire (M)	2005-current
Deluxe Big Block Stratocaster (M)	2005-06
Deluxe Big Block Telecaster (M)	2005-06
Eric Johnson Stratocaster	2005-current

Jaguar Baritone HH (J)	2005-current
Jaguar HH (J)	2005-current
John Mayer Stratocaster	2005-current
Richie Kotzen Signature Telecaster (J)	2005-06
Robin Trower Stratocaster	2005-current
Showmaster FMT-HH (K)	2005-current
Showmaster QMT-HH (K)	2005-current
So-Cal Speed Shop (K)	2005
Standard Stratocaster FMT (M)	2005-06
Strat-O-Sonic HH	2005-06
Tie-Dye Strat HS (K)	2005
Toronado GT HH (K)	2005-06
Toronado HH (M)	2005-06
'67 Telecaster (Closet Classic/N.O.S./Relic)	2005-current
50s Telecaster With Bigsby (J)	2005-06
60s Telecaster With Bigsby (J)	2005-current

Aerodyne Classic Stratocaster (J)	2006-current
American Vintage 70s Stratocaster	2006-current
American 60th Anniversary Stratocaster	2006
American 60th Anniversary Telecaster	2006
Classic Player Baja Telecaster (M)	2006-current
Classic Player 50s Stratocaster (M)	2006-current
Classic Player 60s Stratocaster (M)	2006-current
Deluxe Power Stratocaster (M)	2006-current
Highway One Stratocaster (2nd version)	2006-current
Highway One Stratocaster HSS (2nd version)	2006-current
Highway One Telecaster (2nd version)	2006-current
Jaguar Bass VI Custom (J)	2006
James Burton Telecaster (2nd version)	2006-current
Koa Stratocaster (K)	2006-current
Koa Telecaster (K)	2006-current
Standard 60th Anniversary Stratocaster (M)	2006
Strat Pro	2006-current
Tele Thinline	2006-current
'65 Mustang Reissue (J)	2006-current

American VG Stratocaster	2007-current
American Vintage 1957 Commemorative Stratocaster	2007
G.E. Smith Telecaster	2007-current
J5 Triple Tele Deluxe (M)	2007-current
Tele Pro	2007-current
Vintage Hot Rod '52 Tele	2007-current
Vintage Hot Rod '57 Strat	2007-current
Vintage Hot Rod '62 Strat	2007-current
Yngwie Malmsteen Stratocaster (3rd version)	2007-current

DATING FENDER GUITARS

Finding a method to date a guitar is important. Not only can it help satisfy an owner's natural curiosity about the origins of an instrument but, in the case of desirable instruments, the vintage can have a great bearing on the guitar's value. The Fender brand has its fair share of collectables, of course, and as prices of the more sought-after models often reach very high levels, any corroboratory clues that indicate the year of production will assume increased importance.

Changes specific to each Fender model have been indicated in the preceding instruments listing. Although the respective features for some individual models can provide more dating clues than for others, there are comparatively few aspects that are consistent across all the Fender models – and fewer still that have chronological significance. These few relevant general pointers to the period of production of US-made models are shown during the next few pages, but even these should not be regarded as infallible because, for example, the components in question were not always used in any strict sequence.

NECKPLATE

The standard method used by Fender to fix a guitar neck to its body is with four screws (often erroneously called 'bolts' in Fenderspeak), and this is normally accomplished using a metal neckplate to reinforce the joint. The rectangular four-screw neckplate has been used since the inception of Fender's first solid electric to provide a simple and secure foundation for the neck.

From 1971 to 1981, a restyled, three-screw version (actually two screws and one bolt, but often called the 'three-bolt') was used on the Stratocaster, the Starcaster, and three Telecasters: Custom, Deluxe and Thinline. After 1981, Fender reverted to the four-screw type for most instruments (excluding the glued-neck models, of course).

From 1954 to 1976, the neckplate carried a stamped serial number. (From 1976 onward, the serial appears on the headstock face, except for Vintage reissues and limited editions.)

From 1965 to 1983, the neckplate (both four and three-screw types) was stamped with a large, reversed 'F'.

TUNERS

At first it was not easy for Fender to find machine heads (tuners) to suit Leo's ideal of a small, neat headstock with straight string-pull. They solved the problem by using products supplied by the Chicago-based Kluson company, although even these had to be cut down by Race & Olmsted to squeeze them into the small space available. The Klusons used by Fender each had a 'safety string post', a slotted shaft with a central vertical hole designed to take the end of the string and thus eliminate the unsightly and dangerous protruding string length. These tuners were used from 1950 to 1966. The following variations of the markings on their metal covers can provide an indication of date.

Version 1, used in 1950 and 1951, has 'Kluson Deluxe' and 'Pat. Appld' stamped on the cover.

Version 2, used from 1951 to 1957, has no markings on the cover.

Version 3, used from 1957 to 1964, has 'Kluson Deluxe' stamped in a single, central, vertical line on the cover.

Version 4, used from 1964 to 1966, has 'Kluson' and 'Deluxe' stamped in two parallel, vertical lines on the cover.

Due to supply and quality problems with Kluson, Fender wanted a tuner produced in-house, and in 1965 contracted Race & Olmsted to supply a revised, cheaper design. The result was a tuner with an angled baseplate, 'F'-stamped cover, and a less rounded button. It was used on Fender instruments until 1976 when it was replaced by a more competitively-priced version made by the German Schaller company, which was fitted until 1983. Although ostensibly very similar in appearance, the Schaller unit has a different construction, and can be distinguished by its closed cover, with no visible axle-end on the side.

NECK/FINGERBOARD CONSTRUCTION

From 1950 to 1959, Fender used a fretted one-piece maple neck, with no separate fingerboard.

From 1959 to 1962, the top of the maple neck was planed flat and fitted with a rosewood fingerboard, flat on the base where it met the neck and cambered on top. This type is often called a 'slab-board' because of the appearance of the straight join of fingerboard and neck when viewed from the body end of the neck.

From 1962 to 1983, the top of the maple neck itself was cambered and then fitted with a thin-section rosewood fingerboard which followed the same curve. Again, the appearance of the curved join of the neck-end provides its 'curved' description. A maple fingerboard was offered as an option, officially from 1967 but often supplied prior to that date. In 1969, the fretted one-piece maple neck was reinstated as an alternative to the rosewood fingerboard.

Since 1983, Fender have reverted to a 'slab' rosewood fingerboard, while the all-maple equivalent is still the principal option.

NECK DATES

During production, Fender date various components. One of the most consistent and obvious is the neck. The date is to be found on the body-end, either pencilled or rubber-stamped. There have been times when the neck did not carry this useful information, the longest period being between 1973 and 1981, and for these instruments other dating clues must suffice.

SERIAL NUMBERS

Serial numbers should be regarded merely as a guide to dating, and ideally the production year should be confirmed by other age-related aspects of the individual instrument. As is usual with a mass-manufacturer, Fender does not assign serial numbers in exact chronological order, and number-bearing components such as neckplates were not used in strict rotation. As a result, apparent discrepancies and contradictions of as much as several years can and do occur. Depending on the production period, serial numbers can be located on the guitar's bridgeplate, backplate, neckplate, or on the front or back of the headstock.

The numbers we show in the tables represent the bulk of Fender's US, Mexican, and Japanese production, although there have been and continue to be various anomalies, odd series, special prefixes and the like, but these have no overall dating relevance and are not listed. Also excluded are the series used on vintage replica reissues, limited editions, signature instruments and so on as these are specific to certain models and not directly pertinent to production year.

The listing here does not apply to Fenders that originate from countries other than the US, Mexico, and Japan; these (and Squier-brand instruments) have their own various number series, which unfortunately do sometimes duplicate those in the US system; prefixes include YN for China and CN for Korea (meaning the Cort factory). Any confusion has to be resolved by studying other aspects of the instruments to determine correct origins (often simply determined by a 'Made In...' stamp) and production dates.

Fender Japan production commenced in 1982 and the company have used a series of prefixes to indicate the year of manufacture. We must stress, however, that the information in the table shown here is approximate and again should be used as a general guide only.

Some Japanese series have been used beyond the production spans listed here, in particular the original A-, C- and G-prefix numbers. There was a reversion to an A prefix for recent production, but a change from 'Made In Japan' to 'Crafted In Japan' somewhere on the guitar helps to differentiate between the two sets of numbers.

Again, please bear in mind the need for caution when dating a Fender – and indeed most other guitars – by using only serial numbers.

US number series	Approximate year(s)
Up to 6,000	1950-54
Up to 10,000 (4 or 5 digits, inc 0 or – prefix)	1954-56
10,000s (4 or 5 digits, inc 0 or – prefix)	1955-56
10,000s to 20,000s (5 or 6 digits, inc 0 or – prefix)	1957
20,000s to 30,000s (5 or 6 digits, inc 0 or – prefix)	1958
30,000s to 40,000s	1959
40,000s to 50,000s	1960
50,000s to 70,000s	1961
60,000s to 90,000s	1962
80,000s to 90,000s	1963
Up to L10,000 (L + 5 digits)	1963
L10,000s to L20,000s (L + 5 digits)	1963
L20,000s to L50,000s (L + 5 digits)	1964
L50,000s to L90,000s (L + 5 digits)	1965
100,000s	1965
100,000s to 200,000s	1966-67
200,000s	1968
200,000s to 300,000s	1969-70
300,000s	1971-72
300,000s to 500,000s	1973
400,000s to 500,000s	1974-75
500,000s to 700,000s	1976
800,000s to 900,000s	1979-81
76 or S6 + 5 digits	1976
S7 or S8 + 5 digits	1977
S7, S8 or S9 + 5 digits	1978
S9 or E0 + 5 digits	1979
S9, E0 or E1 + 5 digits	1980-81
E1, E2 or E3 + 5 digits	1982
E2 or E3 + 5 digits	1983
E3 or E4 + 5 digits	1984-87
E4 + 5 digits	1987
E4 or E8 + 5 digits	1988
E8 or E9 + 5 digits	1989-90
E9 or N9 + 5 digits	1990-91
N0 + 5 digits	1990-91
N1 + 5/6 digits	1991-92
N2 + 5/6 digits	1992-93
N3 + 5/6 digits	1993-94
N4 + 5/6 digits	1994-95
N5 + 5/6 digits	1995-96
N6 + 5/6 digits	1996-97
N7 + 5/6 digits	1997-98
N8 + 5/6 digits	1998-99
N9 + 5/6 digits	1999-2000
DZ0 + 5/6 digits	2000
Z0 + 5/6 digits	2000-01
DZ1 + 5/6 digits	2001
Z1 + 5/6 digits	2001-02
DZ2 + 5/6 digits	2002
Z2 + 5/6 digits	2002-03
DZ3 + 5/6 digits	2003
Z3 + 5/6 digits	2003-04
DZ4 + 5/6 digits	2004
Z4 + 5/6 digits	2004-05
DZ5 + 5/6 digits	2005
Z5 + 5/6 digits	2005-06
DZ6 + 5/6 digits	2006
Z6 + 5/6 digits	2006-07
DZ7 + 5/6 digits	2007
Z7 + 5/6 digits	2007-08

Mexico number series	Approximate year(s)
MN1 + 5/6 digits	1991-92
MN2 + 5/6 digits	1992-93
MN3 + 5/6 digits	1993-94
MN4 + 5/6 digits	1994-95
MN5 + 5/6 digits	1995-96
MN6 + 5/6 digits	1996-97
MN7 + 5/6 digits	1997-98
MN8 + 5/6 digits	1998-99
MN9 + 5/6 digits	1999-2000
MZ0 + 5/6 digits	2000-01
MZ1 + 5/6 digits	2001-02
MZ2 + 5/6 digits	2002-03
MZ3 + 5/6 digits	2003-04
MZ4 + 5/6 digits	2004-05
MZ5 + 5/6 digits	2005-06
MZ6 + 5/6 digits	2006-07
MZ7 + 5/6 digits	2007-08

'Made In Japan' number series	Approximate year(s)
JV + 5 digits	1982-84
SQ + 5 digits	1983-84
E + 6 digits	1984-87
A + 6 digits	1985-86, 1997-current
B + 6 digits	1985-86
C + 6 digits	1985-86
F + 6 digits	1986-87
G + 6 digits	1987-88
H + 6 digits	1988-89
I + 6 digits	1989-90
J + 6 digits	1989-90
K + 6 digits	1990-91
L + 6 digits	1991-92
M + 6 digits	1992-93
N + 6 digits	1993-94
O + 6 digits	1993-94
P + 6 digits	1993-94
Q + 6 digits	1993-94
S + 6 digits	1994-95
T + 6 digits	1994-95
U + 6 digits	1995-96
V + 6 digits	1996-97

'Crafted In Japan' number series	Approximate year(s)
A + 6 digits	1997-98
B + 6 digits	1998-99
O + 5/6 digits	1997-2000
P + 5/6 digits	1999-2002
Q + 5/6 digits	2002-04
R + 5/6 digits	2004-05

MODEL NUMBERS

Since the 1970s, many Fender catalogues and pricelists have used model numbers, or part numbers, to make the process of ordering and stock-keeping easier for distributors and stores. Each version and variation is allocated a specific number and, for instance, that for a current (early 2007) Fender American Stratocaster might read 010-7400-700. The numbers provide various pieces of information such as model type, fingerboard wood, hardware options, finish colour, and even if a case is included in the price. But the second and third digits (10 in our example) are particularly useful as they indicate country of origin.

CODE	Source (brand)
010	US (Fender, factory or Custom Shop)
011	US (Fender)
013	Mexico or Mexico/US (Fender, Squier), formerly Japan (Fender)
014	Mexico or US/Mexico (Fender)
015	US (Fender, Custom Shop)
025	Japan (Fender)
026	Korea (Fender); formerly Japan (Squier)
027	Japan (Fender, Squier); formerly Korea (Squier)
028	China (Squier); formerly Japan (Fender), then India (Squier II, Sunn)

CODE	Source (brand)
029	formerly India (Squier II, Sunn)
030	India (Squier)
031	China or Indonesia (Squier); formerly Japan (Heartfield)
032	Indonesia or India (Squier); formerly Japan (Squier)
033	Korea (Fender, Squier) or China (Squier); formerly India (Squier II)
034	Korea (Squier)
150/151/152	US (Fender, Custom Shop)
155/156/157	US (Fender, Custom Shop)
927	US (Fender, Custom Shop)

INDEX

Page numbers in **bold type** indicate an illustration, usually a guitar, musician, or catalogue/ad etc. Page numbers in *italic type* indicate a listing in the Reference Section.

acknowledgements

INSTRUMENT OWNERS

Guitars photographed came from the collections of the following individuals and organisations, and we are most grateful for their help. The owners are listed here in the alphabetical order of the code used to identify their instruments in the Key below.

AH Adrian Hornbrook; **AR** Arbiter Group; **BF** Brian Fischer; **BM** Barry Moorhouse; **BW** Bruce Welch; **CC** The Chinery Collection; **CN** Carl Nielsen; **CO** Country Music Hall Of Fame; **DG** David Gilmour; **DM** Dixie's Music; **FJ** Fender Japan; **FG** Fender Great Britain & Ireland; **FM** Fender Musical Instruments Corp (US); **GM** Graeme Matheson; **GR** Gruhn Guitars; **MB** Mandolin Brothers; **MD** Malcolm Draper; **PD** Paul Day; **PM** Paul Midgley; **RB** Robin Baird; **RG** Robin Guthrie; **SA** Scot Arch; **SC** Simon Carlton; **TP** Tim Philips.

KEY TO INSTRUMENT PHOTOGRAPHS

The following key is designed to identify who owned which guitars at the time they were photographed. After the relevant bold-type page number(s) we list the model name followed by the owner's initials (see Instrument Owners above). **18** Esquire DG. **18–19** Broadcaster DG. **22–23** Nocaster GR. **23** Telecaster GR. **26–27** Telecaster BF. **30–31** Stratocaster DG. **31** Stratocaster 0001 DG. **34–35** Bigsby CO. **38–39** Stratocaster CC. **39** Martin CC. **42** Musicmaster RG. **42–43** Duo-Sonic RG. **46–47** Jazzmaster CC. **47** Jazzmaster CC. **50** Stratocaster MB. **50–51** Custom Telecaster AH. **51** Telecaster SA. **54** red Stratocaster BW. **54–55** gold Stratocaster SA. **58** Jazzmaster CC. **58–59** Stratocaster SA. **62–63** Jaguar RG. **66–67** red XII RG. **67** gold XII MD. **70** Marauder GR. **70–71** Mustang RB. **74–75** Jazzmaster CC; Wildwood GM. **75** Coronado RB. **78** Custom RB. **78–79** Thinline Telecaster BF. **79** B-Bender Telecaster CC. **82** Thinline Telecaster CN. **82–83** Rosewood Telecaster AH. **86–87** Telecaster Deluxe PM. **90** Starcaster TP. **94–95** Bullet DM; Stratocaster SC. **98–99** Stratocaster SC; Telecaster DG. **99** Squier Stratocaster BM. **102** blue Stratocaster PM. **102–103** Telecaster PD. **103** black Stratocaster PM. **106–107** Telecaster BF; Performer PM. **107** Katana PD; D'Aquisto FM. **110** Stratocaster PM. **110–111** Telecaster FM. **111** Stratocaster FJ. **114** green Stratocaster FM. **114–115** yellow Stratocaster PM. **118–119** both FM. **122–123** both FG. **126–127** both AR. **130–131** both FG. **134–135** both FG. **138–139** both FG.

Principal guitar photography was by Miki Slingsby. Some additional pictures were taken by Garth Blore, Matthew Chattle, William Taylor, and Kelsey Vaughn.

ARTIST PICTURES were supplied principally by Redfern's, London. Redfern's photographers/collectors are indicated by the following key: **CA** Cyrus Andrews; **CB** Carey Brandon; **ER** Ebet Roberts; **GW** Graham Wiltshire; **ID** Ian Dickson; **JJ** Jens Jurgensen; **JP** Jan Persson; **MO** Michael Ochs Archives; **RC** Rafaella Cavalieri; **RG** Ramerez Gant; **RK** Robert Knight; **RP** Roberta Parkin; **TF** Tabatha Fireman.
Pictures and photographers are identified by bold-type page number, subject, and the Redfern's photographer/collector key: **23** Spaniels MO; **26** Rock 'N Roll Trio MO; **26** Leon McAuliffe MO; **27** Gatemouth Brown MO; **34** Merle Travis MO; **38** Otis Rush MO; **39** Buddy Guy MO; **46** The Ventures MO; **55** The Shadows RB/Redfern's; **62** The Trashmen MO; **63** The Beach Boys CA; **71** Bob Dylan JP; **83** Curtis Mayfield/Impressions MO; **86** Keith Richards GW; **90** Joe Strummer ER; **91** Tom Verlaine ER; **110** Jerry Donahue RP; **111** Eric Johnson RK; **115** Eric Clapton ER; **118** John Frusciante ID; **123** J. Mascis JJ; **127** Kurt Cobain RC; **128** Boyan Chowdhury TF; **134** John Mayer RG; **138** Yeah Yeah Yeahs TF; **139** Jamie T CB.

MEMORABILIA illustrated in this book, including advertisements, brochures, catalogues, colour charts, patents, and photographs (in fact anything that isn't a guitar), comes from the collections of Scot Arch, Tony Bacon, Paul Day, Martin Kelly, *The Music Trades*, The National Jazz Archive (Loughton), Don Randall, Alan Rogan, and Steve Soest (Soest Guitar Repair). These alluring pieces were transformed for your visual enjoyment by Tony Bacon and Miki Slingsby.

ORIGINAL INTERVIEWS used in this book were conducted by Tony Bacon as follows: Joe Carducci (November 1997); Bill Carson (September 1991); Mike Eldred (March 2007); Phyllis Fender (February 1992); George Fullerton (February 1992); Bob Heinrich (December 1997); Dale Hyatt (February 1992); Mike Lewis (December 1997); Seth Lover (October 1992); Bill Mendello (April 2007); Justin Norvell (March 2007); Karl Olmsted (February 1992); John Page (February 1992, December 1997); Don Randall (February 1992); Dan Smith (February 1985, February 1992, December 1997, June 2005, March 2007); and Forrest White (February 1992). The sources of any previously published quotations are footnoted where they occur in the text.

THANKS to the following for help on this and the previous two editions: Julie Bowie; Larry Acunto (*20th Century Guitar*); Ivor Arbiter (Arbiter); Dave Burrluck (*Guitarist*); Joe Carducci (Fender US); Michael Caroff (*Fender Frontline*); Bill Carson & Susan Carson; Walter Carter (Gruhn Guitars); Gayle A. Castro (Fender Custom Shop); Doug Chandler; Cheryl Clark (G&L); Paul Cooper; Merelyn Davis; Jane, Sarah & Simon Day; Nicky Donnelly (Arbiter); André Duchossoir; Mike Eldred (Fender Custom Shop); Phyllis Fender; George Fullerton & Lucille Fullerton; Dave Glover (Arbiter); Jon Gold (Fender US); Scott Grant (Fender Custom Shop); Alan Greenwood (*Vintage Guitar*); Clay Harrell; Bob Heinrich (Fender US); Bob Henrit; Christopher Hjort; Lee Holtry (Fender US); Dave Hunter; Dale Hyatt & Eileen Hyatt; Nina Jackson (September Sound); Tom James; Mike Kaskell; Martin Kelly; Mel Lambert; Mike Lewis (Fender US); Seth Lover & Lavone Lover; Brian Majeski (*The Music Trades*); Neville Marten (*Guitarist*); Charles Measures; Howard Meek; Bill Mendello (Fender US); John Morrish; Jun Nakabayashi (Fender Japan); Justin Norvell (Fender US); Karl Olmsted & Katherine Olmsted; John Page; Gary Peal (Fender Great Britain & Ireland); Steve Preston (Arbiter); Don Randall; Simon Raymonde (September Sound); Julian Ridgway (Redfern's); Jim Roberts; John Ryall; Johnny Saitoh (Fender Japan); Sam Sekihara (Fender Japan); Rich Siegle (Fender US); Dan Smith (Fender US); Richard Smith; Steve Soest & Amy Soest (Soest Guitar Repair); Sally Stockwell; Fred Stuart (Fender Custom Shop); Mick Taylor (*Guitarist*); Phil Taylor (David Gilmour Music); Guy Wallace (Music Man); Jim Werner; Neil Whitcher (Fender Great Britain & Ireland); Forrest White; Spike Wrigley (Arbiter).

SPECIAL THANKS to Paul Day in his polo neck for supreme work in updating the reference section and especially for omitting the Buxted Paxocaster.

BOOKS

Tony Bacon *50 Years Of Fender* (Backbeat 2000)
Tony Bacon (ed) *Electric Guitars: The Illustrated Encyclopedia* (Thunder Bay 2000)
Tony Bacon & Paul Day *The Fender Book* (Balafon 1998); *The Ultimate Guitar Book* (DK/Knopf 1991)
Donald Brosnac *Guitar History I* (Bold Strummer 1986)
Bill Carson *My Life And Times With Fender Musical Instruments* (Hal Leonard 1999)
Phil Carson *Roy Buchanan: American Axe* (Backbeat 2001)
Walter Carter & George Gruhn *Gruhn's Guide To Vintage Guitars* (Miller Freeman 1999)
Scott Chinery & Tony Bacon *The Chinery Collection – 150 Years Of American Guitars* (Balafon 1996)
A.R. Duchossoir *The Fender Stratocaster* (Mediapresse 1988), *The Fender Telecaster* (Hal Leonard 1991), *Guitar Identification* (Hal Leonard 1990)
Fender *Custom Shop Guitar Gallery* (Fender/Hal Leonard 1996)
George Fullerton *Guitar Legends: The Evolution Of The Guitar From Fender to G&L* (Centerstream 1993)
Hugh Gregory *1000 Great Guitarists* (Balafon 1994)
George Gruhn & Walter Carter *Electric Guitars And Basses* (GPI 1994), *Gruhn's Guide To Vintage Guitars* (Miller Freeman 1999).
Guitar Magazine (Japan) *The Fender 1: Stratocaster* (Rittor 1987), *The Fender 2: Telecaster & Other Guitars* (Rittor 1993).
Guitar Trader *Vintage Guitar Bulletin Vol.2* (Bold Strummer 1992)
Ralph Heibutzki *Unfinished Business: The Life & Times Of Danny Gatton* (Backbeat 2003)
Christopher Hjort *Eric Clapton & The British Blues Boom: the day-by-day story 1965-1970* (Jawbone 2007)
Christopher Hjort & Doug Hinman *Jeff's Book* (Rock'n'Roll Research Press 2000)
Steve Howe & Tony Bacon *The Steve Howe Guitar Collection* (Balafon 1994)
Colin Larkin (ed) *The Guinness Encyclopedia Of Popular Music* (Guinness 1992)
Ray Minhinnett & Bob Young *The Story Of The Fender Stratocaster* (IMP 1995)
John Morrish *The Fender Amp Book* (Balafon/Miller Freeman 1995)
Keith Shadwick *Jimi Hendrix: Musician* (Backbeat 2003)
Richard R. Smith *Fender: The Sound Heard 'Round The World* (Garfish 1995)
John Teagle & John Sprung *Fender Amps: The First Fifty Years* (Fender/Hal Leonard 1995)
Tom Wheeler *American Guitars* (HarperPerennial 1990); *The Stratocaster Chronicles* (Hal Leonard 2004)
Forrest White *Fender: The Inside Story* (Miller Freeman 1994)
YMM Player *We Love Fender Guitars* (Player Corporation 1982); *History Of Electric Guitars* (Player Corporation 1988).

We also consulted various back issues of the following magazines: *Fender Bridge, Fender Facts, Fender Frontline, The Guitar Magazine, Guitar & Bass, Guitar Player, Guitar World, Guitarist, Making Music, MI Pro, Music Business, Music Industry, The Music Trades, One Two Testing, Vintage Guitar, 20th Century Guitar.*

Updates? The author and publisher welcome any new information for future editions. Write to: Fender Electrics, Backbeat, 2A Union Court, 20-22 Union Road, London SW4 6JP, England. Or you can email: fenderelectics@backbeatuk.com.

THE FENDER ELECTRIC GUITAR BOOK – you won't part with yours either.

"The Fender people hope to always be close to the feelings of those who buy, sell and play electric instruments, because that is the greatest source of information for the development and improvement of instruments."
Fender Catalogue No.2, 1950.